# WE WERE THE FIGHTING IRISH

## Will Notre Dame Reclaim the Glory of Her Name?

## Patrick Xavier

Kindle Direct Publishing
A Division of Amazon Digital Services LLC

In Memory of Marion Casey
1922 – 2009

and

For My Kids

Luke Thomas
Mary Catherine
Michael Angelo
Elaine Rose
Joseph Patrick
Francis Xavier

# Table of Contents

# Prologue

*We are Stardust. We are Golden.*
*We are caught in the Devil's Bargain.*
*And we've got to get Ourselves*
*Back to the Garden.*
**Joni Mitchell, Woodstock, 1969**

When I was six years old, my teacher asked me to carry a small ring of flowers on a pillow in a procession around our school. It was a gorgeous day in May. Deep shades of blue filled the sky, brilliant streams of sunlight warmed our backs, and cool steady breezes soothed our smiling faces. When the procession stopped, we stood and sang before a beautiful statue of a barefoot lady dressed in blue and gold, and my classmate took the ring of flowers and placed it on the lady's head. They said her name was Mary, and that she was the Mother of God.

Seven years later, my dad invited me to see Notre Dame play Michigan State in "the game of the century" for college football's 1966 national championship. When I asked him what "*Notre Dame*" meant, his answer brought back to mind that special day in May, and instilled in me a life-long love for Our Lady, her school, and her famous football team.

Like the millions of other members of that vast national network of faithful Fighting Irish known as the "subway alumni," I am not an alumnus of Notre Dame (and neither is my father or my wife). However, this regrettable deficiency on my part made the enrollment of my two kids there just that much sweeter to savor.

That is, until May of 2009, when instead of a procession to that immaculate woman to whom it owes so much more than its name, Notre Dame paid homage to Barack Obama, and broke a whole legion of hearts, including mine.

This book sees that sad event as the shameful capstone to the conflicted way in which Irish Catholics - themselves once the objects of brutal degradation - have addressed the two most divisive social justice issues of the last two centuries: slavery and abortion.

Saint Patrick, the former slave who spent his life freeing souls from their enslavement to mortal self-interests, surely saw slavery and abortion as equally degrading acts, both born of the same spiritual enslavement, both dismissive of God and his gift of eternal life.  But some from St. Patrick's flock would wander away, both in the Civil war fought not long ago, and in the culture-war being waged today.

With Notre Dame as its primary vehicle, this book visits both of those wars, and in the end examines the tragic irony of a Catholic university – dedicated to Mary the Immaculate Conception and built by the Fighting Irish - bestowing an honorary doctor of laws degree on an African-American whose pro-abortion actions as a legislator and legal executive have dishonored the memory of Martin Luther King Jr., who penned these prophetic words in "A Letter from a Birmingham Jail" on April 16, 1963:

> *I would agree with St. Augustine that "an unjust law is no law at all." Now, what is the difference between the two? How does one determine whether a law is just or unjust? A just law is a man-made code that squares with the moral law or the law of God. An unjust law is a code that is out of harmony with the moral law. To put it in the terms of St. Thomas Aquinas: An unjust law is a human law that is not rooted in eternal law and natural law. Any law that*

*uplifts human personality is just. Any law that degrades human personality is unjust...*

*There was a time when the church was very powerful—in the time when the early Christians rejoiced at being deemed worthy to suffer for what they believed. In those days the church was not merely a thermometer that recorded the ideas and principles of popular opinion; it was a thermostat that transformed the mores of society. Whenever the early Christians entered a town, the people in power became disturbed and immediately sought to convict the Christians for being "disturbers of the peace" and "outside agitators." But the Christians pressed on, in the conviction that they were "a colony of heaven," called to obey God rather than man. Small in number, they were big in commitment. They were too God-intoxicated to be "astronomically intimidated." By their effort and example, they brought an end to such ancient evils as infanticide and gladiatorial contests. Things are different now. So often the contemporary church is a weak, ineffectual voice with an uncertain sound. So often it is an arch-defender of the status quo. Far from being disturbed by the presence of the church, the power structure of the average community is consoled by the church's silent —and often even vocal — sanction of things as they are.*

*But the judgment of God is upon the church as never before. If today's church does not recapture the sacrificial spirit of the early church, it will lose its authenticity, forfeit the loyalty of millions, and be*

*dismissed as an irrelevant social club with no meaning
for the twentieth [and twenty-first] century.*

# 1

## THE IMMACULATE CONCEPTION OF NOTRE DAME

**Edward Sorin**

On November 22, 1842, the University of *Notre Dame du Lac* ("Our Lady of the Lakes") was founded in a frozen Indiana forest by a French priest with a child-like devotion to a holy little Hebrew girl named Mary, whom he knew by heart to be the blessed mother of God's Word made flesh.  To spread that Word, Father Edward Sorin of the Congregation of Holy Cross had traveled all the way from Le Mans, across the sea by steamship, up the Erie Canal by barge, and over miles of uncharted terrain on foot.  Upon his arrival, he would write that the virgin snow, softly blanketing that Indiana forest, had moved him to meditate on Mary's perfect nature, and filled him with a very special peace.

For eighteen centuries before Sorin, from the moment the crucified Christ first cast his gaze upon his beloved disciple John and urged him to "behold thy mother," millions of men and women of good will, Catholics and Protestants alike, were given to wonder about Mary, and what she's meant to man's salvation.

Then, a mere sixteen years after Sorin's snow covered inspiration, Mary herself made a startling revelation for those who would believe. On March 25, 1858, she appeared to a simple French peasant girl in a grotto at Lourdes, and uttered these extraordinary words: "I am The Immaculate Conception."

Coincidentally, the Catholic Church, after centuries of study, had found this profound notion about Mary's unique nature to be worthy of acceptance as official Church doctrine just four years before her alleged appearance at Lourdes.  And so, the Church's eventual acceptance of the authenticity of Our Lady's apparition came as little surprise, especially for those who had visited Lourdes, and witnessed the many healing miracles there.  However, explaining Mary's unique nature to others was another matter, and much misunderstanding still abounds about the doctrine of her Immaculate Conception after all these years.

Even among faithfully practicing Catholics, there are still some who mistakenly assume that the Immaculate Conception refers to Mary's virginal conception of Christ, rather than to her own Immaculate Conception, that is, her freedom from original sin within the womb of her own mother.  But the more unfortunate misunderstandings are those which have persisted among protestants who've rejected Catholicism largely on account of what it teaches about Mary.

First, with respect to the doctrine itself, the prudent protestant asserts, and understandably so, that Mary could not have been free from original sin at her conception because she herself rejoiced in God her "savior." Luke 1:47. However, as explained by John Duns Scotus, the Scots-Irish mystic who first proposed the doctrine of Mary's Immaculate Conception around 1308 A.D., there was certainly nothing to prevent God from saving Mary from the stain of original sin *before* her physical conception, if He'd chosen to do so. In fact, asserted Scotus, it made perfect sense for God to do just that, given that Mary was to be the bride of God's Holy Spirit, and the vessel who would nurture and birth His Son.  Hence, the angel Gabriel's greeting to Mary as "full of grace" by one translation, and "so highly favored" by another. Luke 1:28. (It's no accident that the Church celebrates the Feast of the Immaculate Conception on December 8th, the date of Scotus' death, and beyond ironic that his name is now a commonly used acronym for the Supreme Court of the United States.)

But another misunderstanding among protestants is more generic, inasmuch as it relates to Mary as but one among many "saints" to whom Catholics pray for help.  On this point, Deacon Eddie Ensley relates a poignant story.

Eddie had been raised in Georgia, where Catholics were a relatively rare commodity for which one needed a hunting license. He was studying to become a Presbyterian minister, but was curious about Catholicism.  He'd been intrigued by what he'd seen at services in Catholic churches, but found the fervent Catholic devotion to Mary (and other saints) to be a major stumbling block.  Maybe his uncle had been right after all when he explained to Eddie that he needed to know only two things about Catholics:  they're all alcoholics, and they worship statues.

In any event, Eddie had occasion to discuss these matters with a Catholic priest one day over a couple of Bloody Mary's. Eddie actually had one without the vodka, which the priest called a Bloody Shame.  The conversation went something like this:

"Eddie, do your Presbyterian friends ever ask you and their fellow parishioners to pray for them?"

"Well, sure."

"And do you and your Presbyterian friends believe that death is merely a passing from this life to the next, where we all remain part of the Body of Christ."

"Of course, they do."

"Well, then why is it so hard to understand when Catholics ask other members of the Body of Christ, who have led a good life here on earth, but have moved on to the next, to pray for them?  Especially someone as good as Mary?"

Suffice it to say that Eddie was unable to offer good answers to these last couple of questions, and converted to Catholicism some time later.

Now these observations are by no means offered to offend Presbyterians or encourage their conversion, but simply to shed more light on Mary's unique role in the mystery of man's salvation, and how she became the heart and soul of Sorin's Notre Dame.  He was in fact so taken by the wonder and beauty of what happened at Lourdes that he arranged for the construction of a replica grotto on the Notre Dame campus, where it remains today the site of many pilgrimages and prayers.

Indeed, it is fair to say that Father Sorin intended Our Lady's University and Grotto to be places where one could come to appreciate and embrace the Church's reverence for Mary as the Ark of God's ultimate covenant, the one by which He offered His only

Son, our Lord and Savior Jesus Christ, as the ultimate sacrifice for the forgiveness of our sins.  In full communion with Christ's Church, Sorin surely saw Mary as the woman identified by God Himself as the future enemy of the serpent from the Garden of Eden; as God's hand-crafted replacement for the arks built by Noah and Moses; and as the woman whose womb held fruit so blessed that the moment her greeting reached her cousin Elizabeth's ears, John the Baptist leaped within Elizabeth's womb.  And Mary said:

> "My soul proclaims the greatness
> of the Lord,
> and my spirit rejoices in God my
> Savior,
> for He has looked upon his lowly
> servant.
> From this day forward all
> generations will call me blessed,
> for the Almighty has done great
> things for me,
> and Holy is his Name.
> His mercy reaches from age to age,
> for those who fear Him.
> He has shown the strength of his
> arm,
> and has scattered the proud in
> their conceit.
> He has pulled down princes from
> their thrones,
> and has lifted up the lowly.

He has filled the hungry with good
things,
and the rich he has sent empty
away.
He has come to help his servant
Israel,
mindful of his mercy,
and according to the promise he
made to our ancestors,
to Abraham and his children for
ever."


Mary stayed with Elizabeth about three months and then went back home. <u>Luke</u> 1:41-55

Therefore, these profoundly telling images – of Mary ordained by God from the moment of her conception to be the spotless Mother of Christ; of an Immaculate Mary praising the presence of her unborn child, ordained by God from the moment of His conception to be man's eternal salvation; and of John the Baptist leaping for joy in the womb of the once barren Elizabeth – are precisely the right ones to bear in mind as this book takes a look at what's become of Father Sorin's Notre Dame.

# 2

# HERE COME THE IRISH

**Charles M. Carey**

*"Tomorrow, the world will be green for a day while we honor the patron saint of Erin.  Bighearted people of all nationalities will pause to applaud the contribution of the Irish to the civilization of the world. Best of all contributions made was the faith which they took with them wherever their wanderings took them. Patrick is a great saint of God; and therefore, a great saint of the church.  And if he belongs to the Church,*

*then he belongs to you.  That's why you should pray to St. Patrick, asking him to increase your Faith; bolster it; make it a living reality in your everyday life – keeping you aware that the trials and sufferings of this exile are as nothing when compared to the glory that awaits those who fight the good fight that overcomes the world!*

*Tomorrow you can take this one lesson from the Irish:  that they were never so poor in all their wanderings and sufferings that they bartered their Faith for the comforts of this life.  They had little to take with them wherever they went; but the Faith was always the most precious of their paltry possessions. Their spirit has made it easier for you to practice your Faith here in America today.  May the Fighting Irish always be with us!"*

The Reverend Charles M. Carey, CSC, to the students at Notre Dame, March 16, 1953.


Soon after Father Sorin's arrival in Indiana, fifteen faithful Irishmen joined him in the building of Notre Dame. Several of these men hailed from Ireland's County Meath, home to the sacred Hill of Tara.  Legend has it that scattered remnants of the lost tribes of Israel – in particular the Tribe of Dan - had migrated to Meath over a thousand years before the birth of Christ, and buried the ark of the covenant carrying the ten commandments, together with Jacob's so-called Stone of Destiny or Ladder to Heaven, deep into the Hill of Tara, turning it into the seat of power for many a pagan high king to come.  Legend further has it that Tara is also where Saint Patrick first took his 5th century stand against the Irish high kings of his time by igniting a bright Easter bonfire in open defiance of their pagan customs. No surprise, then, that Tara would in time become the site of several historical events involving the quest of Saint Patrick's Catholics to free themselves from centuries of brutal British oppression.

Patrick's love for the Irish had first arisen from what he'd witnessed of poor women – how they'd been abused by brutal slave-masters in the worst of ways, objects of unbridled lust in animals masquerading as men. Largely on account of that same lust, which corrupted King Henry the Eighth eleven centuries later, Patrick's Catholics would gather at Tara to take their first true stand against British persecution in 1641.

Unlike the pagan slave-masters confronted by Patrick, Henry was a sophisticated misogynist who clothed his abuse of women in the sacrament of marriage, six times, ending them with an annulment here, a beheading there. In 1509, He married Catherine of Aragon, his brother's widow, with the express permission of the Pope. However, when Henry grew tired of Catherine and began his affair with Anne Boleyn (after screwing Anne's sister Mary for a while), he went back to the Pope with bible in hand and annulment on his lips. But the Pope declined this time, explaining to the king that annulments required some failure to unite in the first place, and that his case just didn't qualify. Henry therefore sought the intercession of his Chancellor, Sir Thomas More, to persuade the Pope to change his mind. Thomas had helped Henry defend the Catholicism of his kingdom against the protests of men like Calvin and Martin Luther. But Thomas too declined to help him with the annulment, compelling Henry to choose which head would be his guide, the one which held his crown and once honored his Catholicism, or the one he longed to poke between Anne Boleyn's legs. Henry chose the latter, at least until he beheaded Ms. Boleyn in favor of wife number three, and thus by "virtue" of his crown began the Protestant Reformation.

Commencing in 1559, Queen Elizabeth, the only child of Henry and her beheaded mother Anne, aimed to end Catholicism in the British Isles by means of Penal Laws. At first, the penalty for being a bloody papist was mere imprisonment and loss of property, but when that didn't work, one was sometimes drawn and quartered. Priests were a particular target. While the laity could surrender their faith and stay (in fact they were forbidden to travel), the priests had to go, for their mere existence was an act of high treason punishable by brutal public execution. Meanwhile, confiscated Catholic property was transferred to implanted protestants, such as Scottish Presbyterians implanted in northern Ireland's Ulster region.

These penal laws and "plantations" persisted for 80 years before Patrick's Catholics finally found their fighting spirit by forming a confederation at the Hill of Tara on Christmas Eve, 1641, and launching their first Rebellion. From there, they fought for their freedom until 1649, when Oliver Cromwell seized power by executing England's King Charles and crushing Ireland's Confederacy by the bloodiest of massacres. In sum, he murdered most of the Catholic land-owning class and incinerated all visible remnants of the Roman Catholic Church.

Then, except for a brief respite from oppression under the reigns of Charles II and James II, the fate of Patrick's Catholics was sealed in 1690 for yet another century at the infamous Battle of the Boyne, not twenty miles from Tara. There, at the behest of the British, an imported Dutch puritan named William of Orange, together with his overwhelming army of Orangemen, would outnumber the Irish and French allied forces of his own father-in-law, James the Second, seizing for himself the triple crown of England, Scotland and Ireland.

Under Cromwell and William, then, came ugly enhancements to Elizabeth's Penal Laws. Patrick's Catholics were forbidden from functioning in any meaningful way. They were severed from whatever might lend them a little dignity, and reduced to starving beggars made to turn on friends and fellow family members for the sake of their own survival.  In fact, the injustices visited upon the Irish were so awful that Britain's own Sir Edmund Burke was moved to proclaim before Parliament that no greater "oppression, impoverishment and degradation of a feeble people and debasement in them of human nature itself [had] ever proceeded from the perverted ingenuity of man."  Indeed, the fate of Ireland's eighteenth-century Catholics was similar to that of African slaves in some respects, and likewise did some find themselves stuffed into the bellies of wretched ships bound for America.

But most would endure on the old sod, with *Erin go bragh* on their lips, at least until yet another Battle at Tara took its toll on May 26, 1798, marking the end of one more ill-fated Irish Rebellion, this one with its roots in those who'd already gone abroad as much as those who'd stayed at home.  For as Cromwell, William, and lastly George the Third, had each overplayed their hands, they'd unwittingly sown the seeds of revolution in the colonies across the sea.  There, a Jesuit-educated Irishman by the name of Charles Carroll, whose great grandfather had lost his land to Cromwell, and whose brother had lost his life to William at the Battle of the Boyne, would proudly join his protestant brethren as the sole Catholic co-signer of their Declaration of Independence from King George.  As Carroll would later put it, they had in fact declared "not only our independence of England but the toleration of all sects professing the Christian religion and communicating to them all equal rights."

This spirit of religious freedom found in Mr. Carroll and his friends became infectious, influencing the pro-Catholic French (on the verge of their own revolution) to join their struggling American brothers in arms against the bloody British, who'd recently roughed them up in the Seven Years War.  Consequently, King George was compelled to defend his hold on Ireland from threat of invasion by

France, and promised penal reforms for the Catholic Irish if they'd
make up militias to defend the Emerald Isle.  This they did, and in
return saw a series of concessions come their way, culminating in the
Catholic Relief Act of 1793.  Many of their rights and religious
freedoms were restored, but their participation in Parliament
remained strictly prohibited, as were their places in other positions of
power; and therein lied the last rub.  Without civil or political powers,
they'd remain without the means to make up for the fact that their
lands and livelihoods had been systematically stolen from them over
the last two centuries.

Oddly enough, it was some Scottish Presbyterians out of
Ulster, of all places, who would seek vindication for Irish Catholics
with whom they'd once waged war over the implantations first
instituted by Queen Elizabeth some 240 years earlier.  They called
themselves the Society of United Irishmen, professing Catholic
emancipation and Irish independence as their goals, though some of
them seemed interested mainly in the latter.  Notably among the
lukewarm was their leader, Theobald Wolfe Tone, who apparently
perceived the Pope as an "incarnation of evil," the Mass as
"abominable nonsense," and in his published *Argument on Behalf of
the Catholics of Ireland,* opined that it was British oppression alone
that kept the hopes of foolish papists invested in their priests.  In
other words, he believed that once Ireland gained independence, its
Catholics would come to their senses and join Protestant ranks.

Tone never got the chance to test his theory.  Instead, his ill-
conceived Battle at Tara in 1798 resulted in such a rout that it
enabled the British Parliament to adopt the Acts of Union which
created the so-called United Kingdom and ended Irish claims to
independence in the summer of 1800.  But there was one notable
bright side to this loss.

William Sampson had been one of Tone's United Irishmen,
and as fierce an advocate for Irish independence as any in the ranks.

But he was not an Ulster Presbyterian, and was by no means anti-Catholic.  Sampson hailed from Derry in County Cork - about as far away from Ulster as an Irishman can get - and was a member of the Church of Ireland (child of the Anglican Church of England after Henry the Eighth).  However, as a student of English Common Law in London, and then as a member of the Irish Bar, he had grown greatly troubled by the treatment of Catholics at the hands of his fellow Anglicans, and bravely began to speak out about it.  In fact, he was among the most formidable of advocates for Catholic emancipation during the Rebellion, and all the more so afterward when he came to the States.

Sampson hadn't planned to trade Ireland for America any more than the many starving souls forced to sail across the seas for survival, but in his love for them fell victim to the very same tyranny.  Arrested for his role in the insurrections, he was banished from Ireland to roam about Europe, embittered by his exile for eight years before landing in the port of New York, poetically, on July 4, 1806.  There, he must have been all the more moved by what he witnessed on the docks, day after day, month after month, as more and more of his sorely pressed brethren disembarked from near-death with barely more than their next breath.  No, the horrid Potato Famine hadn't hit them yet.  For that, those still at home would have to wait another forty years.  But history has had a way of obscuring the fact that owing to centuries of Anglican oppression, Patrick's Catholics had been living well below the poverty line long before the bloody potato went black with blight. Forced to farm ever smaller sections of what were once their own estates, they had already reached the point, well before the official famine, where the only crop that could sustain them was the more-per-plot potato.  Hence, the bitter end was but a matter of time, and only the most self-absorbed of god-forsaken bigots could have failed to see it coming.  Consider here the comments of one Charles Kingsley, an oft-quoted Anglican historian who had witnessed the impact of the Potato Famine upon the Irish: "I don't believe they're our fault. . . [T]hey are happier, better, and more comfortably lodged under our rule than they ever were. But to see white chimpanzees is dreadful. If they were black, one would not feel it so much, but their skins, except where tanned by exposure, are as white as ours."

Sampson himself would be spared his bonnie Erin's darkest days, and the shame of his fellow Anglican's awful bigotry, for he died in December, 1836, but not before breathing his very life into the cause of his Catholic brothers and sisters in Christ.

After arriving in the United States, Sampson had become a noted New York barrister, and the landmark legal case that providentially crossed his path was the People vs. Philips. However, neither the people nor Mr. & Mrs. Philips were Sampson's clients. Instead, he offered himself as a "friend of the court" ("*amicus curiae*") on account of the paramount "catholic question" that had come to light. (In cases of great legal importance, it is not unusual for attorneys to offer, and for courts to accept, the special assistance of outside counsel acting as *amicus curiae* in the interests of justice).

Daniel and Mary Philips had been charged with receiving stolen property. After their indictment, however, Mr. James Keating, the victim of the theft and apparently a member of the same Irish Catholic parish as the defendants, withdrew his complaint against them when his property was suddenly restored to him by Father Anthony Kohlmann, the French Jesuit pastor of the parish (St. Peter's - the first and only Roman Catholic parish in New York City as of 1813). Father Kohlmann, it seems, had heard someone's confession, and counseled restitution to the kind Mr. Keating. The prosecutor responded to this turn of events by trying to compel Father Kohlmann to tell what he'd heard in the confessional. When Father Kohlman refused to violate his sacred oath of secrecy, William Sampson stepped forward with the claim that compelling Father

Kohlman to testify, or punishing him for his refusal to do so, would curtail the Catholic sacrament of confession and thereby infringe upon the free exercise of religion protected by the First Amendment.

Sampson poured his heart and soul into the argument, reciting for the court the whole sordid history of anticatholic bigotry to which he'd been privy for all of his 50 years. In sum, he told the court that "[t]he rights, lives [and] liberties... of Catholics had been assailed through successive ages, in every wanton form that avarice, vengeance and malignity could devise," including their ongoing oppression right here in the former British colonies, not quite aired of the stench from overseas.

Listening intently was one Dewitt Clinton, the Irish protestant Mayor of the City of New York, who also served as Magistrate of the Court of General Sessions.  This Mr. Clinton, not unlike the 42nd U.S. President who would one day share his name, was a politically savvy member of what would eventually evolve into the Democratic Party about a decade down the road.  In fact, he had just been his party's nominee for president, losing the general election to James Madison (author of the 1st Amendment, ironically enough).  Now, with the rolls of Irish Catholics ever on the rise, and his plans to run for governor already in the making, Dewitt didn't have to wonder where his bread was buttered.  Besides, the esteemed Mr. Sampson had made matters easy.

"Ireland," lamented Magistrate Clinton, ". . . has been divided into . . . oppressors and the oppressed.  The Catholic has been disenfranchised of his civil rights, deprived of his inheritance, and excluded from the common rights of man."  But here in the land of liberty, he proudly declared, "[t]hey are protected by the laws and constitution of this country, in the full and free exercise of their religion, and this court can never countenance or authorize the application of insult to their faith, or of torture to their consciences." Dewitt's resounding decision earned him the abiding loyalty of Irish Catholics, who would help him get elected, and re-elected, as Governor of New York from 1817 through 1822. In return, he would successfully press the flesh to fund construction of the Erie Canal, an enormous public works project that was right up the unskilled Irishman's alley, putting thousands to work for a very long time.

Regarded by some, once done, as the eighth wonder of the world, the Erie Canal wove the waters of its Great Lakes namesake at Buffalo to their wedding with the Hudson River at Albany, a span of some 363 miles carved through all kinds of testy terrain. A full forty feet wide and four feet deep, three high-spirited lads of Irish folk lore are said to have shoveled a fifty-foot length of it in under six days at the first phase of construction, setting the stage for the legions of legendary Irish laborers who would follow for the next seven years. Indeed, a retired Ivy professor named Payson, who'd passed his younger years along the canal, would one day look back on those "wild Irish bog trotters," working "knee deep in the wet muck" by day, and "fighting drunk" with their shillelagh sticks come Saturday night. One group, digging by day and boarding by night on the farmlands of a Presbyterian Scot by the name of Mary Archibald, had so endeared themselves to her that she invited them to a family wedding, then went to bail them out when a riot at the reception hall had landed them in jail.

Some had been recruited right off the docks. Others serving time for questionable convictions were pardoned by Governor Clinton and put to work. They were the "shanty Irish," shoveling through leech-filled muck enough to make a grown man shudder, then off to sleep in their shacks full of flies and mosquitoes. Their pay was little more than a dollar a day (less if they took some in food, washing and whiskey), but this was ten times the wage of an unskilled man in search of work on the Old Sod, so for them 'twas something to sing about (not that an Irishman ever needed an excuse). This, then, from *Paddy on the Canal*:

*When I came to this wonderful empire,*
*It filled me with the greatest surprise.*
*To see such a great undertaking,*
*On the like I never opened my eyes.*
*To see a full thousand brave fellows,*
*At work among mountains so tall.*
*A dragging a chain through the mountains,*
*To strike a line for the canal, So....*

*I entered with them for a season,*
*My monthly pay for to draw.*
*And being of very good humor,*
*I often sang "Erin go bragh."*
*Our provision it was very plenty,*
*To complain we'd no reason at all.*
*I had money in every pocket,*
*While working upon the canal.*

*When at night we all rest from our labor,*
*Sure, but our rent is all paid.*
*We laid down our pick and our shovel,*
*Like-wise our axe and our spade.*
*We all set a joking together,*
*There was nothing our minds to enthrall.*
*If happiness be in this wide world,*
*I am sure it is on the canal.*

From <u>The Canaller's Songbook</u>, Hullfish
Verses from The American Vocalist (1853).

The "great undertaking" was completed in 1825, providing the
preferred way west for many an immigrant settler until the trains
took over.  Included among these courageous canal-riders out to
manifest their destiny (and ours) was the indomitable Reverend
Edward Sorin and his band of Irish brothers, beneficiaries of the
back-breaking efforts of their Irish Catholic brethren before them.  To
be sure, Sorin had also come with some of his French countrymen,
and their contributions to North American Catholicism are
incalculable, but 'twas the Irish who'd help Sorin long sustain Notre
Dame, and make it the mystical marvel that it is to this day.  Here,
then, are their Irish Christian (and Holy Cross congregational)
names, those first novitiates who would trim the timber, build the
bunks, farm the fields, and minister to the first young minds who
made up the first student body.  Sons of Erin all, listed first are the lot
that came from County Meath, home to the sacred Hill of Tara -

Mr. Michael Connelly (Brother Patrick) – Born
circa 1798 in *County Meath* (where and when the Battle
of Tara must have told his parents it was time to go), he
entered the novitiate in 1842 and helped Sorin found,

farm and forge Notre Dame, where he remained until he died on April 18, 1867.  Nineteen when the canal's construction started, he may well have been one of the men who carved the way to South Bend;

Mr. James Tully (Brother Peter) – Born in 1808, also in *County Meath*, and also entering the novitiate in 1842 and helping Sorin found, farm, and forge Notre Dame before finding another vocation in 1847;

Mr. John Bray de la Hoyde (Brother Paul) – Born in 1816, also in *County Meath*, and also entering the novitiate in 1842, he arrived at Notre Dame in February of 1843 and was the first of the pioneer Brothers to die there, on May 27, 1844;

Mr. Thomas Everard (Brother Ignatius) – Born in 1817, also in *County Meath* (at Drogheda, site of the Battle of the Boyne), and also entering the novitiate in 1842.  He arrived at Notre Dame in 1843, and died there in April of 1899;

Mr. William Coffey (Brother Timothy) – Born in 1804, also in *County Meath*, he entered the novitiate in 1845 and labored there until his death in 1873.

Mr. Felix Riley (Brother Jerome) – Born in 1815, also in *County Meath*, he also entered the novitiate in 1845 and also labored there until his death in November, 1871.

Now, the nine other inaugural Irishman, no less important, who came from other counties, or from counties unknown, to help Sorin forge a strong foundation for their mother, Notre Dame -

Mr. Patrick Day (Brother Alexis) – Born in 1819 in County Limerick, he entered the novitiate in 1849 and died at Notre Dame in 1854;

Mr. Thomas Dowling (Brother Anthony) – Born in 1780 in Ireland, (County unknown), he entered the novitiate in 1844 and took his final vows on his death bed in August, 1846, dying at Notre Dame in 1847;

Mr. Dennis Rogan (Brother Augustine) – Born in 1793 in County Down, he entered the novitiate in 1849 and was a baker at Notre Dame until his death in 1876;

Mr. Timothy O'Neil (Brother Basil) – Borne in 1810 in Ireland (County unknown), he entered the novitiate and help Sorin found and forge Notre Dame in November of 1842, where he remained until his transfer to Fort Wayne in 1846;

Mr. William Rodgers (Brother John Baptist) – Born in 1815 in County Kildare, he entered the novitiate in 1845 but died in October of 1846;

Mr. James Flynn (Brother Michael) – Born in 1810 in County Connaught, he entered the novitiate in 1845 and served as Notre Dame's laundryman, fire chief, boiler man and night watchman, respectively, until his death in 1884;

Mr. Finton Moore (Brother Stephen) – Born in 1811 in County Queens, he entered the novitiate in 1844 and served as Notre Dame's porter, sacristan, fundraiser, supervisor of apprentices and assistant postmaster, respectively, until his death in 1869;

Mr. Thomas John Walsh (Brother Victor) – Born in 1810 in County Dublin, he entered the novitiate at Notre Dame in 1848 but was transferred to New Orleans not long before his death in 1852;

Mr. John O'Sullivan (Brother William) – Born in 1815 in Ireland (County unknown), he entered the novitiate in 1842 and helped Sorin found and forge Notre Dame until he changed vocations in 1847.

Today, there's an all but obscure little cemetery near the northwest corner of the campus that is home to many of these fifteen men, and others who'd come after, including one very special man by the name of Patrick Connors (Brother Paul of the Cross, about whom there'll be more a bit later in this book.)  Legend has it that early in the morning, on six or seven Saturdays each Fall, if one listens very closely in the quiet, one can hear them in the breezes that blow through the trees, singing softly but surely for the ears of all the Fighting Irish faithful to hear:

*Well I remember the leaves a fallin'*
*And far off music like pipes a callin'*
*And I remember the golden morning*
*I saw the long ranks as they were forming*

*And there's a magic in the sound of their name*
*Here come the Irish of Notre Dame*

*The pilgrims follow by sacred waters*
*And arm in arm go the sons and daughters*
*The drums are rolling and forward bound*
*They're calling spirits up from the ground*

*And there's a magic in the sound of their name*
*Here come the Irish of Notre Dame.*

(Here Come The Irish, by Jim Tullio and John Scully)

# 3

# THE WAGES OF WHITENESS

In 1843, right around the time that their brothers from County Meath were arriving in Indiana to help build Notre Dame, a hundred thousand Irishmen had come to County Meath and swarmed the Hill of Tara to attend a "monster meeting" on behalf of another six million of their fellow countrymen scattered throughout Ireland. They'd come to hear Daniel O'Connell assure them of what their hearts had longed to hear - that *Erin go bragh* belonged to them, and 'twould one day be returned to them, don't fear.

Born in County Kerry about a year before Charles Carroll claimed colonial independence from the English King, Daniel O'Connell would spend the whole of his adult life staking the same claim of independence for the colony called Ireland. No fan of the Irish Rebellion, O'Connell strived for Catholic emancipation and Erin independence by brave but peaceful means. He would pick up where William Sampson left off when he was banished in 1798. O'Connell turned barrister that very same year, having studied English common law at London's ancient Lincoln's Inn, the same *alma mater* of Sir Thomas More some three hundred years earlier. How poetic and providential, then, that O'Connell would strive to complete the task that his colleague St. Thomas had started – Roman Catholicism saved from destruction by royal tyrants.

In a speech echoing Patrick Henry's heart-leaping "liberty or death," O'Connell began his heady days in Dublin on the heels of the Acts of Union in 1800, declaring that his fellow Catholics would sooner suffer the penal laws than surrender their Erin.  It was a battle cry that would carry him to unrivaled leadership in the Irish Catholic community for nearly fifty years, until his death in 1847.  He died while on pilgrimage to Rome, with the wish on his lips that his heart would complete the journey to eternal rest in the Eternal City, but that his body belonged to dear Dublin.  He'd succumbed to a cerebral disease which first plagued him when he was prosecuted and imprisoned for sedition soon after that so-called "monster meeting" he'd convened on the Hill of Tara in 1843.  His conviction was eventually reversed, resulting in his release, but not before the whole affair had taken an awful toll.  Then came the infamous Potato Famine, whereupon he would summon what remained of his wits and wherewithal to beg before bloody Parliament on behalf of his perishing people.  It was the last public act of his selfless, legendary life.

Given that he failed to foil the Union in his lifetime, and died departing Erin in the midst of her worst misery, one wonders whether in weaker moments he thought himself a failure, this man who'd tirelessly summoned, one by one, the whole of Erin's Catholics into common cause.  From a single "Catholic committee" convened in 1810 Dublin, he'd spawned a close-knit network of local committees that evolved into a national Catholic Association come 1823.  With membership dues put at a penny per month, an army of peasants some six million strong would pool their pence into a powerful force for freedom.  Six years later, in 1829, the long-reigning Orangemen "struck their colors" in surrender to the cause of Catholic Emancipation, and Daniel O'Connell took his seat as the first Catholic member of British Parliament.  Twelve tumultuous years later, in 1841, he took office as the Lord Mayor of Dublin, and from that perch pressed for Union Repeal, a push that reached its fateful peak at Tara. There the battle would end once again, in tragic irony.

In 1833, a mere four years after he'd so proudly assumed his seat in Parliament, Daniel O'Connell had been equally proud to help pass the Slavery Abolition Act, forever ending that scourge of humanity in all the British Empire. O'Connell abhorred slavery with no less fervor than he'd brought to the Irish Catholic cause, and was an outspoken supporter of its abolition, both in the UK and the USA. However, while his American brethren were poised to help him break the UK Union, they wanted no part of O'Connell's appeals for abolition in their own backyard.  Irish-American Catholics, children of that former slave named Saint Patrick, and themselves just freed from centuries of servitude, cared not for the cause of African-American emancipation. O'Connell called to them, in the name of Patrick, but they could not hear, his cries drowned out by the dins of a democratic republic in danger of self-destruction. Nevertheless, he could not bring himself to retreat from so seminal an issue as the cardinal sin of slavery, even if it meant losing crucial overseas support for his long-cherished goal of Irish independence.  And that is in fact what happened.  As a consequence, America would wage a bloody civil war, while Ireland would wait another 80 years, and see the loss of thousands more lives, before achieving independence in 1922.

Why wouldn't Irish-American Catholics support abolition, and if they had, would a civil war over slavery have been averted, as it had been in every other nation in the civilized world?  Moreover, if they'd stood fast with O'Connell when he'd needed them most, would an Irish Free State have come quicker and cleaner, without the strife of another 75 years, the bloody Irish Rising of 1916, or the three-year War of Independence ending in 1921?  How could their trips on the famine ships have sent them reeling backward? How could they have failed to see the stains and smell the blood that had soaked into the bellies of those very same ships, once crude shuttles for so many slaves?  How could they have clung to their Catholicism through three centuries of brutal British oppression, only to ignore Christ in the cries of the shackled black man?

One answer lies in the failed leadership of five American bishops, each pivotal in their patronage to and influence over the politically-driven dictates of a Democratic party that was dead set against abolition.  Listed from North to South, they were:  John Bernard Fitzpatrick, Bishop of Boston, 1846 – 1866, the son of Kings County Ireland immigrants; John Joseph Hughes, Archbishop of New York, 1842 – 1864, born in County Tyrone;  Francis Patrick Kenrick, Bishop of Philadelphia from 1842 to 1851 and Archbishop of Baltimore from 1851 to 1863, born in County Dublin; John England, born in County Cork and from 1820 to 1842 the Bishop of Charleston (an enormous diocese that included all of North Carolina, South Carolina and Georgia); and Patick Neeson Lynch, born in County Monaghan and also Bishop of Charleston from 1858 to 1882.

Each failed to advocate for abolition despite centuries of encyclicals from Rome in advance of the U.S. Civil War.  In 1850, while beatifying St. Peter Claver for his extraordinary service to black Africans in bondage, Pope Pius IX identified the involuntary enslavement of innocent men as mankind's "supreme villany," capping four hundred years of unequivocal Papal condemnation initiated by Pope Eugene IV in 1435, when he declared slavery to be an illicit and evil sin inviting immediate excommunication; and continued by Pope Pius II in 1462, when he called slavery a "great crime;" by Pope Paul III in 1537, when he attributed slavery to Satan himself; and right through to Pope Pius IX's immediate predecessor, Pope Gregory XVI, whose 1839 encyclical entitled *In Supremo Apostolatus,* proclaimed in no uncertain terms that -

*We warn and adjure earnestly in the Lord faithful Christians of every condition that no one in the future dare to vex (or bother unjustly) anyone, despoil him of his possessions, reduce to servitude, or lend aid and favor to those who give themselves up to these practices, or exercise that inhuman traffic by which the Blacks, as if they were not men but rather animals, having been brought into servitude, in no matter what way, are, without any distinction, in contempt of the rights of justice and humanity, bought, sold, and devoted sometimes to the hardest labor.  Further, in the hope of gain, propositions of purchase being made to the first owners of the Blacks, dissensions and almost perpetual conflicts are aroused in these regions.*

*We reprove, then, by virtue of Our Apostolic Authority, all the practices above-mentioned as absolutely unworthy of the Christian name.  By the same Authority, we prohibit and strictly forbid any Ecclesiastic or lay person from presuming to defend as permissible this traffic in Blacks under no matter what pretext or excuse, or from publishing or teaching in any manner whatsoever, in public or privately, opinions contrary to what We have set forth in these Apostolic Letters. (From the current Official Vatican translation.)*

Alas, these Irish bishops had gone as deaf as the rest of O'Connell's tribe, lost in their new land and wrongly trying to reconcile their anti-abolitionist attitudes with what had come from Rome.  They argued, in essence, that while Pope Gregory had certainly denounced the slave trade, he had not denounced mere slavery, a preposterous assertion that some historians have seen fit to sustain all the way to the present day (see, e.g., The University of Notre Dame's Dean of Arts & Letters, John T. McGreevy, in *Catholicism and American Freedom*, W.W. Norton & Co. 2003, at p.50, 52).  Abolition, they urged, was sure to visit greater misery on the black man, not to mention havoc on the economy of the South, and stress upon the unskilled labor market in the North.  Better to leave well enough alone, they said.  Leave these pitifully dependent black creatures to the charitable ministries of a loving Church, and the certain paternal kindness of the genteel South.

Not surprisingly, first among them to advance this nonsense was the South's beloved Bishop England, who squandered much of his earthly time and talents squaring slavery with Catholicism in order to smoothly assimilate Catholics into the Southern culture. Indeed, his eminence saw slavery as quite alright with God, and so did himself and his ilk the dubious service of taking a single word from Pope Gregory entirely out of context, and turning it into the illicit linchpin of a self-delusional argument.  England would emphasize the word "unjustly" in the Vatican's "vex (or bother) unjustly" as supposed proof of Pope Gregory's alleged intention to distinguish the evils of selling slaves from the virtues of merely owning them, whereas Gregory's true intention (as explained in Father Joel Panzer's excellent treatise entitled *The Popes and Slavery* (Alba House, 1996)) was to distinguish the unjust enslavement of innocent men from the "just-title servitude" of criminals, enemy combatants, and those who freely offered themselves in service to others.  Thus, had Bishop England invited his fellow episcopals to explain that it was ok to keep the black man in shackles against his will, even if he'd committed no crime and worn no enemy uniform, so long as his enslavement was purely economic.  In other words, announced Baltimore's Archbishop Kenrick, the treatment of the slave as a thing was unjust, but not the ownership of his labor. Indeed, Kenrick went so far as to call for the recapture and return of fugitive slaves, citing St. Paul's time-worn words to Philomen for support, while altogether ignoring the plight of St. Patrick, for whom he'd conveniently forgotten his kinship. (*Nota Bene:* The Vatican's original translation, from the Latin "<u>injuste vexare</u>" to the English "bother unjustly", has been reduced to "vex" alone, perhaps to signal confused historians that Panzer has it right, and that England and his fellow sub-vicars of Christ had gotten it all wrong.)

Such revolting sophistry must have made O'Connell sick, even as it sanitized the political passions of Irish-American parishioners sitting in the pews. The pews of sacred places like St. Patrick's (Old) Cathedral in New York, where parishioners who'd been meat-hooked by Tammany Hall's tough guys into towing the anti-abolitionist line from the moment they'd stepped off the boats, would look with rapt attention toward their awesome Archbishop and hang on his every word.

There's an old New York joke that, lo and behold, begins with an Irishman raising his glass. "Let's toast to the two greatest institutions in New York – Archbishop Hughes and Tammany Hall," he says, to which his friend drinks and then replies, "Well alright then, but what's the second one?" Now, given the hard-earned reputation of Tammany's men for the strong-armed tactics made famous by Boss Tweed, one would think they'd have had the upper hand when dealing with a cleric. With Hughes, however, dubbed "Dagger John" by the abolitionists within the Whig party who feared more than reviled him, one suspects that the shoe was often on the other foot. Case in point: Catholic schools. It was Hughes who had strong-armed Tammany, from his own hall that he'd named "Carroll" (after Charles Carroll, co-signer of the Declaration of Independence), into helping him pass the Maclay Act, which curbed anti-papist influence over New York's "public" schools in 1841, and paved the way for parochial schools to spread throughout the land.  In fact, Hughes himself founded Fordham University (this author's alma mater) that same year, and later played an important role in the formation of Manhattan, Manhattanville, and Mount St. Vincent Colleges.  In addition, he helped give birth to several Catholic hospitals and orphanages, and recruited scores of Irish sisters to staff them.  Thus, there was much to commend this special man to the hearts of his Catholic faithful, Irish and non-Irish alike.  Even so, the sad fact remains that he railed against abolition, and thus led his flock down the shameful path of prolonging the sickness of slavery in the deep and deeply ill South.

On the other hand, it is not hard to empathize with the bishops' attitudes, but for their misguided paternalistic bigotry toward the black man.  After all, Hughes had spent his first 20 years in Ireland, the son of a dirt-poor farmer persecuted by anti-papists, before coming to America in 1817 to experience only more of the same (his home was ransacked after the Maclay Act), as had his fellow Irish bishops to one sad degree or another.  So, whether it was him telling Tammany, Tammany telling him, or each inciting the other, Hughes undoubtedly harbored some hatred-bred beliefs about what the Whig party really wanted to do, as did an Irish rank and file already wed to a tarnished Democratic party.  The days of Dewitt Clinton, their antidote to Tammany, were long gone, and so there was no one in power to bid them think twice about the virtues of peaceful abolition.  No, if anti-papists favored the Whig party, and the Whig party favored abolition, then their motives must be sinister.  In short, they suspected that the Whigs wanted blacks to take work away from the Irish, if not to bring an end to the Union altogether and return rule to the bloody royalists.  Truth be told, the Whigs were more of a "catch-all" party than Irish Catholics had imagined, appealing to voters with conflicting views on a wide variety of topics, slavery and abolition included.  They were, in a way, an early experiment in the inexact science of so-called "big-tent" politics.

That said, with the fog having lifted over the last hundred and fifty years, there is simply no ignoring the unhappy fact that Archbishop Hughes had advocated for bigotry, softer but shameful nonetheless.  When an editorial appearing in the October 12, 1861 edition of his Archdiocesan newspaper known as the *Metropolitan Record* asserted that slavery existed by "divine permission of God's providence," and is not a crime or moral transgression, but a good way "for human masters to . . . take care of these unfortunate people," it ignited a firestorm of criticism, compelling the Archbishop to speak in his own defense.  For example, here is what he wrote to the French *Journal des Debats,* as republished in the February 20, 1862 edition of the *New York Times:*

> *[A]lthough I have never written or said a word in favor of Slavery, I am decidedly opposed to Abolitionism, as it is understood in America. . .*
>
> *The guiding chiefs of the Abolition movement in the Northern States appear inspired by fanatical zeal on a question which concerns the most-grave interests of the Southern States and the whole country.*
>
> *Slavery is the 'sick man' of the United States. The Abolitionists of the North, where Slavery does not exist, see the situation of the 'sick man' at a distance through a telescope.  Their exaggerated views influence their prescriptions.*
>
> *There are several cities in the South where Slavery is perpetual, and where the yellow fever and the cholera are frequent visitors.  One could not suppose that any archbishop or bishop could wish to*

*make himself the advocate of cholera or yellow fever.
What he would do would be to abandon the treatment
of these maladies to the inhabitants of the cities where
they prevail, and the physicians who know in what
manner they can be cured or mitigated; but our
Abolitionist doctors of the North, who dwell far from
Slavery and these epidemics, would wish, in the
interest of humanity, to burn the cities of the South,
which they would consider as the most prompt means
of purifying the air, of destroying and exterminating
by a single remedy, the cholera, Slavery, and the
yellow fever.*

*There are in the Southern States four million of
slaves. Abolish Slavery all of a sudden, and what will
become of them? What will become of their masters?
What will become of the products of their labor, of
which Europe has such need? The Abolition Party of
North America take no account of all this.*

In reply, the French journal wrote this, also republished in the
February 20, 1862 edition of the *New York Times*:

*While denying that he said a word in favor of
Slavery, the [Archbishop] avows that he is decidedly
opposed to Abolitionism, as it is understood in America
. . .*

*To reconcile this opposition to Slavery with this
antipathy to Abolitionism seems to us a very difficult
task. We believe that there are not two ways of
understanding Abolitionism, and when one is opposed
to slavery, it appears to us that the best way of*

*proving it is to favor and prosecute Abolition by every possible means even at the risk of finding himself accused of a 'fanatical zeal' by the Archbishop of New York, and by those who abhor slavery after a fashion.*

*Our reverend correspondent, who is desirous of engaging in a controversy with us on this subject, ingeniously compares Slavery to the yellow fever and the cholera, which are prevalent diseases in the Southern cities, and thinks that, without making himself the advocate of yellow fever and cholera, the only course he could follow would be to abandon the treatment of the diseases to the populations who suffered from them, and to the physicians who know the manner of treating them.  This reasoning is admirable, but the Archbishop of New York forgets to examine the question to ascertain whether the people of the Northern States should not have the right to take necessary measures for protecting themselves against yellow fever and cholera, when their fellow-citizens of the South are doing all that they can to infect the pure atmosphere, and spread and propagate upon Northern territory the plagues with which they themselves are infested. . .*

Indeed, it was this same sad revelation – that the South was seeking to spread its disease – which led the once wavering Orestes Brownson, perhaps the most widely read and respected lay Catholic intellectual of his time, to argue at last for abolition.  He saw that an increasingly aggressive South, no doubt emboldened by the complicity of an entire corporation of Irish Catholic bishops, had proved itself responsible for causing the war.  Brownson's epiphany had finally come after four years of agonizing over the conduct of his fellow Catholic, Chief Justice Roger Taney, in ruling that the black man was not a whole person entitled to protection by the US Constitution in *Dred Scott v. Sandford*, 1857. Here is how Brownson had reacted to Taney's decision:

> *Mr. Chief Justice Taney is a Catholic, and knows that from 1462 the Popes have condemned on pain of excommunication, the reduction of African negroes to slavery . . . We regret that in giving the opinion of the court the learned judge did not recollect what he is taught by his religion, namely the unity of the race, that all men by the natural law are equal, and that negroes are men, and therefore as to their rights must be regarded as standing on the same footing with white men. Brownson's Quarterly Review. April, 1862*

As Brownson aligned himself in philosophy with that of the Frenchmen from the *Journal des Débats*, he also found a friend in Edward Sorin, that other Frenchman of Notre Dame fame. When Brownson turned abolitionist, subscriptions to his once successful *Quarterly Review* magazine suffered, and so did his income. So, in November of 1862, six weeks after Lincoln's first Emancipation Proclamation, in stepped Sorin to invite the heady Brownson to teach at Notre Dame. Sorin would thus seem to have been another French abolitionist at heart, though he was never outspoken on the subject, and counseled the same circumspection among his Notre Dame staff and students, who hailed from both the Northern and Southern states alike. That said, one surmises that he'd harbored heartfelt sympathies for Brownson, especially at the news of his rebuke by Archbishop Hughes for having voiced the virtues of abolition at Fordham's Commencement Exercises of 1861. After all, as Sorin was reaching out to Brownson, the "Bulla House" across the street from Notre Dame's campus Biology building was serving as a way station for fugitive slaves enroute to freedom in Canada, and the great Union General William Sherman of Marching Through Georgia fame was settling his family in South Bend and sending his sons to Notre Dame.

In any event, Brownson at first responded to Sorin's offer with enthusiasm, but due to his declining health and advancing age, would balk at the ambitious curriculum which Sorin had in mind for him. Still, Sorin kept up their correspondence, persuading Brownson to publish work on one of Sorin's favorite topics, the Blessed Virgin Mary, for Notre Dame's brand-new *Ave Maria* magazine, circa 1866. Of Mary, Brownson wrote:

> *She was conceived without original stain, but . . . could no more enter the kingdom of heaven without [redemption] than the meanest of Adam's posterity. The redeeming . . . grace was as necessary in her case as in ours; but in her case was applied in the first instant of her . . . Immaculate Conception. . .*
>
> *Mary's . . . great merit is in willing only what [Jesus] wills, and in doing only what He . . . enables her to do . . . He makes her the channel or medium of His grace and favors to men because He loves and delights to honor her by granting them at her request, but it is He who grants them. . .*
>
> *In honoring Mary as the mother of God we honor maternity elevated to its highest possible dignity. . . . It is mainly to the low estimate in which maternity is held among the heathen that we must attribute in both ancient and modern times the prevalence of child-murder . . . in China, India, and perhaps in all nations on which the light of the Gospel sheds no ray. . .*

*. . . Under Christianity this estimate is corrected, and motherhood, as a necessary consequence of elevating marriage to a sacrament, is elevated in some sense to the spiritual order, and made a holy function. . .*

*. . . When God himself condescends to be born of woman, and woman becomes the mother of Him who is the Creator of heaven and earth, and the Redeemer and Savior of mankind, motherhood becomes almost a divine function, and something to be treated with reverence and awe, for not only did Mary bring forth Him who is Christ the Lord, but every human mother brings forth a child destined, if true to the law of his Maker, to be one with Christ, one with God, and a real partaker of the divine nature. . .*

*. . . Every human mother may chant with Mary: "My soul doth magnify the Lord . . . For he that is mighty hath done great things to me, and holy is his name." It is a great and sacred thing to be the mother of a child, if we look to the destiny to which every child may aspire. . .*

*Now, devotion to Mary . . . brings all these great and solemn truths home to our minds and our hearts. We are led to reflect on the great mysteries of the Incarnation . . . and dignity of motherhood, the sacredness and worth of every child born of woman, and the obligation to reverence the mother, to provide for the child's present and future welfare, and to conform society itself . . . to the virtues honored in the maternity of Mary. From this it is easy to see that devotion to Mary has and must have a most salutary influence on all domestic relations, and on the manners*

*and morals, and therefore on the progress of society
itself. . .*

*The nations are in need of this influence still.
Christendom is lapsing anew into heathenism, and the
abominations I have referred to as existing in heathen
nations are reviving in nations that profess to be
Christian . . .*

No doubt these profound and prophetic words were but one
reason why, when Brownson died in 1876, Sorin saw fit to bring his
body to rest within the crypt of the memorial chapel that still bears
his name beneath Notre Dame's Basilica of the Sacred Heart.  In
addition, aside the Basilica stands an early dormitory, since
converted to different use, but ever to be known as old Brownson
Hall.

Returning, then, to that other slavery - not of women for the
sake of lust, but of men for the sake of money - Brownson must have
wondered, in his waning years, whether war would have been averted
if only Hughes and his fellow bishops had worked in careful unison to
curtail that cardinal sin, and reconcile the nation, north to south.
Witness: what happened in New York.  The weight of historical
evidence is that up until the 1840's, when Tammany took over
Manhattan's "old Sixth Ward" in earnest, emancipated African
Americans and the recently arrived immigrant Irish shared a dirt
poor but for the most part peaceful coexistence in the so-called "Five
Points", that same wretched, rough and tumble neighborhood which
*The Gangs of New York* would soon enough make famous.  It was, in
its way, the prototype - the petri dish and the melting pot of liberty's
promise, that alas became a study in the ravages of bigotry.  What if,
while Hughes was in power from 1842 to 1864, he had heard the cries
of O'Connell and assumed the great mantle of advancing the cause of

peaceful abolition and shared assimilation?  Instead, he would rail against it as early as the eve of his elevation to bishop in 1842, and for the next two decades inspire his Irish flock to earn, in the words of David Roediger, "the wages of whiteness," by putting ugly distance between themselves and their black brothers.  Indeed, it was not until the bloody Irish wake at Gettysburg had backwashed over the remains of his New York flock that the Archbishop would at long last act, not six months before his own death, to help bring the beginnings of an end to the murderous bloodshed that his complicity and intransigence had surely aided.  It was July of 1863.  Tens of thousands of Irish-faithful had already slaughtered each other at Antietam, then Fredericksburg, and finally Gettysburg, and now New York was deeply under siege in its own war known as the Draft Riots .

. . .

# 4

# We Were the Fighting Irish

***Absolution Under Fire***
**(Reverend William Corby at Gettysburg)**
**By Paul Henry Wood, Notre Dame: 1891**

After the Civil War started, Archbishop Hughes had voiced
support for President Lincoln in his quest to preserve the Union, and
so agreed to serve as his overseas ambassador in that regard.
However, he would mince no words with Lincoln when it came to
emancipation, declaring that "[w]e Catholics, and a vast majority of
our troops in the field, have not the slightest idea of carrying on a war
that costs so much in blood and treasure just to gratify a clique of

Abolitionists in the North." In hindsight, his mixed message of partial patriotism may be seen as emblematic of more than just one man's tortured mindset, but of the war being waged within all Irish as they wrestled with what was right, a war that would spill itself out from their insides and onto bloody battlefields from Richmond to Atlanta and back. In *The Irish Americans, A History,* University of Notre Dame Professor Emeritus Jay P. Dolan poignantly profiles this bitter conflict:

> *"Once the Civil War began, the Irish joined the armies of both the North and the South. As many as 140,000 Irishmen were found under the Union flag. Another 30,000 wore the colors of the Confederacy. In terms of their proportion to the general population, the Irish were also the most underrepresented immigrant group fighting for the Union. A major reason for this was their allegiance to the Democratic Party and their opposition to Republican support for emancipation. Those in the North, where the bulk of the Irish lived, would fight to preserve the Union, but their ardor cooled considerably once President Lincoln emancipated the slaves. This coolness, if not outright opposition to the abolition of slavery, was not only a trademark of the Democratic Party, but also a distinctive characteristic of the American Catholic Church, which claimed the allegiance of the Irish.*
>
> *During the war many regiments in both the North and the South were predominantly Irish. One of the most famous was the Irish Brigade, led by the charismatic Thomas Francis Meagher. Meagher was an Irish rebel whom the British had imprisoned because of his involvement in the movement for Irish independence.*

*After doing time in an English prison, Meagher was sent off to a penal colony in Australia in 1849, banished for life from Ireland. Three years later he escaped to the United States, where he found success in New York as a noted orator and lawyer. Once the Civil War broke out, he joined the Union army. Before long he organized a brigade made up of Irish recruits whom he persuaded to join the battle with him to preserve the Union. Known as the Irish Brigade, they fought in several bloody battles. At Antietam, where the casualties were the worst for any single day of the war – some twenty-three thousand men – the Irish Brigade lost as many as 60 percent of its soldiers.*

      *Next was Fredericksburg, where Meagher led the Irish Brigade against Irish Confederate soldiers, one of whom was Willy Mitchel, son of John Mitchel, a renowned Irish nationalist. In the 1840s John Mitchel had abandoned a career in law to join Meagher and other young Irishmen in a campaign to gain independence for Ireland. A fierce nationalist, Mitchel discovered a new career as a publicist, writing for the Nation, the voice of Young Ireland, the name given to his band of nationalists. Mitchel wrote, 'The people's sovereignty – the land and sea and air of Ireland for the people of Ireland – this is the gospel that the heavens and earth are preaching, and all hearts are secretly burning to embrace . . .It is the mighty, passionate struggle of a nation hastening to be born into new national life.' Such language was too much for the authorities, who arrested Mitchel for treason. Found guilty, he was transported to Australia in 1848. Five years later he escaped, fleeing to the United States.*

*Eventually he settled in Tennessee, where he became a staunch defender of slavery, believing 'negro slavery the best state of existence for the negro, and the best for his master.' Supporting the Confederacy, he wrote dispatches on the war for a Richmond newspaper. All three of his sons joined the Confederate army; two of them, John and Willy, died in battle, and their brother, James, was wounded. One of the ironies of Irish history is that Meagher and Mitchel, two renowned nationalists joined in a common struggle for Ireland's independence, ended up in the United States on opposite sides during the Civil War.*

*At Fredericksburg, the Union army suffered a disastrous defeat. As at Antietam, the Irish Brigade endured heavy losses. One soldier described the scene: 'The Irish Brigade . . . comes out from the city in glorious file, their green sunbursts waving . . . every man has a sprig of green in his cap . . . They passed just to our left, poor fellows, poor, glorious fellows, shaking good-bye to us with their hats! They reach a point within a stone's throw of the stone wall. No farther. They try to go beyond, but are slaughtered.' The Confederate soldiers who did the slaughtering belonged to the Georgia Irish brigade.*

*At Gettysburg the tide turned as the Union army was victorious in the largest battle ever fought during the Civil War. The human cost was, once again, terribly heavy, with as many as fifty-one thousand killed, wounded, or missing during the three days of battle. John Mitchel's youngest son, Willy, died fighting at Gettysburg. According to one report, his body was 'buried with a note attached: Private Mitchel, son of an*

*Irish patriot.' Many other Irish, from both the North and the South, died at Gettysburg. Today a number of monuments at the Gettysburg National Military Park display the Irish shamrock, reminding visitors of the sacrifice these young men made on the field of battle.*

*Not long after Gettysburg the Irish were involved in another bloody battle. This time it was on the streets of New York, where the infamous Draft Riot of 1863 took place. By the spring of 1863 the Union army was facing a manpower shortage. To overcome this, Congress passed a conscription law to enforce a military draft. If a man's name was drawn in the lottery, he could avoid military service by hiring a substitute or paying a fee of three hundred dollars. The Democrats vehemently opposed the draft, viewing it as 'an unconstitutional means to achieve an unconstitutional end of freeing the slaves.' They inflamed the debate by framing it as a 'rich man's war/poor man's fight' since all a man needed was three hundred dollars to avoid military service. Such a sum was far beyond the reach of an Irish laborer. Opposition among the Irish surfaced in the Pennsylvania mining region and in Boston as well. But the most virulent opposition erupted in New York City.*

*Irish workers in New York were particularly hostile to black laborers because of their competition in the labor market. This resentment was heightened when black strikebreakers were used to counteract a strike by Irish longshoremen in June. This hostility, as well as opposition to Lincoln, was simmering below the surface by the time the draft lottery took place in early July. On Saturday, July 11, the first day of the lottery passed peacefully. Much discussion took place in the saloons and working-class neighborhoods on Sunday, especially of the unfairness of the three-hundred-dollar waiver. Workers threatened to attack the draft office when it opened on Monday. When Monday came, they not only attacked the draft office, burning it to the ground, but they roamed the city burning, looting and killing. For four days rioters, most of whom were Irish, went about the city attacking the homes and businesses of prominent Republicans. The Colored Orphan Asylum was destroyed and at least 11 blacks were murdered, some savagely lynched. The mob even turned on Irish cops and soldiers who tried to quell the riot. One such victim was Colonel Henry O'Brien, who was brutally murdered and his body dragged through the streets. When it was all over, as many as 105 people were dead. The New York Draft Riot has gone down in history as one of the nation's bloodiest urban riots. Moreover, the behavior of the Irish during these fateful days and the racism they exhibited reinforced their reputation for violence. In the aftermath of the riots, a number of the Northern elite produced 'some of the most sustained and virulent anti-Irish sentiment in American history.' The New York Times condemned the Irish as 'brutish' and 'animal' while the New York Tribune called the rioters a 'savage mob', a 'pack of savages', and a mob of 'incarnate devils'[reminiscent of Tone's attitude toward the Pope]. In this way, the racist Irish were themselves reduced to the level of the animal kingdom."*

In the days leading up to the outbreak of the violence, the New York press accused the Archbishop of contributing to the tension by a lack of charity and leadership, to which Hughes responded by fanning the flames in a letter no less muddled than his earlier messages.  Then, when word of the riots reached the Archbishop's ears, he showed himself a beaten man.  Riddled with rheumatism and approaching death, he would appear in public for the last time in his life to address an estimated 5,000 Irish assembled in front of his residence.  From his balcony window, he begged them to disperse, and that is exactly what they did, a bittersweet proof that he'd had it within his power to prevent all their bloodshed in the first place.  This was the legacy he would take to his grave, as would each of his fellow Irish bishops.  Like O'Connell, they would leave the world with *Erin go Bragh* in their hearts, but unlike him would risk no skin to bring an end to slavery. Instead, they left their calling to the blood and sweat of others.  Others like the army of angels who were sent by Edward Sorin from their homes near Notre Dame to horrific field hospitals full of soldiers in pain.

They went by the name which Blessed Basil Moreau, founder of the Congregation of Holy Cross, had given them some five years before he'd first sent Sorin to the States - The Sisters of the Holy Cross, circa 1837.  But to the broken soldiers of both the North and South, they were indeed an army of heavenly angels, attached to no cause but the love of Christ.  In fact, before their four long years of fighting for dear life had finally come to an end, they'd heard the whispered words of over eighteen hundred wounded, begging from their deathbeds for mercy and baptism.  In all, it has been estimated that eighty such Sisters had served in the Civil War (along with many others from different religious orders), though the names of some have been lost in the shuffle.  Here, then, out of respect and admiration, are the names of the seventy who've officially been verified by the War Department in Washington (The M. stands for Mary, the Mother of God):

1.  Sister M. Adele (Catherine Moran);

2.  Sister M. Aglae (Anne Wixet);

3.  Sister M. Agnes (Bridget Nevils);

4.  Sister M. Alice (Bridget Flannery);

5.  Sister M. Aloysius (Mary Caren);

6.  Mother M. Angela (Eliza M. Gillespie);

7.  Sister M. Angelica (Bridget O'Brien);

8.  Sister M. Angeline (Virginia Blake);

9.  Sister M. Ann (Mary Dorsey);

10.  Sister M. Anthony (Mannix);

11.  Sister M. Athanasius (Margaret O'Neill);

12.  Sister M. Augusta (Amanda Anderson);

13.  Sister M. Augustine (Anne Flanagan);

14.  Sister M. Aurelius (Mary Leavy);

15.  Sister M. Bartholomew (Frances Darnell);

16.  Sister M. Bernard (Mary Peacord);

17.  Sister M. Bernard (Winifred Shanley);

18.  Sister M. Callista (Esther Pointan);

19.  Sister M. Calvary (Mary Ann Stace);

20.  Sister M. Catherine (Anne Kilkenny);

21.  Sister M. Celeste (Mary Duffy);

22.  Sister M. Celestine (Bridget Cavanaugh);

23.  Sister M. Christina (Sophia Anselma);

24.  Sister M. Compassion (Margaret Gleeson);

25.  Sister M. Conception (Mary McIntyre);

26.  Sister M. De Chantal (Julia Hale);

27.  Sister M. Edward (Mary Murphy);

28.  Sister M. Elise (Unity O'Brien);

29.  Sister M. Eusebia (Anne McIntosh);

30.  Sister M. Faustina (Anne Morrissey);

31.  Sister M. Felicity (Margaret Molloy);

32.  Sister M. Felix (Mary Kelly);

33.  Sister M. Ferdinand (Agnes Bruggerman);

34.  Sister M. Fidelis (Bridget Lawler);

35.  Sister M. Flavia (Bridget Smith);

36.  Sister M. Francis (Malloy);

37.  Sister M. Francis De Sales (Hanorah O'Neil);

38.  Sister M. Francis De Paul (Joanna Sullivan);

39.  Mother M. Genevieve (Barbara Gaengel);

40.  Sister M. Gregory (Mary Barry);

41.  Sister M. Helen (Catherine Fitzpatrick);

42.  Sister M. Henrietta (Mary McLaughlin);

43.  Sister M. Holy Angels (Catherine Muldoon);

44.  Sister M. Holy Infancy (Madeline Gate);

45.  Sister M. Holy Cross (Ellen Walsh);

46.  Sister M. Irene (Anne Keough);

47. Sister M. Isidore (Mary Conlin);

48. Sister M. Jane Frances De Chantal (Barbara Knoll);

49. Sister M. John of the Cross (Catherine McLouglin);

50. Sister M. Josephine (Mary Reilly);

51. Mother M. Liguori (Anne Chretien);

52. Sister M. Lydia (Mary Clifford);

53. Sister M. Macrina (Annie Snow);

54. Sister M. Magdalen (Ellen Kiernan);

55. Sister M. Martha (Catherine Reddy);

56. Sister M. Matilda (Margaret Hartnett);

57. Sister M. Mount Carmel (Ogilvie);

58. Sister M. Odelia (Hanora Higgins);

59. Sister M. Passion (Anne Crowley);

60. Sister M. Patrick (Bridget McGookin);

61. Sister M. Paula (Winifred Casey);

62. Sister M. Placidus (Bridget Sullivan);

63. Sister M. Providence (Marie Daget);

64. Sister M. Rita (Mary Brennan);

65. Sister M. Rose of Lima (Mary McDermott);

66. Sister M. Theodore (Mary Kearns);

67. Sister M. Theodosia (Mary McCushing);

68. Sister M. Veronica (Regina Scholl);

69. Sister M. Victoria (Mary O'Keefe);

70. Sister M. Winifred (Catherine McGinn)

As their surnames suggest, the vast majority of these extraordinary women were of Irish origin, tending to the terrible fates of many an Irish warrior.  In response to General Grant's appeal that they deal with the wounded where North met South along the Western border of the war, Sorin sent scores of them to Cairo and Mound City in southern Illinois, where the mighty Mississippi and Ohio Rivers met and - depending on what path you took - where a one-day walk would take you into Tennessee, Arkansas, Kentucky or Missouri.

Mother Mary Angela to them all was the extraordinary Eliza Gillespie, big sister to the Reverend Neal Gillespie (a graduate of Notre Dame) and first cousin to Ellen Ewing, the wife of General William Sherman.  Years earlier, Eliza and Ellen had been at the heart of an East coast relief effort for the Irish of the Potato Famine, and it was in this work that Eliza first felt her calling to the religious life.

Mother Mary Angela took Sister Mary Patrick (Bridget McGookin), Sister Mary Athanasius (Margaret O'Neill), and Sister Mary Frances De Sales (Hanorah O'Neil), to organize and operate the military hospital at Mound City, where they and a host of additional sisters would soon take on the supernatural task of treating over 1400 soldiers who arrived at their doors within a matter of days from the battles at Forts Donelson and Henry.

At Donelson, a blizzard stormed the battlefield after the fighting, and many who had fallen when the ground was still soft, found themselves "frozen into the earth" at battle's end.  By the time relief arrived, the only way to give them any chance to survive was to saw off and abandon their limbs, frozen there in the ground, in order to transport what was left of them to the sisters at Mound City.  Once there, they would be the beneficiaries of another brand of bravery, to which Sister Mary Frances would one day bear witness:

> *"[S]oon after the battle of Fort Donelson, Mother Angela was assisting the Chief Surgeon on the lower floor. He was performing a difficult operation, the accuracy of which would determine the life of the soldier. His head and that of Mother Angela were bent over the poor boy. Suddenly from the ceiling a heavy red drop fell upon the white coif of Mother Angela, who . . . did not move. Another, and still another, drop after drop came till a little stream was flowing. At last, the final stitch had been taken, and the two heads . . . rose simultaneously. Not 'til then did the doctor know that a stream of blood, trickling through the [boards} of the upper floor, had fallen steadily upon the devoted head of Mother Angela, who now stood before the surgeon with her head and face and shoulders bathed in the blood of some unknown soldier."*

The mayhem at Mound City was so overwhelming that it led to the spread of deadly disease and claimed the precious lives of Sister Mary Fidelis (Bridget Lawler, 31, of Queens County Ireland), and Sister Mary Elise (Unity O'Brien, 24, of County Donegal).

Equally bad were the conditions at Cairo, where the sisters would attend to the aftermath of Shiloh, a brutal battle in which more lives were lost than in all of the previous American wars combined, nearly 24,000 from both sides. Sister Mary Augusta (Amanda Anderson) described the horrid scene:

Many of these wounded made their way to Mound City and
Cairo by way of the Mississippi River, as patients given aid and
passage aboard the U.S.S. Red Rover, the Navy's first hospital ship.
Originally a Confederate barracks ship until captured by the Union,
the Red Rover served as an essential "treat and transport" vessel for
the last three years of the war.  From the day of its commissioning on
Christmas Eve (1862), until the end of its faithful service late in 1865,
you could find Catherine Moran of County Mayo (Sister Mary Adela)
and Regina Scholl of Prussia (Sister Mary Veronica), shuttling fore
and aft on Red Rover's decks as the ship weaved its way through war
zones up and down the Mississippi, cannon balls and bullets whizzing
past their heads.  Two such cannons from the ranks of the
Confederacy, christened "Lady Polk" and "Lady Davis", had
mysteriously malfunctioned in the heat of battle.  After the war, they
were given to Mother Angela and taken to St. Mary's, where they
would serve as a reminder of the Sisters' heroic service until returned
to the military and melted back to ore at the start of World War II.

In addition to these many beloved Sisters, Sorin sent seven of
his precious-few priests into the terrible fray: three fine Frenchmen -
Bourget, Leveque and Carrier - and four whose names read like the
letterhead of an Irish law firm - Gillen, Dillon, Cooney and Corby,
Chaplains-at-War.

Like the two young sisters who succumbed at Mound City,
Father Bourget lost his life to malaria there, four days shy of his 31st

birthday, while a sickly Father Leveque would give his all until "exhaustion" took him at the age of 56.

Father Carrier was chaplain to the forces at Vicksburg, where he served Generals Grant and Sherman with great distinction, and then parlayed the friendships he had made with these two men into exemptions from the draft on behalf of the small band of Holy Cross Brothers who were sorely needed to remain at Notre Dame and aid the short-handed Sorin.

Father Paul Gillen of County Kerry served throughout the war. A robust man in his early fifties, he rigged himself a horse-drawn wagon, traveling from regiment to regiment, offering spiritual comfort to the troops.

Father James Dillon of County Galway was chaplain to the men of Corcoran's Irish Legion, until a steadily debilitating lung disease had forced his early retirement. His death four years later, at the age of 35, was largely due to his sacrificial service during the war.

For nearly four years, Father Peter Cooney of County Roscommon was attached to the troops of Tennessee and Kentucky. So strong was the bond between him and the men that they wept like children when they learned he was leaving.

But the most memorable war figure of them all was the incomparable Reverend William Corby, for he'd slogged through marsh and slept in mud with Meagher's brave Irish Brigade, men from the Fighting 69th, mustered along the Potomac, awaiting their marching orders. He'd survived on sea biscuits basted by the sweat of his sorry excuse for a horse. He'd endured infestations of gray-back lice as fearsome as any enemy, as awful as Egyptian plagues. He'd smelled the powder of many guns, and seen the bloodshed of many sons. He'd prayed with the wounded and agonized over the dying on battlefields strewn with slaughter. He had been to Antietam, where two hundred thousand men had tried to mutilate each other for twelve straight hours.

Born on October 2, 1833, the Feast of Guardian Angels, he stood now on Cemetery Ridge, July 2, 1863, three months shy of his thirtieth birthday.  Peering across the pastures of Gettysburg, at the grey-coats amassed in the distance, he inhaled the heavy, fear-laden air of a terrible battle about to begin.  Shedding his blue cloth coat, he revealed the black linen cassock beneath, ever their chaplain, ever their priest.  Then he put 'round his neck a purple stole, the same one he'd packed in his pocket, perhaps, on the day that he'd left dear Notre Dame in order to serve the North.

Maybe he scaled the boulder by himself.  More likely some men helped hoist him up there, when the cannon fire first filled the air.  From there, he saw the great numbers, gripped with fear but ready to fight.  He cleared his throat, and their attentions turned.  The colors dipped, and time stood still, suppressed by the will of a great brigade, bending as one at the knee.  Colonel Mulholland remembers the moment well:

> *"Father Corby stood on a large rock in front of the brigade.  Addressing the men, he explained what he was about to do, saying that each one could receive the benefit of absolution by making a sincere act of confession and firmly resolving to embrace the first opportunity of confessing his sins, urging them to do their duty, and reminding them of the high and sacred nature of their trust as soldiers, and the noble object for which they fought . . .*
> *As he closed his address, every man, Catholic and non-Catholic alike, fell on his knees with his head bowed down.  Then, stretching his right hand toward the brigade, Father Corby pronounced the words of the absolution: Dominus noster Jesus Christus vos absolvat . . . in nomini Patris, et Filii, et Spiritu Sancti, Amen."*

*. . . [I}t was awe-inspiring. Nearby stood a brilliant
throng of officers who had gathered to witness this very
unusual occurrence, and while there was profound
silence in the ranks . . . yet over to the left, out by the
peach orchard . . . the roar of the battle rose and swelled
and re-echoed through the woods, making music more
sublime than ever sounded through cathedral aisle. The
act seemed to be in harmony with the surroundings. I
do not think there was a man in the brigade who did not
offer up a heart-felt prayer. For some, it was their last;
they knelt there in their grave clothes. In less than half
an hour many of them were numbered with the dead of
July 2. Who can doubt that their prayers were good?
What was wanting in the eloquence of the priest to move
them to repentance was supplied in the incidents of the
fight. That heart would be incorrigible, indeed, that the
scream of a Whitworth bolt, added to Father Corby's
touching appeal, would not move to contrition."*

Corby himself picks it up from there:


*"In performing this ceremony, I faced the army.
My eye covered thousands of officers and men. I noticed
that all, Catholic and non-Catholic, officers and private
soldiers, showed a profound respect, wishing at this
fatal crisis to receive every benefit of divine grace that
could be imparted . . . for all – in quantum possum – not
only for our brigade, but for all, North and South, who
were susceptible of it and who were about to appear
before their Judge. Let us hope that many thousands of*

*souls, purified by hardships, fasting, prayer, and blood,
met a favorable sentence on the ever-memorial field of
Gettysburg. The battle lasted three days, and was the
greatest of the war. . .*

*The Irish Brigade had very many
advantages over other organizations, as it was at no
time during the war without a chaplain; but I was the
only one at the battle of Gettysburg. Often in camp and
sometimes on the march we held very impressive
religious services, but the one at Gettysburg was more
public, and was witnessed by many who had not,
perhaps, seen the others. The surroundings there, too,
made a vast difference, for really the situation reminded
one of the day of judgment, when shall be seen 'men
withering away for fear and expectation of what shall
come upon the whole world', so great were the
whirlwinds of war then in motion. . ."*

Thirty-three years after the war, at the 50th anniversary
celebration of Edward Sorin's priesthood, Archbishop John Ireland of
St. Paul, a son of County Kilkenny and former chaplain of the 5th
Minnesota Regiment in the Civil War, would take to the podium at
Notre Dame and issue this proclamation:

*"Father Sorin, you saved the honor of the
Church. I speak from a special knowledge of the facts,
and I speak from my heart. And could the country's
martyrs speak from the silent earth at Gettysburg, and
a hundred other gory fields, their voices would re-echo
with our own in your praise on this glorious
anniversary."*

That same school year (1887-88), there were two other men, both named Paul, both making history, on the campus of Notre Dame.

One was a 16yr. old prodigy named Paul Henry Wood, in training to paint the only published work of his precious life, that of Corby standing over the Irish Brigade and bestowing *Absolution Under Fire (depicted at the beginning of this paragraph}*.  The poor young artist would then perish in a tragic accident at the age of twenty, but his work would survive to adorn the walls of the Snite Museum, right next door to Notre Dame's football stadium. Indeed, it would inspire a matching statue of Corby, his arm outstretched, to stand at the entrance of Corby Hall and be forever christened by some clever student as "Fair-catch Corby", an irreverently fitting metaphor to what the future held for dear old Notre Dame.

And then there was that other Paul, of the Fighting Irish in a war called football . . .

# 5

## Son of Erin,
## Father of Fighting Irish Football

Conceived amidst the misery of the potato famine, he was - for the in-your-face timing of his arrival alone - an Irishman's answer to the Welsh poet's call that we "not go gentle into that good night, but rage, rage, against the dying of the light."  Born in County Waterford in 1849, he was destined - unlike his fellow Waterford countryman Francis Meagher of Civil War fame – to preside over the strides of happier brigades in that dormitory named after Brownson, his notions about the battle over abolition unknown.  For here was an Irishman 'twas born for love alone, to grace this world when the war was over, and to look over nobler, worthier wars, on battlefields built only for living glory.

His Christian name was Patrick Connors, and though a noted old sportswriter would one day say he was the father of Notre Dame athletics, he was more than that.  He was in fact the Father of Fighting Irish Football.  Yet he became, and has remained, a largely forgotten man, and for this old Notre Dame ought to hang its head in shame.  For where, oh where, 'midst all the Blue-Gold gloss, is the statue and the plaque, to Brother Paul of the Cross?

He'd fled the effects of the famine at the age of five, his father left behind, his mother by his side.  But by the time he'd turned sixteen, they were both already dead, and he'd wandered into the arms of a new mom and dad - Notre Dame *du Lac* and her incoming president, the Reverend William Corby – who would love him for the rest of his life.

On Patrick's application for admission to the novitiate of the Congregation of the Holy Cross - May 1, 1865 - he said his calling had come from "being with the Brothers", a hint that they'd already adopted him as one of their own.  But like our Lord and our Lady, his formative days are hidden away 'midst the treasures of blessed obscurity.  "Why do you quit the world?" inquired the Congregation's form application.  "To save my soul," came his wry and humble reply; and so he did, if ever a man has done.  Perseverant and prayerful as a postulant, he would contemplate his calling for a full twelve years, clothing himself completely in Christ, before committing to Him in earnest.  Here is how he penned his final profession, long hand to paper, on August 15, 1876, the Feast of the Assumption of Mary, body and soul, into heaven:

*"In the name of the Father, and of the Son, and of the Holy Ghost:*

*I, Patrick Connors, Brother Paul of the Cross, unworthy though I am, but nevertheless relying on the Divine Mercy, and earnestly desiring to devote myself to the service of the adorable Trinity, make forever to Almighty God the vows of poverty, chastity, and obedience, according to the sense of the rules and constitution of this congregation, in the presence of our Lord Jesus Christ, of the Blessed Virgin Mary, conceived without sin, of her worthy spouse St. Joseph, and of all the heavenly court, promising to accept with submission every employment it may please my legitimate superiors to assign me.  Given in the [pre-Basilica] Church of Our Lady of the Sacred Heart this 15th day of August, 1876.  Called in the world, Patrick Connors.  Called in Religion, Brother Paul of the + "*

Brother Paul was blessed with athletic zest, noble bearing, and a countenance of courage and kindness.  He would return those blessings many times over to Notre Dame his mother, until he could give her no more.  His superiors would assign to him the task of tending to the welfare of Notre Dame's students, including his use of sundry schemes for helping them wholesomely let off some steam, and boy did he ever run with that.  On September 22, 1879, three years after his commitment to the congregation, they would find him field-side, directing the action as Notre dame played its first officially recorded "football" game.  It was, in fact, an enthusiastic if over-manned (42 to a side!) intramural soccer match between the Reds and the Blues, the Reds prevailing by a score of 2 goals to 1.  Afterwards, with latin echoes of "Rah, Rah, Rah, Nostra Domina!" in the air, the winners would celebrate into the night with a barrel of "aged" apple cider, source of the now age-old adage at ND that "tradition never graduates." Now, we don't know what role the robust Brother Paul may have played in prohibiting (or procuring) the spiritually influential beverage. What we do know, though, is that "[t]he revelry ended after a 'kind but firm' admonition from Father Corby . . . to cut out the carousing and retire to the dormitories."

Today, that soccer match stands much emblematic of an intramural athletic program rivaling that of any other college in the country. In the 2007-2008 academic year alone, for example, Notre Dame campus facilities were accessed nearly 400,000 times by over 19,000 individual participants in the contests, games and classes of over 300 different university athletics and fitness programs. All this a testament to the storied tenacity of one extraordinary man, who served as Notre Dame's first true director of athletics for over 25 years, nurturing student participation in sports such as baseball, crew, tennis, handball, soccer, and so on. But that is only a part of his wonderful legacy. The other part got off to an equally auspicious start:

> *"When a Notre Dame man crashed into the Wolverine . . . after he had signaled for a fair catch, then knocked the ball from his hands, scooped it up and thundered down the field for a touchdown, [the referee] disallowed it and penalized Notre Dame.*
> *In one split second ... 150 wild Irishmen were around [the referee's] neck. Brother Paul of the Cross saved [him], raised his hand, asked for silence, and said: 'These boys are our guests. We invited them to teach us the game. [The referee] knows the rules."*

So marked the birth of Fighting Irish football, and perhaps the greatest rivalry in all of sports: Michigan 26, Notre Dame 6, April 20,

1888.  In truth, the two teams had first played an abbreviated practice game six months earlier, on November 23, 1887, with Michigan prevailing 8 to 0.  An alumnus of Notre Dame and protégé of Brother Paul by the name of George DeHaven had continued his studies at Michigan, where they were playing an Americanized version of football first made fashionable by a Yale man named Walter Camp. It was more a variation of British rugby than it was of soccer, since a player could hold and pass and run with the ball.  DeHaven loved it so much that he wrote to Brother Paul about it; Hence, Brother Paul's invitation for DeHaven to come to South Bend with his friends and get things going.  Down they came by train from Ann Arbor, and the rest is history.

## NOTRE DAME

## FIGHTING IRISH FOOTBALL TEAM 1887

We know from the effort he put into it over the last years of his life that there was something very special about this new sport which had so impressed Brother Paul, but we'll never know exactly how he felt from anything he said because he wasn't a man of many words. So maybe he wouldn't mind too much if we borrowed from the sentiments of some other Irish Brothers to try to get a sense of his own.

In his extraordinarily moving memoir, *Miracle in the Andes,* plane crash survivor and inspirational speaker Nando Parrado explains how the game of rugby, as taught to him and his teammates by the Irish Christian Brothers, had helped them to endure for 72 days in the frozen Andes mountains:

> *"Many of us on the Old Christians [rugby team] had known each other for more than ten years, since our days as schoolboy ruggers playing under the guidance of the Irish Christian Brothers at Stella Maris [Our Lady Star of the Sea] School [in Uruguay] . . .*
> *For the Christian Brothers, the first goal of a Catholic education was to build character, not intellect, and their teaching methods stressed discipline, piety, selflessness, and respect. To promote these values outside the classroom, the Brothers...steered us toward the rougher, earthier game of rugby . . . an Irish passion . . . [They] firmly believed that the qualities required to master the sport were the same characteristics one needed to live a decent Catholic life – humility, tenacity, self-discipline, and devotion to others. . . Most of all the game demanded that teammates develop an unshakeable sense of trust. . .*

The day after Notre Dame's 26 - 6 loss to Michigan on April 20, 1888, the two teams met again, and this time Notre Dame lost by a score of 10 to 4 in a game that ignited the now infamous rivalry in earnest.  It seems that after Notre Dame jumped out to an early 4 - 0 lead by forcing back-to-back safeties, the referee supplied by the Michigan team decided to award it a touchdown on a play in which Michigan's runner may have stepped out of bounds after beginning the play before the players were set.  At the time, a touchdown was 4 points, and a conversion 2, making the score 6 – 4.  Then, Michigan scored again without question, but failed to convert, making the score 10 – 4.  However, Notre Dame came right back with what they thought was a touchdown, only to have it disallowed by the same referee for unexplained reasons, thus depriving Notre Dame of an opportunity to tie the game.  The final score was Michigan 10, Notre Dame 4, though many thought it should have been the other way around.  In any event, the hotly contested outcome is widely believed to be the reason why Michigan couldn't find time in its football schedule to play Notre Dame again for 10 years.

But Notre Dame was undaunted, playing and winning their next two interscholastic games, the first against the visiting Harvard Preps of Chicago, 20 – 0, in the spring of 1888, the next on the road against Northwestern, 9 – 0, in the cold of November, 1889.  However, it was at Northwestern that Brother Paul and his 11 so-called "Specials" (their original name) had first heard both the past and the future calling when a bunch of bigoted Northwestern fans began to chant – "Kill the Fighting Irish!  Kill the Fighting Irish!"  In fact, this would prompt Notre Dame to sound a brief retreat, confining their next two years of football to campus. There, Brother

Paul could be seen, strutting South Bend's unsheltered sidelines, sometimes in the snow and bitter cold, which brings us back to Nando Parrado.

After the plane crash, Nando and his teammates at first hunkered down, braving the brutal elements of winter in the Andes mountains while waiting weeks for someone to find them.  When no one came, Nando and some others summoned the strength and courage to set out from their make-shift shelters and try to hike for help.  After an incredible, death-defying climb to the top of a far-off frozen mountain peak, they discover that they're really in the middle of nowhere, and that no one is ever going to find them there.  But desperation and anger turn to epiphany and peace as Nando experiences the presence of God, and gets an inkling of eternal life:

> *"I felt a moment of calmness and clarity, and in that clarity, I discovered a simple, astounding secret: Death has an opposite, but the opposite is not mere living.  It is not courage or faith or human will.  The opposite of death is love. . . Love is our only weapon. Only love can turn mere life into a miracle, and draw precious meaning from suffering and fear.  For a brief, magical moment, all my fears lifted, and I knew that I would not let death control me.  I would walk through the godforsaken country that separated me from my home with love and hope in my heart. . .*
>
> *In the Andes we lived heartbeat-to-heartbeat. Every second of life was a gift, glowing with purpose and meaning.  I have tried to live that way ever since and it has filled my life with more blessings than I can count.  I urge you to do the same.  As we used to say in the mountains, 'Breathe.  Breathe again.  With every*

*breath, you are alive.' After all these years, this is still the best advice I can give you: Savor your existence. Live every moment. Do not waste a breath."*

Little did anyone but Brother Paul know that he was quietly enduring his own personal suffering as he tended to his boys right to the end.  Indeed, when he died on December 12, 1893, twelve days after his Fighting Irish had finished their first perfect season at 4 and 0, it came as a tragic shock and terrible blow to everyone on campus. This, from the South Bend Tribune, 13 December 1893:

> *"Patrick Connors came to Notre Dame 28 years ago and has since been connected with the University.  His religious title was Brother Paul of the Cross, and he was . . . lovingly called Brother Paul . . .[by] the students [that] personally endeared him, and sadness now claims each one . . . He took an unusual lively interest in athletics, and on the field his stately figure with its dignified, noble bearing was most conspicuous.  He brought athletics at the University to a high plane.  To the students and faculty, his death is a serious blow.*
>
> *For quite some time, Brother Paul had been ill, but no one would have thought that any kind of disease could have fastened itself on such an athletic man.  He doubtless prolonged his life by his vigorous athletic training.  But his recent exposure to all sorts of weather during the football season may have been responsible for bringing on this crisis and the resulting death.*

*Expressions of sorrow are heard from all
sides. No one came closer to the students than did
Brother Paul and no one seemed better liked than he."*

Funeral services were held at Sacred Heart, in the same spot
where the young Patrick Connors had first confirmed his calling to
the Congregation of Holy Cross some 28 years earlier. After a
Solemn Requiem Mass had been sung by Notre Dame's new
President, the Reverend Andrew Morrissey, it was Notre Dame's Very
Reverend Provincial, the one and only William Corby, who
pronounced the absolution of his dear adopted son in the presence of
an overflowing assembly.

Patrick Connors. Son of Erin. Father of Fighting Irish Football.
May perpetual light shine upon you, and may your soul, and the souls
of all the faithful departed, through the mercy of God, rest in peace.
Amen.


(Author's Note: According to Linda Brennan Norris of Fort
Wayne, Indiana, whom I met by extraordinary coincidence while we
were both conducting research on Brother Paul in the Archives at
Notre Dame's Hesburgh Library, the correct spelling of her great
Uncle's name is Conners, not Connors. However, Notre Dame's
archived records have it as the latter, for reasons which remain
unclear.)

# 6

# Daughter of Misogyny, Mother of Blood Money

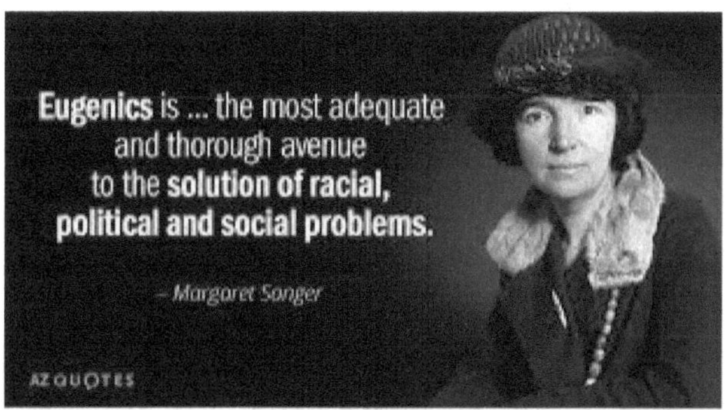


*Fathers, be good to your daughters*
*Daughters will love like you do*
*Girls become lovers who turn into mothers*
*So mothers, be good to your daughters too*

**Daughters, John Mayer, 2003**

Not long before Patrick Connors came into the world, Michael Hennessey Higgins was also born in Ireland.  But while Patrick was preparing to enter the novitiate at Notre Dame, Higgins was enlisting in the Union army.  After the war, he would claim that he had led Sherman's march through Georgia as a drummer boy.  But army records don't support his story, and since Higgins had strong hankerings for drinking and free-thinking, it's hard to hear his little rum-pa-pum-pum ringing true.  On the other hand, a front row seat to the devastation that Sherman's men had visited upon the South would certainly help explain why Higgins had walked away from God and gravitated toward outspoken atheism.  Or maybe it was his childhood flight from British bigotry to Canada in the cavern of some filthy famine ship that did it.  That and the price one had to pay to be Catholic, even in America.  Whatever his actual afflictions, a self-employed tombstone cutter for Catholic cemeteries could hardly afford his kind of open contempt for the Church, and it cost his family dearly in dollars.  No, this was not a drummer boy who'd be banging one out for the baby Jesus any time soon.  This was a boy who would grow to greatly burden his Irish Catholic wife, and teach his daughter to despair her "joyless" life.

Little Maggie Higgins was swimming in her mother's womb while Notre Dame's main building was burning to the ground on April 23, 1879, but by the time she was born in Corning, New York, on September 14, 1879, the unstoppable Edward Sorin had miraculously rebuilt Our Lady's home, complete with Mary's statue and Golden Dome, and just in time for Brother Paul's kids to make their happy plans for soccer and cider in South Bend.

One of eighteen children conceived by her dear mother (seven lost to miscarriage), little Maggie would suffer a childhood "filled with drudgery and fear," largely on account of her foolhardy father. He once slipped into bed with her when she was still dazed by the haze of narcotic medication, and she would always wonder whether she'd been violated.  He mocked her when she searched for solace in prayer, and mortified her among would-be friends with his proud proclamations of apostasy.  He subjected her whole family to the spirit-draining strains of ostracism and poverty, and her mother to the unrelenting trauma of perpetual maternity, until she succumbed to chronic tuberculosis when Maggie was only sixteen.  Thus, did her godless, misogynist father help deprive her, first of her mother's faith, then of her mother's hope, and finally of her mother's love. Indeed, despite the distance life would take her from her childhood home, the mere thought of Corning would turn her stomach.

No great surprise, then, that poor Maggie Higgins would morph into Margaret Sanger. Marrying for the money of two willing men and sleeping with a slew of others, she grew hopelessly devoted to the self-delusion that such was the way to a woman's liberation, rather than the path to her personal ruin. "The marriage bed," she said, "is the most degenerating influence in the social order." Instead, women should strive for "unlimited sexual gratification without the burden of unwanted children." In short, this modern day Eve would put the apple 'tween her legs, and the worst fears of Orestes Brownson would draw nearer to fruition.

Worse than her tortured sense of self-worth, however, Sanger suffered from a childhood disease for which contraception and abortion would become the cure - her disdain for the disabled and poor. An insidiously infectious disease, it persists, however-latent, even to this day, in her many elitist, eugenicist descendants.

Eugenicists: Persons who advocate improvement of the genetic qualities of humanity through the scientific control of procreation.

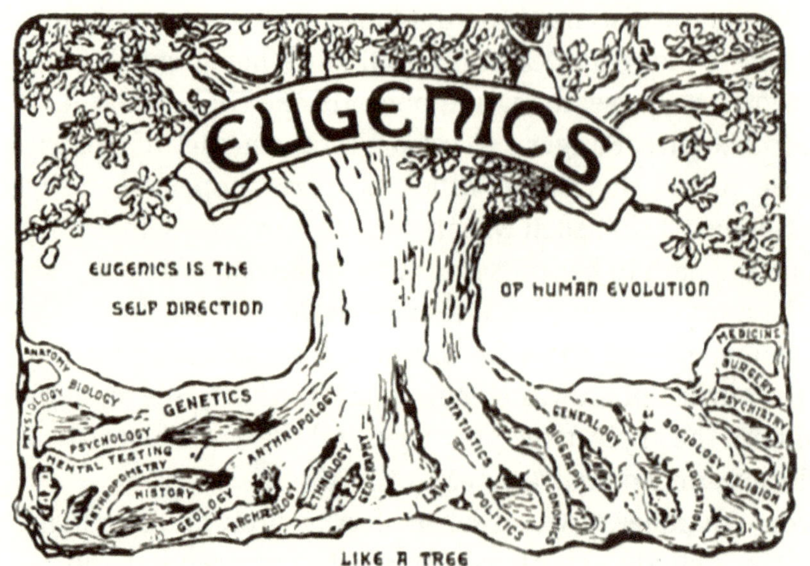


**"Eugenics is the self-direction of human evolution": Logo from the <u>Second International Eugenics Conference</u>, 1921, depicting it as a tree which unites a variety of different fields.**

Make no mistake.  Of the many men for whom Margaret played mistress, whether literally or metaphorically, most were proud eugenicists, not to mention closet misogynists. Notably included among them was a band of godless Brits.  First there was Thomas Malthus, the father of "scientific racism," a forerunner to eugenics. Then there was that atheist descendant of the apes, Charles Darwin, and his cousin Francis Galton, the father of modern eugenics.  And last but not least, there were the three stooges who became Margaret's version of "unlimited sexual gratification without the burden of unwanted children" - Havelock Ellis, who apparently enjoyed urinating on women; Hugh de Selincourt, who seems to have preferred just screwing as many of them as possible; and H.G. Wells, who we're told was somewhat less the misogynist and more the revolting racist. In spirit, they were British subjects of the King of modern misogyny, his highness Henry the Eighth. In fact, they were the philosophical ancestors of Adolf Hitler himself, the 20th century's supreme eugenicist.

Before heeding the admonitions of Havelock Ellis, who urged her to mask her true motives and tone down her fiery rhetoric, Margaret made no bones about the underlying impetus for her Brownsville-based Birth Control Clinical Research Bureau, which would grow to become Planned Parenthood, that enormous octopus of abortion clinics with tentacles today reaching into 134 countries on every continent. For example, Sanger's early writings spoke of a women's "right to destroy" and sarcastically observed that "the most merciful thing that a large family does to one of its infant members is to kill it," whereas her later, Havelock Ellis-inspired Brownsville clinic handbills hawked contraception to avoid abortion. However, as asserted in Dr. Angela Frank's exquisite dissertation, *Margaret Sanger's Eugenic Legacy: The Control of Female Fertility*, MacFarland & Co., 2005, "there is evidence that [this very same Brownsville clinic] referred at least seventy-five women for abortions, some for non-disabling or non-life-threatening conditions." But abortion was merely one means, one tool in the arsenal of control, targeted toward Margaret's eugenic ends. Her overriding goals are illuminated by some of her other utterances that apparently eluded the advice of Havelock Hills:


*"No matter how much they desire children, no
man and woman have a right to bring into the world*

*those who are sure to suffer from mental or physical affliction. It condemns the child to a life of misery and places upon the community the burden of caring for them, [and] probably ... their defective descendants for many generations." Margaret Sanger, Birth Control Review, November, 1918.*

*"More children from the fit, less from the unfit -- that is the chief aim of birth control." American Medicine editorial characterizing a 1919 article by Margaret Sanger entitled "Why Not Birth Control Clinics in America?" Both items reprinted in the May, 1919 edition of Sanger's Birth Control Review.*

*"The campaign for birth control is not merely of eugenic value, but is practically identical in ideal with the final aim of Eugenics." Sanger, The Eugenic Value of Birth Control Propaganda, 1921.*

*"[A] qualitative factor as opposed to a quantitative one is of primary importance in dealing with the great masses of humanity." Sanger, The Pivot of Civilization, 1922*

*"Organized charity is the symptom of a malignant social disease . . . [I}t encourages the perpetuation of defectives, delinquents, and dependents. These are the most dangerous elements in the world community, the most devastating curse on human progress and expression." Sanger, The Pivot of Civilization, 1922.*

*"Our failure to segregate morons who are increasing and multiplying ... demonstrates our foolhardy and extravagant sentimentalism ... a dead weight of human waste. Instead of decreasing and aiming to eliminate the stocks ... We are paying for, and even submitting to, the dictates of an ever-increasing, unceasingly spawning class of human beings who never should have been born at all." Sanger, The Pivot of Civilization, 1922*

*"The government of the United States deliberately encourages and even makes necessary by its laws the breeding – with a breakneck rapidity – of idiots, defectives, diseased, feeble-minded, and criminal classes.  Billions of dollars are expended by our state and federal governments and by private charities and philanthropies for the care, the maintenance, and the perpetuation of these classes . . . The dullard, the gawk, the numbskull, the simpleton, the weakling, and the scatterbrain are amongst us in overshadowing numbers – intermarrying, breeding, inordinately prolific, literally threatening to overwhelm the world with their useless and terrifying get." Margaret Sanger, Editor, International Aspects of Birth Control: The International Neo-Malthusian and Birth Control Conference. American Birth Control League, New York, 1925.*

*"The first step would thus be to control the intake and output of morons, mental defectives, epileptics.  The second step would be to take an inventory of the secondary group such as illiterates,*

*paupers, unemployables, criminals, prostitutes, dope-fiends; classify them in special departments under government medical protection, and segregate them on farms and open spaces as long as necessary for the strengthening and development of moral conduct. Having corralled this enormous part of our population and placed it on a basis of health instead of punishment, it is safe to say that fifteen or twenty millions of our population would then be organized into soldiers of defense---defending the unborn against their own disabilities." Margaret Sanger, A Plan for Peace, The Birth Control Review, 1932.*

In light of all this glaring, irrefutable evidence of her horridly inhumane, indeed holocaustic ideology, one would think Ms. Sanger's movement should have gained little traction or, at the very least, that modern day feminists, made aware of her iniquities, would finally stop extolling the woman's alleged virtues. Yet neither of these two things are true. Instead, her little baby's been exceedingly well-fed and systematically sanitized right down to its new name - Planned Parenthood - while the mother's reputation remains largely if precariously intact, preserved in a state of perpetual rehabilitation at academic clinics across the country. One excellent example is NYU's *Margaret Sanger's Papers Project*, an "historical editing project" at which "[c]reating scholarly editions of historical documents requires training and rigorous attention to detail." Presumably, NYU's "Biographical Sketch" of Ms. Sanger on their Papers Project website exemplifies the sort of creative scholarly editing they have in mind for the whole sordid history of her work. It is, to say the least, a sanitized sketch, wherein poor Margaret's reputation is portrayed as having been permanently tainted, not so much by anything she herself said or did, but "by her association with the reactionary wing of the eugenics movement," from which she allegedly tried to distance herself in favor of "conservative mainstream middle-class values" by the late 1920's.  Apparently, Ms. Sanger's 1932 Plan for Peace, excerpted above, escaped the attention of NYU's biographers, unless of course they viewed her Plan for Peace as consistent with their concept of "conservative mainstream middle-class values," which is certainly possible.

In any event, Margaret Sanger's role in the modern-day birth control movement has been carefully reduced to the old and "honorific" as NYU and others, try as they might, have been unable to hide all her scars.  However, most of Margaret's modern-day feminist friends remain quick to defend her on the ostensibly unassailable, supremely ideological grounds that she single-handedly secured for them the holy grail of a woman's wondrous liberation.  But recently, there have been different voices emanating from feminist ranks, like that of Dr. Angela Franks.

Dr. Franks is every bit the dedicated feminist, but of an enchantingly elevated order.  Her work on Margaret Sanger's Eugenic Legacy, as alluded to above, both rightly recognizes feminist ideology run amuck as an obfuscation of reality, and extraordinarily exemplifies how deliberate detachment from such ideology is essential to the search for truth.  Here are some samplings from her aforementioned work, *Margaret Sanger's Eugenic Legacy: The Control of Female Fertility*, MacFarland & Co., 2005:

> *Sanger's ideology is a . . . sensualism that allows*
> *for injustice to be performed on women [and] lives on*
> *today in the organizations she founded . . .Id at 9.*
> *. . . Planned Parenthood continues . . . to*
> *perpetuate eugenic beliefs about the poor and about*
> *the disabled. . .*

*. . . [For it] the ovaries and wombs of impoverished women are the unceasing source of the bulk of human suffering. This scapegoating is fundamentally anti-woman . . .*

*Feminism ought to be the premier liberation movement. Yet with bedfellows like Planned Parenthood, feminism is threatened with incoherence. As Karl Barth said, with the horror of Nazism full in his mind – 'No community whether family, village, or state, is really strong if it will not carry its weak and even its weakest members . . . On the other hand, a community which regards and treats its weak members as a hindrance, and even proceeds to their extermination, is on the verge of collapse.' The temptation to apply eugenic solutions to human problems is among the gravest threats to feminism today. Id at 19-20 . . .*

*Regarding the question of Chinese women and their subjection to forced sterilization and forced abortion, for example, Planned Parenthood . . . has praised China's coercive activities as being 'at the forefront of family planning.' Id at 61 . . .*

*The pressure exerted on women to conform their reproductive desires to those of Planned Parenthood is still present . . . [Its] overarching anti-natalist philosophy was . . . enunciated by an ad campaign that its . . . affiliate ran in 1996 . . . 'BABIES ARE LOUD, SMELLY, AND EXPENSIVE. UNLESS YOU WANT ONE . . .' The ad indicates the distorted lens through which reproduction is viewed. . . The point of the ad is to dissuade people, especially the young, from wanting to become mothers and fathers . . . Id at 63-64 . . .*

*Eugenics has not really died out; it has just taken on new projects . . . Sanger and Planned Parenthood have effectively inured the American conscience with the control ideology. Id at 127. . .*

*Sanger's complicity with eugenic sterilization, and the complicity of the organizations she founded, is perhaps the most terrifying testimony to the dangerous and misogynistic effects of negative eugenics . . . Id. at 202 . . .*

*By the sixties, Planned Parenthood's much-hoped-for outreach to businessmen was firmly established. . . The message in a nutshell: population growth is bad for business, but donating to Planned Parenthood is good for the bottom line . . . [because according to its 'People and Profits' propaganda] 'Planned Parenthood represents the most effective form of safeguard for U.S. investments abroad. By averting unrest and social upheaval stemming from overpopulation, poverty and famine, family planning can provide a foundation for peaceful progress. The developing nations will become more affluent, their people will become better customers for American products when competent family planning services are available for all.' Id at 209-211 . . .*

*The latest war against women and girls is being fought by means of sophisticated prenatal diagnostic techniques. . . One geneticist, John D. Stephens, who patented a technique that can test for gender quite early, noted that, if a fetus is aborted, it is 'almost always a girl.' . . .*

*Planned Parenthood's capitulation to sex-selection abortion follows logically from it eugenic ideology . . . [and] colludes with the denigration of the female . . .*

*As a result, women and girls, especially the poor, continue to suffer at the hands of an unchallenged misogyny that considers their reproductive powers inherently problematic, if not repugnant, and disposable for the sake of the 'greater good' . . .*

*In promoting consumerist ideology (one that Sanger's own version of the bourgeois lifestyle presaged), Planned Parenthood . . . has allowed itself to become a tool of men more interested in profits than people. Id at 232-236. . . [and by] accepting this radical misogyny, feminism . . . trivializes the damage done to women and girls through violence perpetrated on their bodies.  Id at 239. . .*

*[W]hen the usual misogynist suspects – the self-anointed elite in the mainstream press, big business, Hollywood, the education establishment, the academy, as well as popular culture (the propaganda machine of these elites) – are advocating a plan of action, feminists should investigate the matter, with full critical consciousness, [and] . . .stop making deals with the devil.  Planned Parenthood has a eugenic history and philosophy. . . One need only note the apologies it gives for brutally misogynistic regimes and population-control programs to realize the necessity of a clean break. . .*

*To be free, women must live in harmony with the rhythms of their own bodies, not in spite of*

*them . . . Feminism needs to provide the tools for*
*women and girls to rebuild their fragile sense of self,*
*so that they once again feel at home in their bodies. . .*
*All this does indeed mean that feminism*
*must also shed its inhibitions concerning the defense*
*and even the celebration of motherhood. Id at 246-249.*

In addition to this indictment of their ongoing, profit-driven, eugenic-misogynistic philosophy, Planned Parenthood's public portrayal of itself as the champion of women's choice is further belied by the evidence that it has adhered to a sinister symbiotic business model of selling sex to impressionable young women, and then urgently advocating abortion if anything should go wrong.

"Our goal," asserted one Planned Parenthood newsletter as early as 1953, "is to be ready as educators and parents to help young people obtain sex satisfaction before marriage.  By sanctioning sex before marriage, we will prevent fear and guilt."

"Relax about loving," continued The Great Orgasm Robbery by Sherri Tepper of Rocky Mountain Planned Parenthood in 1977.  "Sex is fun and joyful, and courting is fun and joyful, and it comes in all types and styles, all of which are okay.  Do what gives pleasure, and enjoy what gives pleasure, and ask for what gives pleasure.  Don't rob yourself of joy by focusing on old-fashioned ideas about what's *normal or nice.*  Just communicate and enjoy!"

These admittedly dated examples are in fact an accurate prelude to what Planned Parenthood has been doing with increasing organization and vigor for over 50 years, right up to and including the present time.  Witness, the International Planned Parenthood Federation's November 2009 mission statement, *Stand & Deliver: Sex, Health & Young People in the 21st Century,* wherein its efforts to encourage worldwide unconstrained sexual orientation and experimentation "as a source of pleasure" and "expression of self" in children as young as ten years old are made unmistakably clear.

Echoes of Margaret Sanger here, who declared that abstinence was "positively harmful" to one's health as it could cause debilitating nervous derangement. This, in response to the 1930 Encyclical of Pope Pius XI entitled *Casti Connubii* ("On Christian Marriage"), in which His Holiness cautioned that contraception could lead to a loss of respect for women who, rather than being beloved and respected companions, would increasingly be viewed by men as mere objects of sexual gratification.

Of course, if the contraception recommended by Planned Parenthood didn't do the trick, abortion was the order of the day according to David Reardon's Aborted Women: Silent No More, Crossway Books, 1987, which cites from a survey of women who purchased abortions from Planned Parenthood, 89% of whom said that their counselors had been "strongly biased in favor of abortion," and 80% of whom said that their counselors gave them "little or no information about [abortion's] potential health risks;" This, despite the fact that the risks are significant, and the alternatives available. Indeed, Dr. Horton Dean, a Los Angeles gynecologist, having seen the marked increase in physical and mental abortion-related complications since its legalization in 1973, became "convinced that the Planned Parenthood programs pose the greatest health hazard in America today." The true scale of complications from abortion are, in his view, "a national health disaster." So much for the so-called champions of women's choice.

Nevertheless, Planned Parenthood remains the largest provider of abortion and birth control services in the world, and possibly the most profitable non-profit organization in history, generating an estimated 10 billion dollars in annual worldwide revenues. Of the well over one million surgical abortions performed annually in the United States alone, approximately 25% were said to have occurred at one of Planned Parenthood's 855 US clinics in fiscal 2006, for example, during which its gross income from all services and government grants (our tax dollars hard at work) reportedly exceeded one billion ($1,000,000,000.00) dollars. (From the All-American Life League).

Thus, it would appear that despite pervasive evidence of its perverted philosophies, Planned Parenthood has largely succeeded in continuing to portray itself to the public as a benevolent association interested only in the health and welfare of poor women, thanks to Margaret's successors at Planned Parenthood, notably including Cass Canfield and Alan Guttmacher (more on them a little later in the book).

Margaret Sanger, daughter of misogyny, mother of blood money, died on September 6, 1966, but not before she'd succeeded in seducing half the world, and sown the seeds for its spiritual self-destruction.  Let he that hath wisdom count the number of the beast.

# 7

# Notre Dame Our Mother

**Knute Rockne**

*If you could find a way to bottle the Notre Dame Spirit, you could light up the universe.*

**Joe Theismann**

Shortly prior to the passing of Patrick Connors in 1893, Notre Dame suffered the inestimable loss of Father Edward Sorin, her first and most loyal son, prompting Father Corby to construct a new grotto to honor their Lady of Lourdes in 1896.  Seventy years later, in 1966 (the year of Margaret Sanger's death), the Fighting Irish tied

Michigan State, 10 to 10, and were awarded college football's national championship.  In those seven decades spanning from grotto to glory, Notre Dame's identity acquired extraordinary national importance.  As succinctly summarized by Notre Dame Professor Alfred Freddoso's excellent introduction to his colleague Charlie Rice's groundbreaking book, *What Happened to Notre Dame? (St. Augustine's press, 2009)*:

> Anyone who knows the history of the Catholic Church in America realizes that during the 20th century Notre Dame loomed large in the consciousness of the immigrant Catholic communities that had come to populate the eastern seaboard and the Great Lakes region.  Notre Dame's success, especially on the football field, was symbolic of the aspirations of hundreds of thousands of Catholic immigrants who were struggling to 'make it' in America and to ensure a better future for their many children.

It had all started November 6, 1909, thanks largely to the heroics of Harry "Red" Miller, whereby Notre Dame beat Michigan for the first time, 11 to 3, finally avenging the outcome of that controversial game that had first ignited the rivalry some twenty-one years earlier.  Sportswriter E. A. Batchelor put it this way in the *Detroit Free Press*:

> *Eleven **fighting Irishmen** wrecked the [Michigan coach] Yost machine this afternoon.  These sons of Erin, individually and collectively representing the University of Notre Dame, not only beat the Michigan team, but they dashed some of Michigan's*

If Batchelor's goal was to fan the flames of rivalry, he succeeded wildly. For Michigan coach Fielding Yost was an incredibly sore loser, wrongfully accusing Red Miller of unsportsmanlike conduct and two of his teammates of being ineligible, all the while claiming that his own team had not even taken that "practice" game seriously. For months, debate raged in the press, with those of anti-Irish Catholic inclinations raining on Notre Dame's parade. Result: Michigan cancelled its 1910 game with Notre Dame at the very last minute, and refused to play them again for another thirty-two years, during which time a talented man with the unusual name of Knute Rockne took Notre Dame to a level of football fame never to be matched by Michigan, or by any other team in the entire nation, for the next 100 years.

Rockne was born on March 4, 1888, the very same year that Notre Dame football had in fact been born with the help of Michigan. Rockne then entered Notre Dame as a freshman in 1910 on the heels of its first victory over Michigan. So goes the early evidence of his mythical existence, but there would be more. He was the senior left offensive end for the Notre Dame team which first earned national fame by unleashing the power of the forward pass and beating Army's perennial powerhouse at West Point on November 1, 1913. The passing combination of quarterback Charles Dorais to receiver Knute Rockne made a huge contribution to the final score (Notre Dame 35 - Army 13), and to Notre Dame's first financially profitable football season, a profit that would steadily climb to an astounding $529,420 by 1929. By 2007, Forbes would report that Notre Dame's football program was the most valuable in the nation, with a market value over $100 million dollars, and an annual profit of approximately $46 million.

During his 13 years as coach, from 1918-1930, Rockne would record a won-lost record of 105 to 12 (with 5 ties), which translates to a winning percentage of .801, the highest in college football history to date. He led those thirteen teams, with twenty All-Americans, to six national championships and five undefeated and untied seasons.  His first undefeated team of 1919 played nine games before a total of 56,500 fans.  His national championship team of 1924 played ten games, including the Rose Bowl, before 318,000 fans.  By the end of 1929, despite the stock market's crash, his fourth undefeated team had played nine games in front of 550,000 fans, the one against USC alone attracting 112,000 fans to Soldier Field in Chicago. In other words, the so-called "subway alumni" had arrived on the scene in earnest; or, to paraphrase James Joyce's loving jest about that wonderful thing called the Catholic Church - 'here came everybody.'

Enrollment at Notre Dame tripled during this era in Catholic education, about which Notre Dame Professor and Irish-Catholic historian Jay P. Dolan makes the following somewhat wistful observation in his aforementioned book, *The Irish American: A History* -

> *To most Catholic parents of this generation, it*
> *did not matter that prohibited books were not read*
> *and that certain subjects were not studied in Catholic*
> *schools.  Modern notions of academic freedom simply*
> *were unknown or, if known, not highly valued by*
> *parents or by Catholic colleges and universities,*
> *including Notre Dame.  Parents chose to send their*
> *sons to Catholic schools, and especially to Notre Dame,*
> *because they believed them to be safe, well-supervised*
> *places where education was delivered in a*
> *philosophically and morally secure environment.*
> *Students could be educated for life and work in the*

*contemporary world and in the process become
stronger Catholics and better persons.  That was the
point of it all.*

Indeed, if largely by virtue of their numbers among religious
and lay alike, it was the Irish who would define what it meant to be
Catholic in 20th century America.  In the post-famine era of Ireland
and America dawned a "devotional revolution," where the parish
church took center stage, where being a "practicing Catholic" became
"the coin of the realm," and where "Sunday Mass became the
centerpiece of piety."  By the 1920's, parish church life was in its
glistening golden age as the charitable, spiritual, social, and
educational epicenter of Irish Catholic communities.

The parents in these communities invested heavily in the
elementary and secondary religious education of their children, and
found solace for themselves in their faith, especially during the
depression and through two world wars.  Second only to attendance
at Sunday Mass, they took to congregating in special prayer groups
and service fraternities devoted to such helpers as the Sacred Heart of
Jesus, His Blessed Virgin Mother, St. Joseph the Worker, and the
like, wherein a firm belief in divine assistance was central to their
prayers and tasks.  Together, they waged war against sin, chief among
which was the evil of birth control. Sexual morality was the bedrock
of their faith, all the more so as secular modernists like Margaret
Sanger painted them and their Catholicism as increasingly old-
fashioned.  Indeed, it was Church opposition to birth control, covered
in the forthcoming chapter, which would set it both sadly and
inevitably apart from an ever-swelling "mainstream" of secular
progressive American culture.

Thus, it is in hindsight no surprise that anti-Catholic bigotry
persisted after the 1889 Northwestern game at which the Notre Dame
team had to endure chants of "kill the fighting Irish."  For fully the

next four decades, Notre Dame put up with routine public slurs among the press and general public such as "Papists," "Horrible Hibernians," "Dumb Micks," and "Dirty Irish."  Initially, Notre Dame tried to counter this by calling themselves the "Gold and Blue," the "Notre Damers," the "Warriors" and such, but nothing stuck. Instead, the "Fighting Irish," as if by the force of manifest destiny, acquired an increasingly positive persona of its own as World War I ended, the Free Irish State was firmly established in Erin, and Rockne took a previously unheralded team to ever greater heights and lime-lights.

Finally, in 1927, Notre Dame's then president, the Reverend Matthew Walsh, in response to an inquiry from the New York World about the school's official position on its still unofficial name, declared that "the name 'Fighting Irish' . . . seems to embody the kind of spirit that we like to see . . . on the athletic field.  I sincerely hope that we may always be worthy of the ideals embodied in the term . . .," and from that day forward, it was a name that, while still uttered in hatred, would never again bring shame, or so one thought.

Nevertheless, in the 1920's, the nation experienced an especially strong surge of anti-Catholicism, driven in large part by the resurrection of the Ku Klux Klan.  For the hooded ones would temporarily change their focus from anti-Black to anti-Catholic in order to gain political traction among anti-papist Protestants throughout the heartlands, and especially in Indiana. Catholics, according to the Klan, were unpatriotic, intolerant, and devious people committed to imposing their views on others and undermining all things American.  This propaganda was successful because the power of the press and politicians in general was largely in the hands of intolerant Protestants, and because influential Catholics such as those at Notre Dame were loath to speak out against it for fear of making matters worse.  But its intensity increased anyway, and things were brought to a boiling point in 1924.

In May of that year, some Notre Dame students took matters into their own hands by violently confronting groups of Klansmen in the streets of South Bend, much to the dismay of university officials who had admonished against such action. Their conduct resulted in a backlash against Notre Dame in the surrounding communities of South Bend and Elkhart, upon which the Klan further capitalized by fomenting more hatred and making more plans to capture even greater political power. It became a case of spoiled rotten Irish Catholic brats against poor innocent protestant patriots. This tact would eventually aid the Klan in obtaining a permit to hold a parade in South Bend on October 18, 1924, but not without providence entering the fray.

Father John O'Hara, Notre Dame's Prefect of Religion, reacted magnificently to this sad turn of events by masterfully handling matters on and off the campus. First, he turned his attention to the students, telling them that while he understood their eagerness to defend the honor of Notre Dame by fighting for what they believed in, aggressively engaging in random acts of bloodshed had made them no better than the bigots who had gotten their ire up, and done further damage to the already fragile reputation of their Catholic alma mater in the process.

Then, O'Hara acted with great dispatch to temper that damage and effect some repairs by turning to the most effective weapon he had at his disposal – football. As suggested by one of Notre Dame's historians, O'Hara may have been inspired by a New York Times editorial that had been reprinted in *Notre Dame Alumnus* magazine as the problem was brewing in the months before the bloodshed. "There is in Indiana a militant Catholic organization . . . engaged in secret drills," it facetiously warned. "They make long cross-country raiding expeditions . . . Worst of all, they lately fought and defeated a detachment of the United States Army. Yet we have not heard of the

Indiana Klansmen rising up to exterminate the Notre Dame football team."

Klan-driven anti-Catholicism did in fact incite the Notre Dame football team to prepare for a 1924 campaign that "was looked upon by the players as sort of a spiritual crusade," to hear O'Hara tell it. And to hear historian James Burns tell it: "In truth, this football season was much more than a spiritual crusade.  For O'Hara and millions of American Catholics throughout the country who believed and felt as he did, and especially for the 300,000 Catholics living in Indiana – 11 percent of the population of the state – the performance of the Notre Dame football team in that year gave them all a supreme moment of restored pride and dignity." (excluding George Shuster, who would abandon and betray his alma mater, pouting like a self-absorbed little sop, in 1925.  More on him later.).  The linchpin to restoring this pride came poetically on October 18, 1924, the same day on which the Klan had scheduled its South Bend parade.  Seven hundred miles to the east, in New York's infamous Polo Grounds, Notre Dame would defeat a powerful and previously undefeated Army team, 13 to 7, courtesy of their backfield, about to be made infamous.

Witnessing the win from the press-box above was a Notre Dame intern in journalism by the name of George Strickler, who had recently seen a Rudolf Valentino movie entitled "The Four Horsemen of the Apocalypse."  Strickler remarked that Notre Dame's four-man backfield had reminded him of the fearsome mythical horsemen in the movie.  New York sportswriter Grantland Rice overheard the remark, and the rest is history:

> *Outlined against a blue-gray October sky, the*
> *Four Horsemen rode again.  In dramatic lore, they are*
> *Famine, Pestilence, Destruction, and Death, but they*
> *are only aliases.  Their real names are Stuhldreyer,*

From there, with the help of Rice and a whole lot of other providential public relations assistance, Father O'Hara would expertly parlay Notre Dame's growing national fame past notoriously anti-Catholic opponents like Nebraska, and onward all the way to the Rose Bowl, where Stanford would be its tenth and final victim in an undefeated, untied, national championship season.

In fact, O'Hara was the one who had urged an otherwise reluctant president Walsh to allow the team to trek to Pasadena for the Rose Bowl, national anti-Catholic sentiments notwithstanding. Not only did Walsh relent, but he put O'Hara in charge, the only Holy Cross priest to accompany the team on the trip.  He and Coach Rockne then brilliantly orchestrated a three-week long whistle-stopping, flag waving train trip peppered with pro-Catholic public relations propaganda of celestial proportions, promoting wholesome and gentlemanly gridiron spirituality wherever they went.  Afterward, it was evident to O'Hara and others that the team had taken full advantage of a unique opportunity, traveling from coast to coast exhibiting spiritual and sportsmanlike conduct, extinguishing brushfires of bigotry, and assuring all who would listen that Catholic education in general, and at Notre Dame in particular, was a friend, not a foe, to America's fondest ideals.  Indeed, at least according to the incomparable O'Hara, Notre Dame had found in her football team an essential instrument of the Good Lord's providence, their heroics on the football field comparing happily to King David's dance "before the Ark of the Lord."  Indeed, in the words of another well-respected Notre Dame historian:

> *[E]ven after discounting O'Hara's emotional excesses, one must recognize that the religious spirit informing the football team during the season of 1924 was so powerful and evident that even Coach Rockne, the great motivator, was touched by it.  Although he was normally undemonstrative about religion, sometime after the Rose Bowl victory and triumphant national tour, Rockne asked for religious instruction, was baptized, and was received into the Catholic Church in November of 1925.*

And then there's this from Rockne himself:

> *I used to be impressed deeply at the sight of my players receiving Communion every morning, and I finally made a point of going to Mass with them on the morning of a game. . .*
> *One night before a big game in the East, I was nervous and worried about the outcome the next day, and was unable to sleep.  I tossed and rolled about the bed, and finally decided to get up and sit downstairs.*

*About five or six o'clock in the morning, while pacing
the lobby of the hotel, I unexpectedly ran into two of
my own players hurrying out . . . and I decided to go
along with them.  They didn't realize it, but these
youngsters were making a powerful impression on me
with their devotion, and when I saw all of them
walking up to the Communion rail to receive, and
realized the hours of sleep they had sacrificed, I
understood for the first time what a powerful ally their
religion was to them in their work on the football field.
Later on, I had the happiness of joining my boys at the
Communion rail.*

Eventually, the Klan receded and self-destructed, but not
before it had succeeded in heightening anti-Catholicism enough to
crush the presidential candidacy of the Catholic Al Smith in 1928.
Undaunted, Notre Dame responded to the indignities that Smith
endured by defeating Army before a crowd of 78,000 at Yankee
Stadium four days after the election, the game at which Rockne
delivered his famous "win one for the Gipper" speech (George Gipp
played for Rockne for 5 seasons, 1916 – 1920, before pneumonia took
his life in December of 1920).  The press would call it "Rockne's
Revenge," and Notre Dame would top it all off by awarding Smith its
1929 Laetare Medal, the highest honor that can be accorded to
anyone by the university.

After coaching Notre Dame to victory in each of his last
nineteen games, Knute Rockne perished in a 1931 plane crash at the
age of 43.  Here is how Notre Dame's in-house historian and Holy
Cross priest, Father Arthur Hope, saw Rockne's tragic death:

*. . . It is not untrue to say that no death within the confines of the United States caused more grief and depression in those years than the death of Rockne. When the news of his going had been flashed to the world, men stood in silent groups all over the nation, and the boys of the country were numbed in the knowledge that their hero had been taken from them. On the campus, of course, the blow was absolutely stunning. We will never forget the silence of the students. Once the news was confirmed, they closed their mouths and went to the church or the hall chapels to pray. In silence, they tried to hide their gloom and heart-break, for if they had talked, they would have wept.*

Years later, that old "B movie" actor by the name of Ronald Reagan would also chime in:

*Growing up in the Midwest, as I did in the Rockne years, and loving football as I did, long before I played in high school and college, I was part of the great, nationwide, unofficial Notre Dame cheering section . . .*

*My life has been full of rich and wonderful experiences. Standing near the top of the list is my long and honored association with the University of Notre Dame and its legendary hero, Knute Rockne . . .*

Football revenues would recede in the years after the 1929 market crash and 1931 death of Knute Rockne sent the country into a tailspin, but reserves and careful cutbacks would enable Notre Dame to weather the economic storms until O'Hara took the helm in 1934 and turned things around with savvy business acumen.  Heartley Anderson proved an ineffective substitute for his friend Knute Rockne from 1931 to 1934, so O'Hara replaced him with Elmer Layden, who wrought new fortunes, both on the field and financially, for Notre Dame.  O'Hara also effectively tapped into an increasingly affluent Notre Dame alumni, and successfully solicited funding from charitable institutions.  After the war, these sources would prove invaluable to Notre Dame's financial future as the wealth of the American Catholic community increased enormously in the post-war economic boom.

O'Hara bade farewell to Notre Dame late in 1939 to become the Apostolic Delegate for United States Military forces, followed by his appointment as Bishop of Buffalo in 1945, and Archbishop of Philadelphia in 1951.  Then, in 1958, he became the first priest from Blessed Moreau's 120 yr. old Congregation of Holy Cross to be admitted to the College of Cardinals of the Roman Catholic Church. He died on August 28, 1960, and is buried at the Basilica of the Sacred Heart on the campus of Notre Dame.  Today, Notre Dame's Mendoza School of Business (ranked first in the nation in 2010, according to <u>Business Week</u>), is proud to call its own endowment network of alumni, family, and friends - The John Cardinal O'Hara Society.

Notre Dame also endured the loss of enrollments occasioned by World War II, but at the same time contributed greatly to the war effort by making itself home to thousands of Naval midshipmen for their year-round ROTC training, and by putting the rest of its renovation and construction projects on hold for the duration of the war.  But the war did not keep Notre Dame from playing football.  In fact, its football fortunes increased with the arrival of Frank Leahy and his highly disciplined approach to the "T formation" type offense in 1941.

From to 1941 to 1953, excluding two years for military service, Leahy compiled an extraordinary record of 87 wins and only 11 losses, six out of eleven unbeaten seasons, and four national championships.  He was named nationwide college Coach of the Year five times, producing thirty-six All-Americans, and four Heisman Trophy winners.  Two years prior to his death from Leukemia in 1973, he sent a telegram to his four national championship teams, gathered together for a grand reunion that his health had left him unable to attend.  In that telegram he told them that "[w]ords cannot adequately express the depth of my sadness over not being with you . . . Never lose contact with that famous Lady who reigns so serenely over our beautiful campus . . .You are men endowed with qualities that forged our nation to greatness.  Notre Dame leadership is more important now than ever before."

Coach Leahy needn't have worried, for Notre Dame football players, and students of all stripes, were wonderfully devoted to their "famous Lady," especially at her home in the Grotto, lighting candles there before football games in the Fall and exams in the Winter, processing there for month of May devotions in the Spring, and finding it the perfect place for every heartfelt wish, from prayers for peace to proposals of marriage.  One such student by the name of John Klee stopped there to say goodbye, and to ask Our Lady to protect him as he headed off to war in February of 1943.  Later, as a B-24 pilot, he and his entire crew would miraculously survive an enemy attack that had forced him to crash land his aircraft in Southern Italy.  When he arrived back home on April 30, 1945, his first order of business after greeting family and friends was to hop a train from Newport News to Notre Dame and thank Our Lady for her protection, a personal May procession of sorts that had him back at the Grotto on V/J Day, May 8, 1945, undoubtedly a day of both tears and rejoicing for everyone there at his dear old Notre Dame.

Likewise, would Notre Dame graduate Dr. Tom Dooley - whose medical relief efforts for Southeast Asian refugees would inspire President Kennedy to start the Peace Corps - be inspired to write this from his hospital bed in December of 1960, a month before he died at the age of 44:

> . . . [T]he cancer has spread . . . But . . . peace gathers in my heart. What seems unpossessable, I can possess. What seems unfathomable, I fathom. What is inutterable, I utter. Because I can pray. . .
>
> I realize the external symbols that surround one when he prays are not important. . .
>
> But just now, and just so many times, how I long for the Grotto. Away from the Grotto, Dooley just prays. But at the Grotto, especially now, when there must be snow everywhere and the lake is ice glass . . . if I could go to the Grotto now, then I think I could sing inside. . .
>
> That Grotto is the rock to which my life is anchored. . . my beloved Notre Dame. . .

Indeed, as beautifully portrayed by the father-son alumni team of Jim and Jeremy Langford in their book, *The Spirit of Notre Dame* (University of Notre Dame Press, 2005-2009), "Notre Dame has a mystique . . . that extend[s] far beyond its campus. . . Many who have never . . . set foot [there] feel a close connection," enemies apparently included. For example, in 1937, Notre Dame fullback Mario Tonelli, wearing football jersey number 58, scrambled for seventy yards and then scored the tie-breaking touchdown to beat USC. Then, in 1941, with his Notre Dame Class of 1939 ring adorning his finger, he joined

the US Army and was assigned to General MacArthur in the
Phillipines, right before the outbreak of the war with Japan.
Captured by the Japanese at the Bataan Peninsula, he was one of the
soldiers who'd managed to endure the barbaric Battaan Death March,
trudging through some sixty-five miles of oppressive jungle with
minimal food and water. While en-route, Tonelli's personally
engraved ring was stolen by a Japanese soldier, but a superior officer
who witnessed what had happened would return the ring to Tonelli.
Why? Because the officer had also witnessed something else. While
a student at USC only four years earlier, he had witnessed Tonelli's
special feat on the football field. "I know how much this ring means
to you," he told Tonelli, as he handed it back to him.

Eleven thousand solders had died on that death march, but
Tonelli survived it, along with another thirty months of ungodly
imprisonment to boot. Then, in 1944, weighing not much more than
100 pounds, he was shipped to mainland Japan for slave labor.
Standing in line for processing, he arrived at the intake table to
receive his identification number – 58 – the same as his old football
jersey. "That's when I knew I'd make it," he would say when he told
his story back in the States, where he lived out a life of public service
until his death in 2003, his Notre Dame ring still adorning his hand.

As for the educational experiences of Tonelli, Dooley, Klee,
and the other Notre Dame students of that era, George McClancey
(Class of 52), reflects on Professor Frank O'Malley, who had been
valedictorian of Notre Dame's class of 1932 before teaching the
humanities there for the next twenty years (one of the twenty-six men
and women on Notre Dame's Wall of Fame as of 2009):

> *[His] classes on Modern Catholic Writers and*
> *Philosophy in Literature bordered on the miraculous . .*
> *.[T]here was something . . . that made it an experience*
> *of profound revelation . . . O'Malley's arrival was the*

*occasion for a wave of awe to pass through the classroom . . . [He] was not just a good teacher, teaching an interesting course. He was prophetic. He was a witness to the truth . . . [H]e revealed to us an understanding of things, made available through faith and thought, which was different from and infinitely more profound than the mix of parochial school religion and complacent middle-class values that was the norm everywhere in American Catholic culture. . . O'Malley made us realize that all was not well in Christendom. On the contrary, there was a great misunderstanding abroad which failed to see the "fear and trembling" promised by St. Paul and seemed to offer a false "promised land" of spiritual comfort and material prosperity as the reward of the Faithful . . . It became as though, suddenly, a fire was enkindled deep in the soul and we hung on every word O'Malley uttered. . .*

*There did, indeed, seem to be a strange power in the very sound of his voice, halting and almost inaudible as it often was, much as there may sometimes be in the mere sound of the voice of a great singer or poet or dramatic actor, to move the soul . . .*

*The ancients had no rational answer to account for the superhuman excellence of great art . . .[but] St. Thomas Aquinas informs us that . . . by the power of the Holy Spirit . . . The Gift of Words, which renders the truth lucid to its hearers, is directed precisely at the empowering of utterance, at the spoken word.*

*. . . [H]is influence on generations of Notre Dame students was so profound and so vast in its consequences that it may find no parallel in the history*

*of the University, if not the history of American higher education.*

Then, as if that were not enough, there are these snippets from O'Malley himself:

> *The Catholic College, as a College of Christ, should be a community of students and teachers centered in Christ...[T]he marrow of a Catholic College is not a system of thought, but a saving personality.*

> *. . . [I]n our concern with teaching and with the works of the mind, we must meditate seriously about the final relation of our existence, our relations to God. Man is not a being sufficient unto himself who can acknowledge his relationship to God or reject it, precisely as he thinks and decides. The nature of man is essentially determined by his relationship to God. Man exists only as one related to God: 'where there is no God there is no man.' And the way in which he understands this relationship, how seriously he takes it, and the consequences he draws from it — all this determines the nature of his life, his work, his vocation.*
>
> *. .*

> *These realizations ought to be more firmly and powerfully yours because you have come to this place of Notre Dame, this great and dominant Catholic university of the United States, a place concerned through all the years with integrating a true faith and a true philosophy with the life of culture. In your time here, you must have become better aware of the*

*composition of life, of the nature of true primacy. You
must have considered here and found here the answer
to 'the old question which traverses the sky of the soul
perpetually, the vast, the general question, what is the
meaning of life.' If you are convinced of your answer,
you will not be deluded by the lies and phrases; you
will be able to resist the pressure of the age. Possessed
as you should be of a true spiritual culture, you will
not be too much disconcerted or ravaged by
contemporary civilization; you will not feel yourselves
prisoners of life, scratching on the walls of your cells;
you will not succumb to the sorrows of the savage
world. Instead, you will save yourselves and save all
those who encounter you in your various works and
ways and vocations.*

What a wonderful time it was, then, in the history of old Notre
Dame, when a student could come from O'Malley's class on the eve of
St. Patrick's Day, 1953, and find in his dorm room the extraordinary
essay of Father Charles Carey, in which he answered the age old
question - "Why the Fighting Irish?"  Here, once again, is what that
loyal son of Erin said:

*Tomorrow, the world will be green for a day
while we honor the patron saint of Erin.  Bighearted
people of all nationalities will pause to applaud the
contribution of the Irish to the civilization of the world.
Best of all contributions made was the faith which they
took with them wherever their wanderings took them.
Patrick is a great saint of God; and therefore, a great
saint of the church.  And if he belongs to the Church,*

*then he belongs to you.  That's why you should pray to
St. Patrick, asking him to increase your Faith; bolster
it; make it a living reality in your everyday life —
keeping you aware that the trials and sufferings of this
exile are as nothing when compared to the glory that
awaits those who fight the good fight that overcomes
the world!*

> *Tomorrow you can take this one lesson
from the Irish:  that they were never so poor in all
their wanderings and sufferings that they bartered
their Faith for the comforts of this life.  They had little
to take with them wherever they went; but the Faith
was always the most precious of their paltry
possessions.  Their spirit has made it easier for you to
practice your Faith here in America today.  May the
Fighting Irish always be with us!*

Ten years later, in 1963, the very same spirit that had poured
from O'Malley and Carey must have preyed upon poor Ara
Parseghian as soon as he passed through the gates enroute to that
national championship in 1966 (and another in 1973):

> *The first time I drove up Notre Dame Avenue
after being named head football coach, an enormous
sense of responsibility overwhelmed me.  The Notre
Dame football program had been in a period of decline
. . .*

> *I didn't realize the magnitude of Notre Dame
until I actually came to the campus and began to be
exposed to all it is and represents.  There is a Notre
Dame mystique that defies definition or description.  It
is something special in its combination of religion,*

*education, and athletics.  It is not only national but international in scope...*

Indeed, Ara must have been among those who heard Brother Paul singing softly to the faithful on those Saturday mornings:

*Well I remember the leaves a fallin'*
*And far off music like pipes a callin'*
*And I remember the golden morning*
*I saw the long ranks as they were forming*

*And there's a magic in the sound of their name*
*Here come the Irish of Notre Dame*

*The pilgrims follow by sacred waters*
*And arm in arm go the sons and daughters*
*The drums are rolling and forward bound*
*They're calling spirits up from the ground*

*And there's a magic in the sound of their name*
*Here come the Irish of Notre Dame.*

And then when the battles were over, and the winds washed through the trees once more, he surely heard Brother Paul and his brethren, singing once again, only this time to the heavens, and maybe a wee bit louder:

*Notre Dame, our Mother*
*Tender, strong and true*
*Proudly in thy heavens,*
*Gleams thy gold and blue.*

*Glory's mantle cloaks thee*
*Golden is thy fame*
*And our hearts forever*
*Praise thee, Notre Dame.*
*And our hearts forever*
*Love thee, Notre Dame*
*(Notre Dame Our Mother, by Rev. Charles O'Donnell, CSC &*
*Mr. Joseph Casasanta)*

Alas, whenever their singing would subside in the sixties, one could hear another ominous but unsettling sound all around; that is, the sound of a world that was "changing with bewildering speed, challenging not only the culture of Catholicism but also the continued existence of the Irish neighborhood parish.  Adding to these new changes was the emergence of a new breed of educated Catholics who were in search of a Catholicism more in tune with American culture. . . Within a few short years such a transformation would take place, bringing an end to a chapter in American Catholic history in which the Irish ruled."  But it's not as if it happened all at once.  No, the weeds were surely growing all the while among the wheat.

# 8

# Weeds among the Wheat

*He put another parable before them. The kingdom of heaven may be compared to a man who sowed good seed in his field. While everybody was asleep his enemy came, sowed weeds all among the wheat, and made off. When the new wheat sprouted and ripened, the weeds appeared as well. The owner's servants went to him and said, 'Sir, was it not good seed that you sowed in your field? If so, where do the weeds come from?' 'Some enemy has done this,' he answered. And the servants said, 'Do you want us to go and weed it out?' But he said, 'No, because when you pull out the weeds you might pull up the wheat with them. Let them both grow till the harvest; and at harvest time I shall say to the reapers: First collect the weeds and tie them into bundles to be burnt, then gather the wheat into my barn.'* From <u>Weeds Among the Wheat</u>, Thomas H. Green, S.J. (Ave Maria Press, Notre Dame, Indiana, 1984-86) at 144, quoting <u>Matthew</u> 13:24-30 (New Jersulem Bible version)

On August 4, 1879, as Maggie Higgins moved a little closer to her mother's birth canal, and Edward Sorin built brick upon new brick, Pope Leo XIII, who was lovingly dubbed "the Rosary Pope" for his prayerful devotion to Mary, issued a prophetic encyclical entitled *Eternal Father (Aeterni Patris)*. In it, he cautioned the Catholic faithful, in accordance with the teachings of St. Thomas Acquinas (The Angelic Doctor of the Church and Prince of Catholic Scholastics), that no matter how clever man's earthly endeavors, nor lofty his natural reasoning, he would never fill the needs nor see the full meaning of his own material existence, lest he walk first and always by unwavering faith in the immutable truths of Christ. Sadly, while O'Malley and his students would embrace this lesson, it was lost not only on Ms. Sanger, but also on a man named Shuster, who, to many among Notre Dame's "loyal sons", would turn traitor for what seemed to them his headlong mission to undermine the heart and soul of the school Father Sorin had founded.

George N. Shuster was born in 1894, just a few months after the deaths of Sorin and Connors, and only fifteen years after the publication of *Aeterni Patris*. Five years later, in 1899, Pope Leo would take his encyclical one step further, warning Baltimore Archbishop James Cardinal Gibbons, in an apostolic letter entitled *Testem Benevolentiae Nostrae* ("Witness to Our Good Will"), that America was in danger of reducing truth to a relative term by making each man's individual intellect the judge of what was good and evil. Then, in a 1907 encyclical entitled *Pascendi Dominici Gregis* ("Feeding the Lord's Flock"), Pope Leo's successor, Pius X, would label such heresy as "modernism," and express great anguish over the unhappy fact that such was being spread by none other than prominent church religious and laity who "seize upon chairs in the seminaries and universities" to scatter the seeds of their destructive weeds while good men lay sleeping. Case in point: George Shuster.

In 1919, Notre Dame's president, Father James Burns, saw that there was a special place for the study of the humanities — philosophy, theology, and literature - at Catholic universities and colleges, where Christian insight could help explain "modern culture to a generation of confused and misdirected men and women." Burns believed that in order to fulfill this mission, Catholic universities needed great teachers who were also good Catholics, generally at peace with the Church, tolerant of its institutional eccentricities, and mindful of its hierarchical authority. Ironically, Burns' eventual successor to the presidency of Notre Dame, the Reverend Charles O'Donnell, would recommend his former Notre Dame student - one George N. Shuster - as just the sort of man that Burns had in mind. Shuster had been only a year behind Knute Rockne, and both men had been brilliant students (Rockne had graduated magna cum laude). But Shuster lacked what it took to make the football team and, perhaps as a consequence, came to harbor a bookworm's sort of cynical disdain for the game, and for fellow student Rockne's growing renown. In any event, O'Donnell's recommendation, made in 1919, was one that would profoundly affect the university in many unforeseen ways for fully the next ninety years.

Shuster had been hired by Burns to head the English Department, and correct what then Reverend Father O'Hara, in his capacity as prefect of religion, had perceived from his surveys of the students to be a "woeful neglect" of good Catholic literature in English courses. Shuster responded by constructing a course called "The Catholic Spirit in Modern English Literature." O'Hara was grateful for Shuster's efforts, but suspicious of Shuster's decision to pepper his reading list with protestant, agnostic, and socialistic writers who were, according to Shuster, "Catholic in spirit." O'Hara turned to Father John Talbot Smith for assistance in the assessment of Shuster's book list. This (together with tight administrative restrictions on faculty salary increases in the next four years) would make young Professor Shuster a most unhappy man. For example, Smith and O'Hara had a hard time understanding how eugenically-minded misogynistic atheists such as Henrik Ibsen and George Bernard Shaw could possibly qualify as Catholic in spirit or otherwise nourish much virtue in students. In addition, as already suggested, Shuster was not enamored of athletics in general, nor of Knute

Rockne in particular.  In short, between the rigorous adherence to
ecclesiastical Catholicism insisted by O'Hara, and the athletic
aspirations of football prowess promoted by Rockne, the "anti-
intellectual" atmosphere at Notre Dame would grow just too difficult
for young Professor Shuster to endure.  He needed more sympathetic
outlets for his own intellectual endeavors.  As he put it in a telling
letter to his wife late in 1923:

> *I should really very much like to get*
> *away from Notre Dame.  Even though I love the place*
> *and love the purpose to which it has been dedicated, I*
> *must admit that it seems impossible to expect of Notre*
> *Dame anything like what I had once hoped for from it.*
> *We have an administration now without any vision or*
> *sense of scholarship – much less poetry . . . And of*
> *course, I saw the future as it could have been under*
> *Father Burns – a new Louvain, with dreams steadily*
> *coming true.  I have spent many a bitter hour beside*
> *the ashes of a dying dream . . .*

So much for Shuster's intellectual assessment of eighty years
of blood, sweat and tears from Blessed Basil Moreau, Edward Sorin,
William Corby, Patrick Connors, Eliza Gillespie, and all the other
sons and daughters of Erin and faithful men and women of the
Congregation of the Holy Cross.  So long to a dying Notre Dame.
Thus, it must have filled the poor professor with endless angst and
frustration when, while trying to satisfy his intellectual cravings on
sabbatical at the decidedly non-Catholic Columbia University, he had
to endure the further indignity of seeing endless streams of positive
press in the New York newspapers about that ash heap of a university
known as Notre Dame, as those two Neanderthals known as Rockne

and O'Hara took the undefeated football team on a Catholic-lover's train ride.

Perhaps this is one of the reasons why Shuster went straight from his sabbatical at Columbia to a post on the mixed bag editorial board of the ostensibly Catholic Commonweal magazine, and proceeded to piss on his alma mater in public by authoring two articles that amounted to the wholesale savagery of most American Catholic university efforts at Shuster's version of "scholarship," including especially cheap shots at those associated with Notre Dame - O'Hara, Rockne, and the whole student body.

Later, Shuster would tell a wholly undocumented story about why he had really left Notre Dame, claiming that O'Hara had taken his copy of *The Rainbow* by D.H. Lawrence and torn it up. Apparently, Shuster's version of "scholarship" entitled him to "color" his departure, so to speak, mindful that working class Catholics were unlikely to appreciate his other intellectual excuses for harming his alma mater. Such was Shuster's spin, akin to the reinvention of Margaret Sanger by that elite academy called NYU and her other inventive friends at Planned Parenthood.

Coming only months after O'Hara and Rockne's wonderfully successful goodwill train tour had put such a damper on Klan-driven bigotry and raised Catholic hopes for a better tomorrow, Shuster's articles were seen as high treason by an "unfilial son" against an institutional mother that had given him "whatever culture he possesses." Nevertheless, the Professor was apparently not content to be seen as a mere tabloid traitor, so he decided to make a revolting personal spectacle of himself at the First Annual Convention of National Catholic Alumni convened at the Commodore Hotel in New York City on November 6, 1925 to "celebrate the role of Catholic colleges and universities in retaining and preserving faith in an age of disbelief." Why he even attended such an event in the first place is a wonder, unless of course he had harbored an intention to sabotage it from the very start.  In any event, after having to listen to the likes of Cardinal Patrick Hayes and Coach Knute Rockne extol the efforts of Catholic undergraduate institutions to instill virtue and build moral fiber in their students, Shuster stood up at his table and issued some unrecorded remarks that, suffice it to say, very publicly offended absolutely everyone in attendance, including Cardinal Hayes.  The result, of course, was to make the professor a permanent *persona non grata* among mainstream Catholics in general and friends of Notre Dame in particular, even as he ingratiated himself to the elite liberal academy in New York City, which may have been his motive all along. He became a leading spokesman for various liberal causes and, in 1939, would assume the presidency of the *tre chic* Hunter College where, according to at least one colleague, he would be fully radicalized by the ultra-liberal women who'd come to make Hunter their home.

Then, in 1943, Shuster struck again, only this time at Notre Dame's patriotism, even as she'd made herself home to our military's best and brightest in order to further our nation's objectives in the war.  For it was at this time that Notre Dame was also home to an outspoken professor of philosophy by the name of Francis McMahon, who fervently favored US intervention in the fight against fascism, including close collaboration with anti-Catholic Communist Russia. Unfortunately, McMahon was apparently prone to undiplomatically overstating his case on occasion, and was therefore not without his detractors, both at home and abroad.  And so, Notre Dame soon found itself at the center of heated controversies about whether, how, and when to get embroiled in the war, and how to deal with the likes of Joseph Stalin, etc.  Eventually, a couple of these controversies were brought to a boiling point abroad, prompting an apostolic emissary from Rome to privately pressure Notre Dame's president, Reverend Hugh O'Donnell, to counsel McMahon about the Vatican's concerns, and have him be more careful about future remarks.  Specifically, the

Holy See was none too pleased about the fact that McMahon had slandered the Catholic Spanish nationalist Francisco Franco by likening him to a Hitleresque fascist, while apparently offering no such similar constructive criticisms of the Catholic-killing Stalin.

O'Donnell met with McMahon, and tried to reason with him about the need for diplomacy and discretion under the circumstances. True to his evidently self-centered, defensive, and decidedly undiplomatic nature, McMahon rejected O'Donnell's counsel, and offered him no alternative means by which he could accommodate McMahon while protecting the interests of Notre Dame in the process. Instead, McMahon sought to rally his troops around the idea that Notre Dame was engaging in censorship, and threatened that which O'Donnell least desired, namely, to have the issue tried in the court of public opinion, and thereby do even more damage to Notre Dame. Nevertheless, O'Donnell relentlessly continued to reconcile McMahon's interests with those of Notre Dame, but to no avail. McMahon saw censorship in any and all efforts by Notre Dame to influence his words and actions, and consequently proceeded to become embroiled in yet another controversy. To wit, he recklessly indicted the entire city of Boston on account of some anti-Semitic outbursts uttered by a handful of bigots. Needless to say, McMahon had thereby sealed his own fate, his career at Notre Dame coming quickly to an end.

But Notre Dame's problems did not end there, thanks to George Shuster. After McMahon was terminated, he and his friends on the faculty asked Shuster to stir the pot of public protest against Notre Dame. Shuster was only too happy to oblige. He assembled an entourage of sixty-seven elite "celebrity academics, educators, scientists, writers, journalists, critics, and union leaders" to sign what was tantamount to a "public indictment of O'Donnell's performance as university president." This, despite everything that O'Donnell had done to help the war effort, and deal with a most difficult and delicate

situation engendered mainly by McMahon's inflated sense of
personal importance and juvenile lack of discretion and diplomacy.
Soon, and owing largely to Shuster's injection of the American Civil
Liberties Union into the fray (that great anti-papist protector of the
secular progressive order), the matter got completely out of control.
The reputations of Notre Dame and O'Donnell were systematically
shredded with little regard for the truth, and with the evident
blessings of Shuster, who sat on the ACLU's executive committee.  In
fact, he actively participated in the politics of personal destruction by
egregiously libeling O'Donnell, falsely labeling him a coward for
allegedly capitulating to pressure from anti-Semitic isolationists,
when in fact he'd done no such thing.  Indeed, O'Donnell's only crime
was his courageous loyalty to Notre Dame, and deference to its
friends in Rome.

No surprise, then, that in the immediately ensuing years,
Notre Dame and other Catholic institutions would confront a brand-
new wave of unprecedented American anti-Catholicism, thanks in no
small measure to that loyal son named Shuster.  No surprise either
that thirty-two years after the fact of his first apostasy in 1925, the
sting of Shuster's insults would remain on then Archbishop O'Hara's
mind, as he fretted over them in letters to his good friend Cardinal
Spellman as late as 1957.

Instead, the surprise would come in the Spring of 1960, while
O'Hara the Cardinal was on his deathbed.  That's when the new man
put in charge of Notre Dame – Reverend Theodore Hesburgh - would
find it fitting to award the University's highest honor, the Laetare
Medal, to none other than George N. Shuster - a medal which bears
the inscription *Magna est veritas et prevalebit*, that is, "Truth is
great and it will prevail." (Ironically, as will be evident a bit later in
the book, Cardinal Giovanni Montini, soon to be named Pope Paul
VI, was seen standing next to Shuster on the stage that day.)

Three months later, John Cardinal O'Hara died, and was immediately entombed in Notre Dame's Basilica of the Sacred Heart. But before the cement had cured around his crypt, Shuster was teaching English again at Notre Dame, and serving as executive assistant to ND's President Hesburgh. To get a sense of how such a move was seen by some of Shuster's closest friends (and perhaps by Shuster himself), there is this from the legendary Saul Alinsky, the original, Chicago-based, atheist "community organizer" who admired Karl Marx and would one day serve as an inspiration to none other than Barack Obama:

> *I get torn by ambivalent feelings whenever I think of you in South Bend. First, I am overjoyed at the proximity and to know that I shall be seeing you frequently (and if you avoid Chicago I shall repeatedly invade South Bend) and then I get feelings of melancholia thinking of you trying to do what you will be doing in a matrix controlled by and permeated by 'Cheer, cheer for Old Notre Dame' and 'Hold that line' ... and some say that Paul of Tarsus had a push-over organizing the Roman Catholic Church compared to the ordeal of a scholar faced with the South Bend intellectual **jungle** of tackles, guards, full-backs and T formation. . .*

"Jungle," one supposes, was an appropriate word for someone like Alinsky in 1961. College football integration was still a few years off, and therefore he had found it perfectly acceptable to refer to all football players as ignorant animals, or at least all the white Catholic ones at Notre Dame. Indeed, it is impossible to overstate the significance of Alinsky's influence, on both Shuster and Obama, when one considers the fact that in his ground-breaking book, *Rules for Radicals*, the bible for all committed far-left liberals, Alinsky pays homage to "the first radical known to man who rebelled against the establishment and did it so effectively that he at least won his own kingdom – **Lucifer**."

So, who or what happened between World War II and the start of the so-called "sixties," that Notre Dame would do such a thing as bring back George N. Shuster?

* * *

Theodore Martin Hesburgh was a living legend whose enormous contributions to Notre Dame are in many ways incalculable.  One would expect as much from a man who was effectively at Our Lady's helm for nearly forty years, and who remained an active emeritus for another twenty-eight until his death in 2015.  Indeed, in terms of capital growth alone, he and his full-time team conducted four development campaigns that raised over $300 million dollars between 1960 and 1972, and by 1982, had used those funds to build 40 buildings and increase ND's endowment to $200 million dollars (now in excess of $13 billion). Thus, it is impossible for a few pages in a single book to do the man justice.  Any such snapshots are bound to be inadequate, and possible unfair.  But then Hesburgh himself knew this.  Witness, what he said about academic freedom - "I'm against half the stuff around here, but we're in the world of ideas.  Ideas are going to be discussed and none are out of bounds."

He was the second of his Irish mother Anne Marie Murphy's five children, born in Syracuse, New York, on May 25, 1917, just four days before John F. Kennedy, all of which may help to explain certain aspects of his character.  However, it may have been his highly intelligent, well-educated German grandfather, Theodore Bernard Hesburgh, from whom he inherited much of his energy, discipline and intellect.

118

After attending Most Holy Rosary School from first grade through 12th, where his family-bred fidelity to the one true Catholic faith was firmly reinforced by the exceptionally well-educated Sisters of the Immaculate Heart of Mary, it was off to Notre Dame he went, his plans for the priesthood already well in mind, in September of 1934. Once there, his three successful years in Notre Dame's seminary for the Congregation of Holy Cross won the admiration of his superiors, who sent him off for the further study of theology and philosophy at the Jesuit-run Gregorian University in the heart of Rome in 1937. Needless to say, this was an eye-opening and enriching experience for him, but the eight-year plan for his studies there was suddenly cut short by the emergence of Mussolini's alliance with Hitler, as Nazi troops occupied France and arrived at the doorsteps of Italy. In June of 1940, he would wistfully board a ship out of Genoa and return to America, where he would spend the next five years completing his studies in Washington D.C., first at Holy Cross College, and finally, after his ordination at Notre Dame in 1943, at The Catholic University of America.

So, just who was this brand new German-Irish priest with the great big brain and the even bigger heart, the one who could so easily enamor himself to others as just plain Father Ted? Well, it would undoubtedly surprise many the ignorant bystander (notably including this author) to learn that at least as a young man (and maybe as an old one in his heart of hearts), he was unequivocally a social conservative of the classic Catholic order. Examples especially pertinent include Father Ted's early attitudes and expressions about women, as well as his thoughts about birth control.

Regarding women, soon after his ordination in 1943, while working with the USO in Washington D.C., he prepared a booklet entitled *Letters to Servicewomen*, which he dedicated to Mary, the Immaculate Mother of God, so that she might inspire such women "to give our darkened world a shining example of Christian womanhood." In the booklet, he counseled women that if they wanted the respect of men, they needed to reject a world which ridicules modesty, to respect themselves by always behaving virtuously, and to treat their bodies as "the Temple of God," lest they enslave themselves, and contribute to the collapse of civilization:

> *When Roman and Greek women became dissolute - the mere tools of men's pleasure – the bottom fell out of marriage and the family and the whole Greco-Roman world collapsed. Christianity restored this collapsing world by restoring woman to her rightful place as the inspirer of man, the queen of the home.*
>
> *Since then, whenever women have stepped off their pedestal and sought false freedom and liberty, they have ended in the lowest kind of slavery – without love, without true friends, with nothing but bitter emptiness to their lives.*

In addition, while serving as chaplain to a reform school in Washington, he had seen how many delinquent boys had come from broken homes. So, when he began to teach at Notre Dame in 1945, he developed a course designed to teach his students the exceptional importance of strong families formed and sustained by virtuous marriage. Likewise, he warned these same students, and anyone else within earshot of his speeches on the subject, about the evils of birth control. For example, in 1947, he lectured that the all-important family was "fighting for its life" amidst a deluge of "filthy literature [undoubtedly emanating from Sanger and her pals throughout Planned Parenthood] telling them twenty new ways of practicing birth control." Indeed, he saw generosity toward children as essential to the glory of God, and therefore to familial strength and happiness, and blamed the growing use of birth control for the vast majority of failed marriages:

> *The world today may go its way, turning away by the millions, babies that could and should be born for the glory of God, but let them not call themselves Christian, for it was Christ who said: 'Suffer the little ones to come unto Me, for of such is the kingdom of heaven.' Heartless modern people who are wedded to the dollar may go on, closing their doors and making life difficult for couples with children, but they too will one day face the Christ who said: 'Whatsoever you did unto one of these my least brethren, you did it unto Me.'*
>
> *My dear friends, never forget that God is not mocked. The world may make and break its own rules about marriage, but it cannot find happiness in marriage apart from God and God's way.*

Father Ted would stay wed to these immutable teachings of his Church until the 1960's, defending them against an ever-growing choir in favor of contraception, because to him such teachings were inexorably "based on unchanging philosophical and theological principles regarding the nature and destiny of man, of marriage, and of sexuality too." (Echoes of a century of encyclicals here). But then something, or someone, seemed to happen to Father Ted, something that had likely been lurking, not all that far away nor deep inside, of the enigma known elegantly to history now as just "Hesburgh", the one and only. The "academy", of course, would understandably insist, as would its many friends in the mainstream media, that this something was the holy sacristy of secular freedom, as embodied in saints with names like Shuster.  But for a growing number of disillusioned others, it was nothing but the weeds among the wheat, here to wreak their havoc from now 'til harvest time.  Whether saint or bad seed, here is what Hesburgh would one day say of Shuster:

> *How can one write adequately about another human being whom he loves?*
>
> *. . . [I]n many ways [George Shuster] reminds me of my father and, since my father has been dead for more than a decade, I have more or less unconsciously looked upon George as a father. . . grateful for his love, his words, his kindly wisdom. . .*
>
> *I am particularly indebted to [him] since he stepped in to help . . . [obtain] from outside many millions of dollars of humanistic and social science research.  Almost single handedly, he initiated a wide range of research in Catholic education. . . Overnight, we were rejuvenated.*
>
> *All this happened during a time when Notre Dame passed from clerical to lay control.  As a member of the new lay Board of Trustees, George helped give direction and purpose to the new Board. The enlightened fashion in which it operated was due in no small measure to his wise counsel.*
>
> *I cannot adequately describe what it meant to have George Shuster as a personal assistant during these crucial years. . .*

Putting aside Shuster's substantial contribution to the muddling of Notre Dame's mission - more on that in a moment -even the most conservative of Catholics may read from any one of the man's many writings and get a glimpse of why Hesburgh had held him in such esteem.  In short, George Shuster was a brilliant and breathtakingly articulate academic of the highest order, whose verbal charisma comes out and captures one's attention, if not always one's heart, at the turn of every page.  Like Hesburgh, no snapshots in a chapter can fully do him justice, and one can only imagine what he was like in person, or how rich and rare the air, when he and the younger, eager Hesburgh, sat down for drinks and dinner. (When he returned to Notre Dame in 1961, Shuster was already 67, Hesburgh just 43).

Regardless, Shuster's near forty years of fanning at the flames of anti-Catholic bigotry had done nothing to dissuade Hesburgh (who may not have known Shuster's whole history, although that is hard to imagine), for he surely swallowed Shuster's shallow insistence that it was Notre Dame's love for football, together with its old-fashioned faithfulness to the magisterium, that were the insufferable causes of its most unfortunate standing in the all-important secular intellectual academy.  How else does one explain Hesburgh's hounding of Frank Leahy, while subsequently honoring Shuster?

Specifically, in 1949, when Hesburgh first became Notre Dame's executive vice-president, as if taking his first cues from Shuster and his ilk, he immediately attempted to remedy what he believed to be an unhealthy public perception of Notre Dame as little-more than a football school.  He did this by proceeding to take Leahy to task at every turn for what Hesburgh evidently believed to be Leahy's obsessively unhealthy devotion to the perfection of ND's football program.  Unfortunately, Hesburgh's efforts in this regard were exceptionally successful.  For after Leahy took the team to one more national championship in 1949, their 4th in 7 years, Notre Dame would not see another one for the next 16 years.  In the meantime, Hesburgh would ascend to the presidency in 1952, and turn the formidable force of his undivided attentions, and those of his assistant Shuster, toward altering every aspect of the school's administration, and with it the future direction and focus of all of its educational endeavors.

Hesburgh's slow but steady drift into semi-heretical waters was evident as early as 1954. For that is when a Jesuit named John Courtney Murray first asserted the makings of his "American Proposition." That is, while persons in a pluralistic society have rights, including the right to their own opinion, the dictates of their conscience were crucial. The problem was that loosely translated, Murray seemed to be suggesting, at least to watchful conservative clerics like Cardinal Alfredo Ottaviani, that Catholics were free to publicly conform their consciences to the dictates of civil society, regardless of whether or not civil society conformed to transcendent truth. Now, while this is not exactly what Murray said, Cardinal Ottaviani was not wholly without cause for concern, as evidenced by the fact that Murray's work would later form the linchpin of liberal Jesuit support for politicians like Ted Kennedy turning "pro-choice." This, despite the fact some have come to regard Murray's work as actually advocating the opposite. All of which has made him, much like John Cardinal Newman, one of the most used, and misused, of the Catholicism's many "modernity" conscious theologians. Unfortunately, the worried Cardinal Ottaviani and his friends reacted poorly to Murray's alleged missives, attempting to utterly censor him, instead of just sternly correcting him, or better yet clearly understanding him. And that is when Hesburgh stepped in to aid his embattled colleague. Of course, there is certainly something to be said for Father Ted's insistence on academic freedom in this instance. The problem, however, is that he seems to have sympathized, not only with permitting Murray's words to come out, but with the most liberal interpretation of his words. What's worse, he seems to have misinterpreted the Vatican's eventual apology for their unhappy

Cardinal's misbehavior as some sort of ecclesiastical approval of Murray as Hesburgh saw him, when nothing was further from the truth, as evidenced by Pope John Paul II's later writings on the subject (See Chapter 15).  In short, Hesburgh was beginning to lean overboard on the inter-related questions of conscience and academic freedom, that is, toward freedom from any absolutes or authority, and away from transcendent truths.  (If this is a little confusing right now, things will hopefully clear up as one reads further.)

In 1962, an article in *Time* magazine entitled *Education: God and Man at Notre Dame,* had this to offer on Father Hesburgh:

> *'A Catholic University is a contradiction in terms,' George Bernard Shaw [the atheist] once said. The Rev. Theodore Martin Hesburgh, CSC, president of the University of Notre Dame, can readily see Shaw's point – that religious dogma seems incompatible with the scientific spirit of skeptical, free inquiry.  He can just as readily reply to Shaw. "We must cherish both values.  We must reflect the 'ancient beauty, ever old and ever new," he says.  "There is no conflict between science and theology, except where there is bad science or bad theology. . .*

> *. . . Hesburgh stands for probing all truth on the ground that there cannot be a conflict in truths.  Some Catholics fear that this might push Catholic colleges toward secularism and deprive them of their reason for being.  Yet the faith-and-reason approach might flower in the nation's first significant generation of Catholic intellectuals.  Carefully keeping his claims moderate, Hesburgh forsees 'a possible renaissance' of Catholic education.  'We are men committed to Truth,'*

*says Hesburgh, 'living in a world where most*
*academic endeavor concerns only natural truth, as*
*much separated from supernatural truth, the divine*
*wisdom of theology, as sinful man was separated from*
*God before the Incarnation. If these extremes are to be*
*united, a work of mediation is needed. We must*
*somehow match secular or state universities in their*
*comprehension of the vast spectrum of natural truths*
*in the arts and sciences, while at the same time we*
*must be in full possession of our own true heritage of*
*theological wisdom'. . .*

Now, no reasonable mind would argue with Hesburgh's heady objectives here, if only he had remained ever mindful that "our own true heritage of theological wisdom" was entrusted by Jesus Christ to the teaching authority (Magisterium) of the Roman Catholic Church, and not to him and the other heads of American Catholic universities. But beginning in 1963, as the president of Notre Dame and the International Federation of Catholic Universities, Father Hesburgh would lead his fellow American clerics on a mission to redefine the nature and purpose of the Catholic University and its relationship to the Church, the State, its faculty, and its students. For 9 years, he and other heads of Catholic colleges worked on a document, issued in November of 1972, entitled *The Catholic University in the Modern World.* That document in fact acknowledged the solemn obligation of Catholic universities to demonstrate "fidelity to the Christian message as it comes to us through the Church [by]. . . recognition of the teaching authority of the Church in doctrinal matters," and the right of Church authority to intervene "when it judges the truth of the Christian message to be at stake." But this has not been worth the paper it was printed on, as is evident from Hesburgh's own autobiography (not to mention those of his academic colleagues).

Indeed, he has been openly contemptuous of any such Church authority since at least 1960, including such basic Canon laws as those that retain for the Church the right to define the word "Catholic", and to exercise vigilance to insure that the principles of Catholic doctrine are faithfully observed at universities that call themselves "Catholic." The seminal and pivotal case in point: the issue of artificial contraception.

A few months before his death in June of 1963, Pope John XXIII initiated a papal commission, consisting of three priests and three laymen, to address the so-called "population question".  His successor, Pope Paul VI, continued the commission and, in March of 1964, allowed the expansion of its membership to fifty-five, including thirty-four laity, nine clergy, and twelve representatives of various religious orders.  Known as the Papal Commission on Population, Family, and Birth, the full membership met for the first time on March 24, 1965 in Rome, where John T. Noonan, then a young Professor of Law at the University of Notre Dame, initiated the proceedings with a lecture incorrectly suggesting that the Church's position on contraception had considerably "evolved" over time, and that perhaps it was time for a change in Church doctrine.  In order to understand how Noonan had gained the podium, and why he was making such a controversial statement, one has to trace back about three years.

In 1962, Cass Canfield, the Chairman of Planned Parenthood, made overtures to an outspoken population control proponent by the name of Father John A. O'Brien, a theology professor at Notre Dame, about holding family planning conferences with like-minded liberal Catholics in New York.  O'Brien was a well-known rogue who had devoted most of his adult life to inciting Church controversy and attacking all manner of ecclesiastical authority.  In fact, O'Brien had favored birth control for nearly thirty years, and Canfield had been impressed by what O'Brien had to say during an Eric Sevareid orchestrated CBS documentary entitled "Birth Control and the Law," which was essentially an infomercial for Planned Parenthood. Canfield's plan was to cozy up to liberal Catholics, achieve their consensus, and secure their cooperation with Planned Parenthood's corporate objectives.

O'Brien alerted his soul-mate, George Shuster, to this special opportunity to make more secular progressive pals, and Shuster did not disappoint.  However, Shuster knew that the Archdiocese of New York would never approve of Catholic participation in conferences that were sponsored by Planned Parenthood. Furthermore, he must have known that ecclesiastical objections would be especially strong in light of certain individual participants, notably including Alan Guttmacher, the eugenically-minded, pro-abortion successor to Margaret Sanger, who once astutely observed that "[w]e [at Planned Parenthood] are merely walking down the path that Mrs. Sanger carved out for us."  So, Shuster suggested that they conduct the conferences at Notre Dame, essentially in secret, and obtained funding for them from none other than the Rockefeller and Ford Foundations.

It is clear from a reading of Shuster's introduction to *The Problem of Population: Practical Catholic Applications,* University of Notre Dame Press, 1964, that he had swallowed – "hook, line, and sinker" - the racist Malthusian notion that birth rates, particularly in the poorer nations, were out of control and threatening the survival of the planet, and that Catholics must therefore subscribe to a worldwide effort at birth control (while opposing abortion, of course) through mediums of mass suggestion.  This, despite Shuster's acute awareness that artificial contraception had coincided with a concomitant increase in sexual indulgence, especially in the more impoverished urban areas of the United States.

It is also apparent that he and other liberal minded Catholics at the conference, such as Jesuit Thomas Reese of Georgetown, were equally aware of efforts by the people at Planned Parenthood to liberalize sterilization and abortion laws as part of their population control push.  Yet they were perfectly willing to associate themselves with this movement, making themselves the pawns in Planned Parenthood's efforts to "soften" the traditional position of the Catholic Church on these issues. In other words, they were the precursors to Mario Cuomo's "personally opposed but" theology (See Chapter 12), despite admonitions from another Jesuit committee member by the name of John L. Thomas, about the inevitable increase of sterilization and abortion due to sexual liberation.

That first conference led to several more and, in 1965, the more liberal Catholic members of the conference, including Shuster, signed off on a joint statement directed to the papal commission on population. It complained about the staleness and alleged inadequacies of existing Church teachings on sex and birth control in light of modern social and scientific developments, and explicitly dissented from such teachings insofar as they forbade the use of artificial contraception. The statement was supposed to remain confidential.  However, it was leaked to the *New York Times*, and published on September 28, 1965.  Meanwhile, in private correspondence to various priests before the issuance of Pope Paul's encyclical on the subject in 1968, Shuster said he was "personally persuaded that the pill [or the coil] offers an acceptable solution provided it is really made a matter of moral counseling" and that married couples not "resort to it of their own accord."  And, in an article in Notre Dame's *Alumnus*, he publicly urged Pope Paul to approve artificial contraception (while Hesburgh stayed conspicuously silent on the subject.)

And so, it is hard to escape the conclusion that the Rockefeller-funded team of Shuster and Hesburgh had exercised considerable influence over the none-too-nuanced remarks of their 32-year-old subordinate named Noonan (Indeed, Hesburgh would eventually award him Notre Dame's Laetare Medal in 1984, the very same year in which he would invite Mario Cuomo to come to campus and address the issue of a Catholic politician's proper position on abortion.) In fact, it was only four months after Noonan's sales pitch to the commission that Hesburgh put the Pope and Rockefeller together, in July of 1965, for a 45-minute private pow-wow.  At this extraordinary meeting between modern-day money and God's main man, Rockefeller tried to sell the none-too-skeptical Pope on the brand-new IUD (Intrauterine Device, or "coil"), an invention born of research by Rockefeller's personally funded Population Council. (One has to wonder whether Rockefeller had bothered to explain to the Pope, or to Shuster and Hesburgh for that matter, that the IUD does **not** prevent conception, but in fact induces the abortion of a human embryo by means of a dangerously infective and inflammatory process that has since caused serious physical harm to the reproductive organs of thousands of women throughout the world).

There are, of course, no minutes of this meeting, but hindsight would seem to suggest that Rockefeller, and his friends Hesburgh and Shuster, had not been much encouraged by whatever the Pope had said.  Indeed, if only from the timing of events that unfolded over the next two years, one can reasonably infer that whatever the Pope said, together with resistance likely signaled by conservative members of the papal commission and magisterium, had more than a little to do with Notre Dame's move toward total autonomy from the Magisterium at essentially the same time.

Specifically, just as the papal commission's two years of talks were coming to a close, some twenty-one months after Rockefeller's meeting with the Pope, Notre Dame's Board of Trustees, populated solely by priests, would approve new by-laws, on April 8, 1967, formally forfeiting their exclusive authority over all university affairs in favor a 'fellowship' consisting of six priests and six laity.  Then, just one week later, on April 15, 1987, the Papal Commission's liberal majority report recommending relaxation of the Church's contraception doctrine went public. This was followed almost immediately by the dismissal of Father Charles Curran, one of the commission majority's most outspoken U.S. liberal allies, from his teaching position at the Catholic University of America, despite the unanimous recommendation of its theology faculty that he be granted tenure. Curran, a contributor to Shuster's *Commonweal Magazine*, had friends in the predominantly liberal Catholic media, and so his dismissal set off a firestorm of criticism and protest apropos of the incendiary atmosphere of the sixties. The relentless rise of Modernism's tides appeared unstoppable. After a week's worth of withering protests by a whole bunch of media-excited students and professors, Catholic University's Board of Trustees relented and rehired Curran, granting him full tenure.

So sounded the death knell of clerical control over Catholic University of America in particular, and Catholic universities in general. Indeed, it was only three months later, in July of 1967, that Hesburgh would convene the now infamous conference at Notre Dame's satellite center in Land O'Lakes, Wisconsin. Once there, twenty-six leading educators from the North American region of the International Federation of Catholic Universities - the ones who'd helped Hesburgh produce that worthless document back in 1963 - would adopt what amounted to a declaration of independence from the Catholic Church, insisting that "[t]o perform its teaching and research functions effectively, the Catholic university must have a true autonomy and academic freedom in the face of authority of whatever kind, lay or clerical, external to the academic community itself." And, as in the case of Shuster and Hesburgh's Notre Dame-based population conferences, it was all done, in large part, for prestige, power, and most of all, for the "research" money (more on this a bit later in this chapter). In short, the Fighting Irish were now being led by two heady Germans who, more than a little full of themselves and lost in the weeds among the wheat, were marching them to the tune of autonomy from Holy Mother Church, and teaching them to do exactly what Father Charles Carey had prayed they never would when he wrote to his own young charges on that eve of St. Patrick's Day in 1953. That is, when he prayed that they would never be "so poor in all their wanderings and sufferings that they barter their faith for the comforts of this life."

One year later, on July 25, 1968, Pope Paul VI issued his long-awaited encyclical entitled *Humanae Vitae.* Here is the essence of what he said:

> *The problem of birth, like every other problem regarding human life, is to be considered . . . in the light of an integral vision of man and of his vocation, not only his natural and earthly, but also his supernatural and eternal vocation. . .*

> *In the task of transmitting life, therefore, [men and women] are not free to proceed completely at will, as if they could determine in a wholly autonomous way the honest path to follow; but they must conform their activity to the creative intention of God. . .*

> *Upright men can even better convince themselves of the solid grounds on which the teaching of the Church in this field is based, if they care to reflect upon the consequences of methods of artificial birth control. Let them consider, first of all, how wide and easy a road would thus be opened up towards conjugal infidelity and the general lowering of morality. . . that the man, growing used to the employment of anti-conceptive practices, may finally lose respect for the*

*woman and, no longer caring for her physical and psychological equilibrium, may come to the point of considering her as a mere instrument of selfish enjoyment, and no longer as his respected and beloved companion.*

*. . . It can be foreseen that this teaching will perhaps not be easily received by all: Too numerous are those voices -- amplified by the modern means of propaganda -- which are contrary to the voice of the Church. To tell the truth, the Church is not surprised to be made, like her divine Founder, a "sign of contradiction," yet she does not because of this cease to proclaim with humble firmness the entire moral law, both natural and evangelical. . .*

*The teaching of the Church on the regulation of birth, which promulgates the divine law, will easily appear to many to be difficult or even impossible of actuation. . .*

*[I]t demands first of all that husband and wife acquire and possess solid convictions concerning the true values of life and of the family, and that they tend towards securing perfect self-mastery. . . [T]his discipline which is proper to the purity of married couples, far from harming conjugal love, rather confers on it a higher human value . . . bestows upon family life fruits of serenity and peace, and facilitates the solution of other problems; it favors attention for one's partner, helps both parties to drive out selfishness, the enemy of true love; and deepens their*

*sense of responsibility. By its means, parents acquire the capacity of having a deeper and more efficacious influence in the education of their offspring; little children and youths grow up with a just appraisal of human values, and in the serene and harmonious development of their spiritual and sensitive faculties.*

*On this occasion, we wish to draw the attention of educators, and of all who perform duties of responsibility in regard to the common good of human society, to the need of creating an atmosphere favorable to education in chastity, that is, to the triumph of healthy liberty over license by means of respect for the moral order.*

*Everything in the modern media of social communications which leads to sense excitation and unbridled customs, as well as every form of pornography and licentious performances, must arouse the frank and unanimous reaction of all those who are solicitous for the progress of civilization and the defense of the common good of the human spirit. . .*

*Christian married couples . . .must remember that their Christian vocation, which began at baptism, is further specified and reinforced by the sacrament of matrimony. By it husband and wife are strengthened and as it were consecrated for the faithful accomplishment of their proper duties, for the carrying out of their proper vocation even to perfection, and the Christian witness which is proper to them before the whole world. To them the Lord entrusts the task of making visible to men the holiness and sweetness of the law which unites the mutual love of husband and wife with their cooperation with the love of God the author of human life.*

*We do not at all intend to hide the sometimes-serious difficulties inherent in the life of Christian married persons; for them as for everyone else, "the gate is narrow and the way is hard, that leads to life." But the hope of that life must illuminate their way, as with courage they strive to live with wisdom, justice and piety in this present time, knowing that the figure of this world passes away.*

*Let married couples . . . implore divine assistance by persevering prayer; above all, let them draw from the source of grace and charity in the Eucharist. And if sin should still keep its hold over them, let them not be discouraged, but rather have recourse with humble perseverance to the mercy of God, which is poured forth in the sacrament of Penance. In this way they will be enabled to achieve the fullness of conjugal life described by the Apostle: "husbands, love your wives, as Christ loved the Church . . . husbands should love their wives as their own bodies. He who loves his wife loves himself. For no man ever hates his own flesh, but nourishes and cherishes it, as Christ does the Church . . . this is a great mystery, and I mean in reference to Christ and the Church. However, let each one of you love his wife as himself, and let the wife see that she respects her husband. . .*

*Beloved priest sons, by vocation you are the counselors and spiritual guides of individual persons and of families. We now turn to you with confidence. Your first task -- especially in the case of those who teach moral theology -- is to expound the Church's teaching on marriage without ambiguity. Be the first to give, in the exercise of your ministry, the example of loyal internal and external obedience to the teaching authority of the Church. That obedience, as you know well, obliges not only because of the reasons adduced, but rather because of the light of the Holy Spirit, which is given in a particular way to the pastors of the Church in order that they may illustrate the truth. You know, too, that it is of the utmost importance, for peace of consciences and for the unity of the Christian people, that in the field of morals as well as in that of dogma, all should attend to the magisterium of the Church, and all should speak the same language. Hence, with all our heart we renew to you the heartfelt plea of the great Apostle Paul: "I appeal to you, brethren, by the name of Our Lord Jesus Christ, that all of you agree and that there be no dissensions among you, but that you be united in the same mind and the same judgment.*

*To diminish in no way the saving teaching of Christ constitutes an eminent form of charity for souls. But this must ever be accompanied by patience and goodness, such as the Lord himself gave example of in dealing with men. Having come not to condemn but to save, he was indeed intransigent with evil, but merciful towards individuals.*

*In their difficulties, may married couples always find,
in the words and in the heart of a priest, the echo of the
voice and the love of the Redeemer.*

*And then speak with confidence, beloved sons, fully
convinced that the spirit of God, while He assists the
magisterium in proposing doctrine, illumines
internally the hearts of the faithful inviting them to
give their assent. Teach married couples the
indispensable way of prayer; prepare them to have
recourse often and with faith to the sacraments of the
Eucharist and of Penance, without ever allowing
themselves to be discouraged by their own weakness. .
.*

Shuster publicly criticized the Pope's conclusions (despite the
fact that the encyclical specifically admonished Catholics to refrain
from doing so), arguing that artificial contraception was required to
control the population of the poor, and urging the Pope to grant an
indefinite indulgence until some other satisfactory solution presented
itself.  He and Hesburgh then attempted to obtain papal approval of a
Notre Dame research institute for the scientific study and
improvement of the rhythm method of birth control, but their efforts
(perhaps in light of their misguided loyalties) were overshadowed by
a competing endeavor initiated by Cardinals John O'Boyle of
Washington and John Wright of Pittsburgh (which paved the way to
an improved post-rhythm method of birth control now known as
NFP, or Natural Family Planning).

Hesburgh nevertheless won more favor, and more financing, from the Rockefeller Foundation.  He was made a member of its executive committee and accepted its funding of cooperative service projects such as the study of family and fertility in Latin America, motivated by his belief that "Notre Dame is in a good position to exert a liberalizing influence on certain sectors of intellectual life in Latin America." (Hesburgh also secured another $6 million from the Ford Foundation, circa 1960.)

For his part, Shuster gained prestigious appointment to the family planning panel component of President Lyndon Johnson's White House Conference on Health, where he sat side-by-side with Margaret Sanger's successor, Alan Guttmacher, as he called for $65 to $95 million in federal funding to curb high birth rates among poor American women by affording them "adequate contraceptive advice" as a routine part of health care by hospitals, obstetrical office and home-visiting social workers.  To be fair, Shuster softened his criticism of the Church after Pope Paul issued his encyclical, acknowledging in private correspondence to priests that the Pope had made "a strong case for the sacredness of life and against unrestrained libidos."  However, he continued to publicly argue for official and indefinite indulgence of artificial contraception, obviously thinking himself such an expert on this subject that he need not heed the Pope's pleas against public dissent.

All of this, of course, portended poorly for future relations between Catholic universities such as Notre Dame and ecclesiastical authority.  Here is an excerpt from Hesburgh's seminal statement on the subject, that is, his *Vision of a Great Catholic University in the World Today*, delivered during Notre Dame's 125th anniversary celebration in 1967 (shortly after Land o' Lakes):

In light of these words, it is no wonder what was about to
unfold before John Paul the Great would reclaim the seat at the head
of the table. To hear one "veteran campus observer" tell it, *circa* 1968,
Father Hesburgh had started moving the university into the
mainstream, but - "[h]e did that just about the time all hell broke
loose in the mainstream. And by this time, Hesburgh himself was so
caught up in the mainstream [that he became] . . . trapped in the
backwater of the very freedom of thought he encouraged . . ." Then
there was this from Notre Dame's Alumnus Magazine in March of
'68: "[T]hat aspect of a Notre Dame education which has meant most
to alumni from the days when Notre Dame was a model Catholic
university," namely, "respect for the institutional church, spiritual
fervor, and virtue producing discipline, is dead, and the alumni are
stunned."

The funny thing is, however, that while Shuster had undoubtedly played a pivotal role in converting Hesburgh to whatever one might call it, Shuster himself had also started out as more or less conservative, giving one to wonder what too much academic intellectualizing can do to men, if not cause them to take too much comfort in a sense of self-enlightenment. Here is something of how Shuster had evolved, starting circa 1935, when he had this to say, in *Like a Mighty Army*, about birth control in the context of his prophetic concerns about that ungodly eugenic-minded madman by the name of Hitler:

> *Manifestly the doctrine[s] of the Catholic Church. . . are not relished . . . by those who feel that modern science has 'emancipated' humanity from various 'moral taboos.' Since prophylactic medicine has altered the consequences of sexual intercourse, and since nomadic habits have undermined the ideal of home stability, the old Christian ideal of the married state appears to be narrow and unsatisfying . . . [A] 'creed of science' which guarantees both indulgence and health has an even greater chance to succeed than did the erotic faiths of centuries past. If we are candid, we shall admit that most of the so-called fundamental challenges to the Church have their origin in sexual desire. No human life can fail to be enriched by trust in a God whose Providence is fatherly and whose mansions dot the endless shores of eternity. But if this God is a barrier of love – well, love often argues that he does not exist. . .*
>
> *Those of us who understand this central modern danger to religion are aware also of the grave difficulties which an era like our own places in the way*

*of him who desires to realize the normal Christian
ideals. . . When one weighs all of this carefully, one
comes within an inch of thinking that the religion of
the future will be the concern of a few who have
withdrawn from the world; and that the masses will
turn to the Church only occasionally when, by reason
of the everlasting sadness that no human heart can
remedy, the choice confronting everyone is . . . between
the mouth of a pistol and the foot of the Cross. . .*

    *I say "one comes within an inch" of doing so.
For the religion of no-religion does for some curious
reason fail to function. It is brutal, treacherous, unjust
and vile. The human being can stand being uprooted
just so long and no longer. . . [So if] for a few years the
Church can be loyal to itself, preferring a thousand
sacrifices to one compromise, there will be a
resurrection of belief such as has not been witnessed in
many hundreds of years.*

*Then, in 1948, he would echo the conservative John Cardinal
Newman while musing on American Catholics in a secular society:*

    *In my time the gulf which separates the
educated American Catholic from his fellow-men in
this country . . . has widened . . .The reason why this is
so . . . is the ever-increasing secularization of the
environment in which we live. It . . . changes its
husbands and wives seemingly without reflection.*

    *. . . and believes it has found wonderful new
drugs for social malformations . . .*

    *Sometimes I find it quite agonizing to
observe the disintegration of an era with a sense of*

*absolute powerlessness to do anything about it. The
fact that one may be attacked, vilified, slandered, and
abused meanwhile, is then almost a relief. There are
so many matters of which a Catholic is believed to be
ignorant – science, the higher criticism, psychology,
democracy, economics. Yet it is not so much
unawareness of which one is found guilty, but rather a
chronic disposition to be out of date. . . [For the anti-
Catholic modernist] one good thing about the fading
out of the Christian gospel must be . . .that it has made
room for Marx, who in turn is already out of date,
even if the doctrine to follow his is still awaiting a
publisher. The fact that the Gospel is, as Newman
made us see it, a continuously unfolding panorama of
insight, and that the wisest word ever spoken of faith is
that it can move mountains, is apparently the least
well realized of possibilities. . .*

*Shuster stayed enamored of Newman for at least another
decade, asserting in 1949 that "[a] student of modern literature can
encounter no more stimulating mind than that of Newman secure in
the possession of ripe wisdom . . .," and in 1958 that –*

*[o]f one thing I am certain at any rate after
many years of association with academic life. The
attempt to evaluate higher education from the pastoral
point of view is always bound to come-round to
endorsing what Newman said a hundred years ago.
Knowledge will not make people better, just as
ignorance will not make them more educated. The
sovereign justification of a Catholic university, he held,
is that it can and ought to have a school of theology. . .*

Indeed, it was Shuster's favorite pontiff, Pope Piux XI, who had said that "there can be no true education which is not wholly directed to man's last end." Yet, it was at this same time (1958) that Shuster began to believe that the "mighty force" of "materialism" tearing millions "from their spiritual moorings" might best be effectively combated by a scholarly sharing in the sanctification of Christ through an immersion into all things secular. In addition, while he saw some progress in Catholic scholarship "in recent decades," admitting that "the university has come of age in our land and there is no dearth of scholarly activity," he was essentially unrepentant about his past criticisms. And in light of a growing social democracy, Shuster saw priests as woefully inadequate administrators of Catholic participation in true scholarly activities, and pointed the way to the laity's takeover of the task:

> *If, then, there were a Catholic university
> in which Catholic lay men and women could live and
> work on a level of equality with the best scholars in the
> most reputable non-Catholic institutions, and if such a
> university had grown to maturity during a hundred
> years, I am sure the many colleges which have
> struggled into being under the auspices of religious
> orders would have a lifeline to a center of intellectual
> activity which would immensely hearten and
> strengthen them.*

This sentiment would seem to have been central to the Shuster-Hesburgh connection. The problem, however, is that they also seem to have shared in the incorrect assumption that Catholic lay faculty could and would continue to be faithfully Catholic without firm religious leadership informed by an intimate collaboration with the Church's magisterium.  One indication of this faulty reasoning, at least on the part of Shuster, was that while he had been fond of quoting one of John Cardinal Newman's famous observations about education – "Knowledge is one thing, virtue another; good sense is not conscience, refinement is not humility, nor is largeness and justice of view faith" – he'd apparently taken this to mean that what was needed was more knowledge, whereas one wonders whether what Newman himself was trying to say was that knowledge was no substitute for virtue.

In fact, after Vatican II (which Hesburgh and others of his ilk had sorely misinterpreted as the Magisterium's advocacy of unconditional autonomy for Catholic universities), Shuster no longer subscribed to Newman's *Idea of a University,* believing it antiquated, inadequate and inferior to his own increasingly secular view of *Catholic Education in a Changing World,* and predicting that "the traditional Catholic state of mind which led to the choice of a Catholic college *primarily* to safeguard the faith, can be expected to survive no more than twenty years longer", that is, until no later than 1987 (which happens to be the year in which Hesburgh retired). Expounding upon this subject circa 1967-68, Shuster said:

> *The older Catholic college did not permit its*
> *students to wander far from the contemplation of*
> *eternity.  Through daily Mass and the annual retreat,*
> *the spotlight was thrown on the eternal destiny of life*
> *with God, and the vocation to the religious life was*
> *thought of as the highest and noblest of all callings.*

*Today, although the Council schema on 'The Church in the Modern World' does not reduce the hope of eternal union with God, it adds a new this-worldly dimension to man's search for salvation. The climate of the Catholic college is changing and will change further; the moment has come for it to develop its own climate of freedom. . .*

*In short, the men who direct Catholic universities of the future, or teach in them, will take freedom of inquiry and expression for granted, because only the unfettered mind can be unimpeachable. But on the other plane they will understand that of necessity a part of their institutional liberty must be auctioned off. A university can no longer be what in a Platonic or Newmanistic sense it should be. It is inevitably part of the contemporary scene, and quite as necessarily in the public domain. . . And so for this reason one must frankly admit that the farther the Catholic university moves into the public domain the less individualized its character will be, and perhaps even the less discernibly spiritual its orientation will become. For the sake of parity with others it will acquire similarity. . .*

*That there are grave risks here may not be as evident as perhaps it should be. Being in the public domain – being chained, where the research is concerned, to tasks which are of direct, immediate interest to the body politic – can act as a curb, or even as a stone around the waist. Let us state the problem at a low level of materialistic concern. A private university always needs more money than it has. After having dealt with the student as a tax-collector*

*does with the citizen, it passes the collection-box
around to the corporately or individually wealthy.
Then, of course, there is always the state. The
university which agrees to do things just because
money is available may well be venal. Must the
galleon always reach port with the gold? Or should
one be squeamish about the blood on the gold? No
kind of prostitution could be worse than the
prostitution of the university, for this is the real
treason of the clerks. Accordingly, one must say that
although the Catholic university should not shirk its
duty within the public domain, it must never be for
sale. It is a holy place. It must for weal or woe bear
witness. I am convinced that the Catholic people sense
this deeply, no matter how like other universities
institutions such as Louvain or Notre Dame may
become. For this reason, the real, abiding why a
Catholic university should exist, the university comes
alive and stays alive. It grows mysteriously out of the
experience, the desire, the affection, and the awe of the
people who are the Church.*

If this single statement of the man named Shuster does not by
its profoundness give one pause, perhaps it belongs in some later
section of this book. But here it stays, because it was said in 1967,
and again in 1968, and thus this is exactly where it tragically belongs.
It is the reader, not the statement, that must be moved, even if this
means that the reader must first finish the book, and then come back
and read it again.

What a wonderful window into the soul of George Shuster.
What evidence that he knew, in his heart of hearts, even as he
plunged headlong into the public domain, that danger was right

around the corner.  Indeed, it was already upon us, and mostly of his own making, and yet he did not see it as corrupting him and Hesburgh, but only as some "academic" threat, if you will.  Or, perhaps he did see it, in his heart of hearts, and his statement was not so much wistfulness, or warning, but a prayer for forgiveness, having failed already to obtain permission.

What is meant by this ought to be evident in the timing of things.  He and Hesburgh had already decided it was full steam ahead with artificial contraception and academic freedom, the church's teaching authority now an old inept torpedo, lost in the waves they were churning in their wake, thanks to modern-day vessels designed by their friends in high places like Planned Parenthood and the Rockefeller Foundation.  Their conferences on contraception and academic freedom had already come to a close, and the papal encyclical en-route from Pope Paul was already an annoying *non-sequitur*.  What an incredible, crying shame.

One need only read Hesburgh's autobiography to know that this is absolutely so. In it, he relates a little something about Pope Paul, post-encyclical, that is telling, not so much for what actually happened, but for what seems to have been lost on Hesburgh himself. For he tells the quaint story of how one Canadian Bishop by the name of Gerald Carter had reacted to the Pope's encyclical, telling his local church constituents in the pews that it was pretty much ok if they couldn't always find the personal fortitude required to comply with Church teaching on contraception.  Hesburgh then goes on to happily explain how, at a later meeting with the Pope, the Bishop (who would soon become a Cardinal) had gone hat in hand to the Pope about the incident, and how the Pope had pretty much let him off the hook, telling him that "I said what I had to say as Pope, and you said what you had to say as pastor of your own people.  I take it that you respect me and are not upset by what I had to say as Pope and I respect you and am not upset at what you had to say as pastor to your people."

It is a heart-warming story, and Hesburgh tells it in a heart-warming way.  In fact, when one reads Hesburgh's autobiography, as well as any of the many third person stories about him, one cannot help but be enchanted by the man, and wishing one could sit down with him, if only for a burger and a beer.  But charm does not the whole man make, and thus, the distressing part of the story is that while Hesburgh tells it to illustrate what an extraordinary man was his beloved Pope (indeed, in other contexts Hesburgh called him "complex" and "highly intelligent"), he fails to seize upon the starkly apparent opportunity to extol the extraordinary wisdom and virtue of the man's *Humanae Vitae*.  For in it, as we read above, it was the Pope himself who pointed out to all the faithful that artificial birth control is an intrinsically ungodly idea, and that the sacraments were there (particularly Penance and Communion) to help comfort and strengthen them in what he knew, as well as anyone, would be a constant struggle to please God perfectly in a world gone increasing astray from its Maker.  What better metaphor could Hesburgh and Shuster possibly need to help see the perfect wisdom of the Church's magisterium?  In other words, what the Church was saying, and what it has always tried to say throughout the centuries, is that pleasing God perfectly is pretty darned hard, but that doesn't mean we shouldn't strive for it.  And it certainly doesn't mean that the Church should be a democracy, denying its own origins of Immaculate Conception and changing God's rules to suit man's conscience. Father Hesburgh, of all people, a man of the cloth of the Congregation of Holy Cross, should have clung to that same Cross as the Sign of Contradiction that it is, even at the expense of secular criticism, or isolation from the so-called "academy."

Instead, from where some sit, he stayed silent on the encyclical and, in effect, sold out, bought by the riches of Rockefeller money, and tied to the lies that would go with it.  Weeds among the wheat indeed.  But what's worse, when he finally opened his mouth about

what birth control wrought – abortion - one could hardly
comprehend what came out . . .

# 9

## Who Wrought Roe & What Roe Wrought

*Endowed with a spiritual soul, with intellect, and with free will, the human person is from his very conception ordered to God and destined for eternal beatitude.  He pursues his perfection in "seeking and loving what is true and good."*

**Gaudium et Spes ("Joy & Hope")**
**His Holiness Pope Paul VI**
**Conclusion of the Second Vatican Council**
**Vigil of the Feast of the Immaculate Conception**
**December 7, 1965**

In 1894, the same year in which George Shuster was born, John D. Rockefeller, Jr., as a young man destined to inherit his German-blooded Protestant father's enormous oil empire ( valued at a billion dollars in 1891, or about $325 billion in today's dollars, according to Forbes ), penned an essay for his Brown University eugenicist professor, in which he denounced ignorant immigrant "scum" (such as Irish-American Catholics) as "hardly better than beasts" (echoes of Charles Kingsley, that bigoted Brit of famine era fame).

Fast forward to 1964, and one finds Shuster helping Hesburgh award Notre Dame's Laetare Medal to Phyllis McGinley, an artsy Irish Catholic woman (with a German mother) who once lived in Larchmont, New York.  Just four years later, she would serve as one more willing pawn in the Rockefeller family's long-term plan to legalize eugenic abortion across the country, ultimately accomplished by their wholesale engineering of *Roe v. Wade* in 1973.

The eight decades of developments that span and connect these events are unveiled in an exceptional dissertation entitled *The Long Road of Eugenics: From Rockefeller to Roe v. Wade,* penned by pro-life attorney Rebecca Messall.  It was published in *The Human Life Review* in the Fall of 2004, right around the time that the United States Conference of Catholic Bishops finally found the courage to formally request that Catholic universities refrain from giving any more platforms, awards, or honors to those who stand in public opposition to the teachings of the Church on such fundamental matters as abortion.

After offering his ugly little essay, the sophomoric John Jr. proceeded to surround himself with like-minded men and women, and to use his formidable fortune to build institutions intended to target the causes, rather than the symptoms, of man's earthly misery. Negative eugenics, that is to say, reducing the excessive number of "feeble" persons on the planet, became a particular obsession.  Thus, "Junior" viewed birth control much like Ms. Sanger, as the veritable "pivot of civilization." And so, starting in the 1920's, she and her Brownsville-based Birth Control Clinical Research Bureau became one of his pet projects.  Junior provided her with "crucial" and sustained financial support, much to the dismay of New York's Archbishop Patrick Hayes, who decried Sanger's onslaught of the innocent:  "Even though some little angels in the flesh, through the physical or mental deformities of their parents," he lamented, "may appear to human eyes hideous, misshapen, a blot on civilized society, we must not lose sight of this Christian thought that under and within such visible malformation, lives an immortal soul to be saved and glorified for all eternity among the blessed in heaven."

Sanger would react vitriolically to such sentimental sop by batting it right back at the Bishop, having learned well from her father how to attack all things Catholic.  But Rockefeller and his erudite business associates had learned how to operate by more sophisticated measures, adhering to the Don Corleonesque adage that one should keep his friends close, and his enemies closer.  How else to explain the fact that one of the other institutions on Junior's charitable giving list with Sanger was none other than Notre Dame, whose then president, the Reverend James A. Burns, was the first to take Rockefeller money, right on the heels of his hiring George Shuster, circa 1920.  Then, just to round things out, last but not least on Rockefeller's wish list was the Kaiser Wilhelm Institute, in essence Hitler's holocaust laboratory in training, committing medical murder, working on batches of euthanized brains, and loving all manner of good racial hygiene.  Rockefeller-style eugenics, it seems, sought the strangest of laboring bedfellows.

But stranger still is how a well-versed, German-blooded, geo-political intellectual such as Shuster could have seen it all coming in 1935 when he penned *Like A Mighty Army,* as alluded to in the last chapter, only to ignore what was lapping our own shores in 1943. For while he and his fellow ACLU execs were so zealously defending that anti-Nazi firebrand by the name of McMahon, it apparently escaped their attention that the anti-trust section of the U.S. Justice department was pressing criminal charges against Rockefeller's oil interests for being far too cozy with I.G. Farben, the Nazi chemical conglomerate that supplied the gas used to exterminate the Jews. This is not so much to suggest that the Rockefellers had a hand in the Holocaust, though the links in that chain are all too evident.  Rather, this is to say that Shuster, of all God's people, should have known better. Yet he remained no less oblivious, or so it would seem, some twenty years later, when the barbarians began waltzing through Notre Dame's front gates (not to mention the Pope's place of business), thanks to the engraved invitations that he and Hesburgh had given them.  One has to wonder what he and the good father were thinking, for God's sake, assuming they were thinking at all.

The sad fact of the matter is that for much of the 20th century, the Rockefeller family provided substantial financial and corporate support to a continuous network of eugenically obsessed social scientists originally known as the American Eugenics Society (AES). To get a sense of this society, one need only heed what its founders had said in 1916: " Mistaken regard for what are believed to be divine laws and sentimental belief in the sanctity of life tend to prevent the elimination of defective infants and the sterilization of such adults as are themselves of no value to the community," and so compulsory sterilization legislation was required to combat "the shiftless, ignorant, and worthless class of anti-social whites in the South" (One has to wonder how they felt about the "blacks").

Of course, after Allied forces unearthed the horrors of Hitler's Holocaust, eugenicists had to go underground, so to speak, emerging on the other side of the war in cosmetically respectable organizations such as John D. Rockefeller III's Population Council, incorporated in 1952.  But one needed to look no further than John D. III's appointment of Frederick Osborn as president of his Population Council to appreciate that the change was in name only.  Indeed, just before his appointment, Osborn had been a member of the board of directors of the AES, from which he had first been heard singing the praises of the Nazi eugenic program circa 1937.  Therefore, absent some supporting evidence, one does not imagine that Osborn found religion after the war, or that John D. III had shown it to him. In fact, all evidence is quite to the contrary.

First of all, while a student at Princeton University, John D. III's own eugenicist professor had taught him what one might rightfully cite as the seminal operating principle of his Population Council - that "[p]rogress is threatened unless social institutions can be so adjusted as to reverse this process of multiplying the poorest, and extinguishing the most capable families."  Also, after a meeting with Osborne in 1938, John D. III noted that Osborn had told him "about his work in the fields of population and eugenics.  It was all exceedingly interesting.  Do feel that he is doing a good job and should be encouraged.  His two fields tie in, of course, very directly with birth control."  Then, in 1940, Osborn himself was telling Time Magazine, in an article entitled *Eugenics for Democracy,* that in order to achieve "superior heredity," doctors should sterilize the "feeble-minded," whether they wanted it or not, while normal parents should be free to have children, unless of course they were "not wanted" for some reason (eugenic abortions, here we come).  Then again, in 1946, as if to signal that the spirit of Adolf Hitler was still alive and well, Osborne took it upon himself to republish the so-called "Geneticists' Manifesto" of 1939, a "biological blueprint for a better humanity" by means of the manipulation of the worthy and unworthy components of the world-wide population through contraception, sterilization, abortion, artificial insemination, etc. And finally, as late as 1968, Osborn published a book entitled *The Future of Human Heredity,* in which he called for the calculated quarantine of "eugenic terminology" in light of the Holocaust, even as he unabashedly extolled the goal of genetically improving the social and biological qualities of future generations by reducing the birth rates of poor, unintelligent, and unemployable persons "at the lower economic and educational levels."  In short, Frederick Osborn was one chronically ill individual, and his illness was contagious.

Not only had eugenics survived the war, it was now going global, thanks in large part to the Rockefellers, their money, and their friends; but not without a fight.  In fact, the ultimate failure of eugenicist efforts at state-by-state involuntary sterilization legislation was largely on account of *angry, organized, and vigorous economic and political opposition orchestrated by church-going Catholics and their clergy, all across the country.*  So score one for the good guys, but not without remaining mindful of the unhappy fact that it was just this sort of show of force that must have riveted the Rockefellers' attentions toward more liberal Catholics, whom he needed in his corner as the fight shifted fronts from sterilization to contraception and, ultimately, to abortion.

In fact, one could argue that the single most significant step which John D. III took toward creating "acceptability for the new field" among Catholics was to rub elbows with the liberal Catholic academy assembled on his dime at Notre Dame for the aforementioned population conferences of the early 60's.  As alluded to earlier, pro-abortion activist Alan Guttmacher of Planned Parenthood (which may not even have survived had it not been for Junior Rockefeller's faithful patronage of Ms. Sanger) attended that conference.  At the time, he was also an important member of Rockefeller's Population Council, as was his fellow conference attendee, Frank Notestein. As such, both men were the Population Council colleagues of the chronically ill Fred Osborn, whom they apparently kept in strategic quarantine when they went off to visit South Bend.

And so, one is given to wonder, once again, how the savvy Shuster and the well-traveled Hesburgh could have mistaken the identities of all those they had brought to dear old Notre Dame; or, if they did know the whole truth, how both men could have wandered so far from their religion as the first source of wisdom when it came to birth control.  Professor Freddoso, in his aforementioned introduction to Charlie Rice's book, *What Happened to Notre Dame?*, explains it as "impatience, infidelity, ingratiation, and

impenitence," in that order.  And so it was.  But such would seem to
overlook the ample credit clearly owing to the other side, the side that
was slowly seducing them into a not so temporary insanity.  In any
event, an example of sorts:

It just so happens that Ms. Phyllis McGinley and Mr. John D.
Rockefeller III were born exactly one year apart on March 21, 1905
and 1906, respectively.  About six decades later, the two would come
together, but not quite in the way one might imagine.  Theirs was not
an affair of hedonism or the heart.  In fact, they may have never even
met. However, he used her nonetheless, for John D. III had a brother
named Nelson, whom McGinley most certainly did meet.  Nelson was
the Governor of New York, while she was that aforementioned artsy
Irish-German Catholic woman from Larchmont, the one who stuck
her neck out, so to speak, while Shuster and Hesburgh hung Notre
Dame's Laetare Medal around it in 1964, thanks in part, one
suspects, to her Shuster-Rockefeller connections.  As such, she serves
as a near perfect metaphor for the emerging age of faithless reason,
and an appropriate seguey into the short-term future, to abortion a la
the Rockefellers and *Roe vs. Wade.*

By the time she received her Laetare Medal in 1964 at the age
of 59, Phyllis McGinley was a Pulitzer Prize winning author of
immensely popular poetry, essays, and children's books.  It was a
body of work that eloquently reflected her *nouveau* persona as a
happily domesticated, self-styled soft feminist, who embraced a
wholesome version of emancipation while praising the virtues of
raising a family.  Referring to her first child, she told Time Magazine:
"I have never felt so divine in my life as the time before [Julia] was
born.  I was so full of euphoria, I was practically immune to all
human illnesses!"  And yet, as a left-leaning Irish Catholic Democrat,
she was, not surprisingly, ok with contraception.  All of which made
her an ideal candidate for meeting George Shuster (at one time a
fellow literary New Yorker with whom she had chance to interact),

and for one day finding her way to Notre Dame as his model of the modern day cultured Catholic woman.  What's more, she'd made friends in high places, including close encounters with John Kennedy and Lyndon Johnson.  But the friendship that best suggests her emerging function as an important political figurehead is an old and obscure one with another Larchmont New Yorker by the name of Nina Jones, who would one day fill the post of personal press secretary to Margaretta "Happy" Rockefeller, wife of New York Governor Nelson Rockefeller.

Just who among McGinley's many friends and connections would be first to make the suggestion is uncertain, but it would seem to be a lead pipe cinch that it was someone who knew just how she felt, about abortion that is.  Otherwise, it's unlikely that Nelson would have taken the suggestion seriously.  No point putting a famous Irish Catholic female champion of the family on his Select Committee to review New York's anti-abortion laws unless she were firmly in favor of "pro-choice" reforms – which she was – the perfect answer to the Rockefeller family's pro-life Catholic adversaries:  "I hate the idea of abortion," she would say from her seat on the Select Committee, "but ours is a pluralistic state, and I don't expect the state of New York to administer [any longer than the last three centuries] the laws of my church."  In other words, she was the mother of the "personally opposed, but" platform.  (As discussed later in this book, Rockefeller's eventual successor, New York Governor Mario Cuomo, would come to Notre Dame and say essentially the same thing, with Father Hesburgh's blessing, in order to influence the outcome of the 1984 presidential election.)

Nelson Rockefeller's efforts at "reform" in New York, which were essentially directed at encouraging doctors to rid the world of disabled babies while still in their mothers' wombs, was part of a larger Rockefeller family funded initiative to adopt such legislation state-by-state under the rubric of the American Law Institute's Model

Penal Code.  Part of the family's funding paid for criminally fraudulent research conducted by a sexually psychopathic atheist named Alfred Kinsey, whose Kinsey Institute "studies" were cited by the ALI in support of the Model Penal Code.  What's more, they were touted by Planned Parenthood in its nationwide push for the sexual reorientation of schoolchildren (a program that has since been statistically proven to have substantially exacerbated problem teen pregnancies owing to unbridled sex for pleasure, as plainly prophesied by Pope Paul VI).  Kinsey was more than just your run-of-the-mill eugenicist, mind you.  He was apparently a despicable child pornography lover who was keenly interested in displacing the traditional family in favor of eugenically selective breeding, with plenty of sexual deviancy on the side.

If the Model Penal Code was the Rockefeller family's cake, *Roe vs. Wade* was the icing on that cake, for not only did it take the issue away from the several states, and legalize abortion without due regard for regional political proclivities, it greatly expanded the limited justifications for abortion that were incorporated into the Model Penal Code, namely rape, incest, and fetal disability.

The fingerprints of the Rockefeller family, and the odor of its money, are all over Justice Harry Blackmun's majority opinion in *Roe v. Wade*.  This, by reason of Blackmun's heavy reliance on eugenic propaganda advanced over time by a spider-web's worth of black widow Margaret Sanger's minions from the AES, each of whom were associated with one or another of the Rockefellers.  Here now an attempt to navigate this spider-web without getting too tangled up in it.

First, recall that John D. Rockefeller Junior had provided Margaret Sanger and her birth control clinic with sustained financial support starting in the 1920's.  Well, Dr. Robert L. Dickinson had been Sanger's clinic colleague, and received similar funding from Junior for his own National Committee on Maternal Health.  After

Dickinson died, Christopher Tietze, who had been Glanville Williams colleague in the British Eugenics Society, took over Dickinson's committee.  Williams and Tietze were both dedicated eugenicists, deeply concerned with "the problem of eugenic quality" being increasingly compromised by "excess births among the lower and uneducated classes." But not to worry; Justice Blackmun's opinion cited books by these two men five separate times in support of the Court's decision to legalize abortion on demand.

Also cited by Blackmun was an organization known as the American Public Health Association (APHA), which had applauded Germany's Sterilization Program in 1934, received a grant from the Rockefeller Foundation to expand its operations in 1957, and was waiting with anticipation for the nationalization of legalized abortion in order to aggressively approach "the problem of overpopulation" in 1962. Then, in October of 1972, as Blackmun and his brethren were deliberating over the decision they would make three months later, the APHA published an article asserting that the "legalization of abortion is probably the single most effective practical measure that can be taken to lower the birth rate, and by doing so, preserve the environment from further deterioration."

Then there was Lawrence Lader, whose book entitled *Abortion* was cited seven separate times by the Court for support.  Lader had been a founding father of NARAL (National Association for the Repeal of Abortion Laws) in 1968, right around the time he took his seat next to fellow dedicated eugenicist Alan Guttmacher, and across from the not so divine Phyllis McGinley, on Nelson Rockefeller's reform commission. The following year, Nelson's brother John D. III personally prophesied to Lader and his fellow board members at the Association for the Study of Abortion (ASA), funded by both Rockefeller brothers, that "a broad interpretation of [the expectant mother's] mental health . . . would allow many if not all women to qualify" for "therapeutic" abortions on demand (which is precisely how the *Roe* Court would soon render any restrictions, in effect, illusory).  In addition to *Abortion,* Lader had also authored a biography of web-spinner Margaret Sanger, and one other book, *Breeding Ourselves to Death,* in which he and his sick friend Fred Osborn had bragged that eugenicist propaganda portraying overpopulation as "the greatest menace of our time" had "helped change the climate of public opinion, enabling great foundations like Ford and Rockefeller together to concentrate over $100 million dollars on the population problem."

But the most sinister Court citations consisted of six separate references to law review articles that had been discreetly funded by the Rockefeller brothers, and authored by an attorney named Cyril Means (A trusted NARAL lawyer, Means had also been on Nelson Rockefeller's commission with Lader, Guttmacher, McGinley, and friends.)  In these pieces of legalized prostitution, as painstakingly explained by Fordham University Law Professor Robert M. Byrn in his own outstanding article entitled *An American Tragedy,* Means distorts eight hundred years of history and tradition to come to the absurd conclusion that civilized society had never seen fit to find that the fetus was a person entitled to protection, when the great weight of authority indicates that this couldn't be further from the truth.  In essence, Byrn traces precedent beginning with Bracton, the thirteenth century English jurist who helped father fundamental concepts in our criminal laws, and continuing all the way through to nineteenth and twentieth century American cases, statutes, and medical literature.  In them, he finds that the law consistently strived to protect an unborn child's personhood and fundamental right to life "from the moment science was able to establish the child's individuated, living, biological existence," which, after the technological advancements of the 1830's, was conclusively determined to be at the moment of conception as a matter of scientific fact.  And coming, providentially, on the eve of the Civil

War, the import and impact of this discovery is described by Professor Byrn in a way that could hardly be more profound, or poignant to this book's essential purpose:

> *Whatever may be said of the common law and the early nineteenth century, it is evident that in the period from 1859 to 1871, spanning a war fought to vindicate the essential dignity of every human being and the subsequent ratification of the fourteenth amendment [fundamental right to life] in 1868, the anti-abortion mood prevalent in the United States can be explained only by a desire to protect live human beings in the womb from the beginning of their existence.*

In fact, in the five-year period preceding *Roe*, that desire was widely reiterated across the country, as 18 states reaffirmed their anti-abortion legislation, 4 made limited reforms, and only 3 significant reforms, while the other 25 saw fit to leave well enough completely alone.  And it was in this pre-*Roe* period that Byrn had been equally profound when he wrote that –

> *. . one of the predominant characteristics of the abortion philosophy is the substitution of the quality of life for the sanctity of life; so that, under the influence of advanced technological know-how, the right to life is reserved only for those whose lives are useful, with the result that euthanasia fits as naturally into the jurisprudence of permissive abortion as does abortion itself.*

This philosophy is now imbedded in *Roe.* In short, the Roe Court, as the appalling self-appointed "social engineers" for us all, evidently viewed abortion as "a viable solution to such quality-of-life problems as pollution, poverty, population growth and race," and therefore took it upon itself to do what they felt was best for us, in spite of how we ourselves had felt about the matter. Equally appalling, as observed by one of Blackmun's own law clerks, is the fact that as "[a]s a matter of constitutional interpretation and judicial method, <u>Roe</u> borders on the indefensible [because] Justice Blackmun's opinion provides essentially no reasoning in support of its holding. And almost 30 years since *Roe's* announcement, no one has produced a convincing defense of Roe on its own terms." Indeed, Justice Byron White, in his dissenting opinion, put it this way:

> *I find nothing in the language or history of the Constitution to support the Court's judgment. The Court simply fashions and announces a new constitutional right for pregnant mothers and, with scarcely any reason or authority for its action, invests that right with sufficient substance to override most existing state abortion statutes. The upshot is that the people and the legislatures of the 50 States are constitutionally disentitled to weigh the relative importance of the continued existence and development of the fetus, on the one hand, against a spectrum of possible impacts on the mother, on the other hand.*

Roe has made America the world's worst aborter of babies, with few signs this will ever cease to be the case. As pointed out by

Ramesh Ponnuru in his powerful indictment of today's leading liberal Democrats entitled *The Party of Death, Roe* puts no real restrictions on abortion in America, unlike any other nation in the civilized world. Many Americans still think that abortion may be restricted in the 2nd trimester, and banned altogether in the 3rd trimester, or after the baby kicks, but this is not what *Roe* really says (nor is it what America has ever wanted, according to a long line of polls).  The ruling in Roe does not allow States to restrict abortion if the health of the mother is at stake at any time, right up to the end of her term, and defines that health by reference to Roe's companion case of *Doe v. Bolton*, wherein Justice Blackmun writes that —

> *- the medical judgment may be exercised in the light of all factors – physical, emotional, psychological, familial, and the woman's age – relevant to the well-being of the patient.  All these factors may relate to health.  This allows the attending physician the room he needs to make his best medical judgment.  And it is room that operates for the benefit, not the disadvantage, of the pregnant woman.*

That this is a complete canard ought to be self-evident, especially to expectant mothers.  Indeed, a doctor who might otherwise be the object of criminal inquiry is the same one, indeed the only one, capable of exercising "his best medical judgment" about what he and he alone was able to observe about his patient, including such subjective things as attitude, demeanor and other expressions of emotion.

But the greater shame of *Roe* really falls upon us all, for we've permitted a few fools in long black robes to take away not one, but two, of our most fundamental rights, and flush them like so much waste.  That is, not only have they stolen our right to life, they've also taken away what we have to say about it by silencing all State by State debate, as eloquently lamented by the late great Justice Antonin Scalia a little later in this book.

# 10

# Kennedy the Queen of Angels

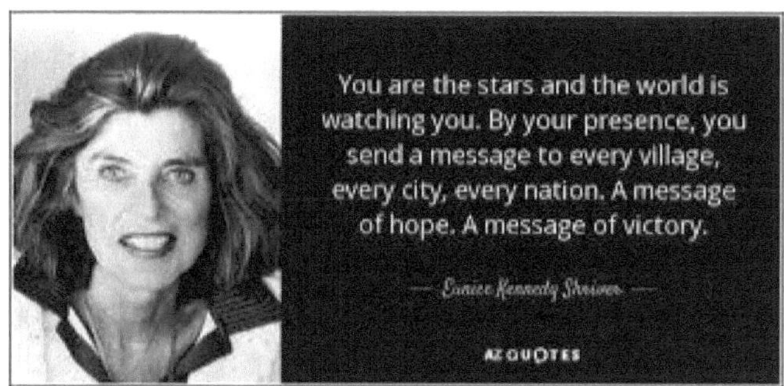



***People were bringing little children to him, for him to touch them.  The disciples turned them away, but when Jesus saw this he was indignant and said to them – "Let the little children come unto me, and do not hinder them; for it is to just such as these that the Kingdom of God belongs.  I tell you solemnly, anyone who does not welcome the kingdom of God like a little child will never enter it."  Then he put his arms around them, laid his hands on them, and gave them each his blessing.  <u>Mark 10:13-16</u>.***

In 1849, as the potato famine approached and Father of Notre Dame Football Patrick Connors came into the world, Patrick Kennedy and Bridget Murphy emigrated from County Wexford to Boston, Massachusetts, where they were married and raised five children. Their last was Patrick Joseph ("PJ") Kennedy, who became a successful purveyor of whiskey, as well as a powerful politician. PJ and his wife, Mary Hickey, had two daughters and two sons. Their second son, Francis Benedict, died when he was only 10 months old, but their first, Joseph Patrick, lived to find even greater fortunes than his father, through shrewd investment in the markets, and most likely through some Prohibition whisky trade as well. It was this Joe Kennedy who married Rose Fitzgerald, and by her sired nine children, including Joe Jr. (#1), John Fitzgerald (#2), Rosemary (#3), Eunice (#5), Bobby (#7), and Teddy (#9).

In 1944, Joe Jr. was killed in the war, while his kid brother John manned the Navy's PT 109, swimming his way to heroism and history. After the war was over, Joe Sr. formed a charitable foundation in Joe Jr.'s name, and dedicated it to addressing disabilities of the brain such as those which had hindered the intellectual development of his beloved daughter Rosemary from birth. From this foundation, and the wellspring that was Rosemary's loving little sister, Eunice, came what is now known the world over as the Special Olympics (But first, Eunice would marry Sargent Shriver in 1953, a few months before her big brother John married Jackie).

Now, unlike George Shuster and his friend, Saul Alinsky, Eunice Kennedy Shriver had always loved football, and indeed all things athletic, dating back to her days in Hyannis Port. That's where she and her two sports-loving brothers, Bobby and John (Teddy was just a tike), would put together family pick-up games while growing up. And it's also where Eunice learned to love those like Rosemary, her learning-disabled big sister by three years. Sad to say, Shuster's eugenic society friends from the Rockefeller Population Council would hardly have approved of someone like Rosemary, surely finding her too "unfit," and unworthy of any future. However, the way that a Marxist like Saul Alinsky had felt about such children, assuming that he felt anything at all, is less certain. But if his philosophically like-minded legacy student out of Chicago is any indication, Alinsky's attitude was likely less than inspiring.  One only says this because Barack Obama, on the two month anniversary of his assuming the presidency, took the opportunity to slight some three million disabled members of the Special Olympics – by likening his lousy bowling skills to theirs -  during his historic appearance on none other than the Tonight Show.  In doing so he became, rather ironically, the first sitting President to lend the dignity of his office to pedestrian entertainment, while exposing himself as the ugly epitome of cold-hearted elitism in the process.  Tellingly enough, this episode aired on the very same day the University of Notre Dame announced that it had invited President Obama to appear there as well, so that he could speak to its graduating class about things like faith, and the call to Christian service, while receiving an honorary law degree for epitomizing social justice, even if only to some, and for some, it would seem.

Obama, of course, quickly apologized for his appalling indifference toward the disabled (apparently just as soon as someone pointed it out to him), and of course, his apology was graciously accepted, at least in public.  However, there is no denying that this was precisely the sort of infuriating indifference to her own sister's dignity, and to the millions of children like Rosemary, which angered Eunice to no end, beginning long before Barack Obama was even born.  Such, that she would devote nearly the last five decades of her life to fighting it, her Irish ever up, and ever the unabashed "extremist" in defense of human dignity, for the unborn as well as the born.  Perhaps it was her own daughter, Maria Shriver, who most graciously expressed how Eunice herself might have felt if she'd the sad misfortune of hearing Obama:

*While I am confident that President Obama never intended to offend anyone, the response that his comments have caused, coupled with the reaction of a primetime audience, demonstrate the need to continue to educate the non-disabled community on the issues that confront those with a developmental disability. My mother has dedicated her life to fighting stereotypes and ridicule for this community, and there is still much work to be done.*

*The President's apology for his comments and his commitment to bringing the Special Olympics to the White House are important first steps in shedding light on this important issue. Often times we don't realize that when we laugh at comments like this it hurts millions of people throughout the world. People with special needs are great athletes and productive citizens, and I look forward to working with the President to knock down myths and stereotypes about this community.*

On the other hand, one is given to wonder whether Eunice, evidently not above the role of angrily indignant mother, would have preferred to slap President Obama's face, as one might any other deserving juvenile delinquent, rather than merely on the wrist, as her First Lady of California daughter had done.

In any event, it was Eunice's enormous affection for her sister Rosemary, and her love for all sorts of sports, that together conspired and inspired her to start the Special Olympics, circa 1968, just two years after the death of the malevolent Margaret Sanger.  But it actually all started a bit earlier than that, in the summer of '62.  That's when Eunice and her husband Sargent had first visited the Southbury Training School in Waterbury, Connecticut, a wonderful place where children with intellectual disabilities were being given a fighting chance to exhibit their inestimable worth, contribute to the community, and preserve their God-given dignity.  It was a far cry from most of the other "mental institutions" in the United States, indeed in the world, and it moved Eunice and Sargent to turn their own Timberlawn farm in Maryland into another Southbury of sorts that same summer. There, some 34 children from various nearby clinics, together with their largely inexperienced but equally large-hearted high school and college kid counselors, would become the beautiful embryo of what would slowly but steadily grow into one of the greatest triumphs of good over ignorance and outright evil in all of human history. And all on account of the unadulterated joy that comes from the spirit of competitive athletics. Indeed, there is hardly a doubt, that had he lived to see the day, Patrick Connors would have been awfully proud of Eunice Kennedy, his kindred spirit from Erin.

For on July 20, 1968, six heart-warming years after the start of her little Timberlawn experiment, and six heart-breaking weeks after the tragic assassination of her beloved brother Bobby, Eunice assembled a thousand kids from 26 States at Soldier Field in Chicago for the first-ever Special Olympics. From there, she proudly championed their cause, and boldly threw down her own gauntlet, challenging the rest of the world to follow her lead for the sake of the millions of other kids whom she knew were out there, hoping and waiting to show their worth, if only they were given the fighting chance.

There were only about a hundred people in the 85,000-seat stadium that day, and not that many more who would learn what had happened in the immediate weeks afterward. But like the IQs of the kids, the numbers just didn't matter. What mattered was the enormous love in their hearts, the truly unconditional kind. The kind that first infected Eunice, and slowly but surely would infect the whole world, like some kind of wild and incurable plague. Such that today, there are over three million Special Olympics athletes training all year-round, for all sorts of events, in all 50 States, and in 180 countries throughout the world.  And, as if that were not enough, as Executive Vice-President of the well-funded Joseph P. Kennedy Jr. Foundation, Eunice parlayed her work with the Special Olympics into a multi-layered paradigm shift toward an increasingly positive awareness of the issues by the public, greater research initiatives in the scientific community, and an improved quality of care in medical and residential facilities across the country and throughout the world.  Largely as a result of her efforts, we would eventually learn that nearly 95% of those with intellectual disabilities can make real contributions to mankind's cause, if only they'd all receive the right care and education.

What's more, Eunice was deeply attuned to the Divine wisdom and mercy of her mission, and so understood that by urging us to love those to whom the kingdom of God belongs, she was offering us the opportunity to keep company with His angels.  "From all I have learned," she once said, "it is clear that life does not begin at birth, it begins at conception."  So, "when God's blessings arrive in your life, it is my hope that you will be open to them, embracing the unexpected with a caring heart and a belief in the mystery of the sublime" because "risking pain to experience indescribable joy is a worthwhile chance to take."  And, as if that were not enough to reveal what was ever in her own heart, Eunice was fond of referring to the touching words of Dr. Maria Egg in *When a Child is Different* (John Day Company, 1963), when she said that "[t]hese little flames we must shield with our hands - for these little flames radiate warmth and quiet joy; they shine on the road that leads to the wisdom of the heart, to human maturity and to true wealth."  In other words, to hear Eunice once again, these children have more to teach us about "peace and hope and faith and love" than we have to teach them, and therefore "[w]e should come away with a new respect for them as persons; a new respect for what they can contribute to their families, to their communities, and the nation." In short, she saw that the Special Olympics had the capacity to teach even the most cynical among us "that all human beings are created equal in the sense that each has the capacity and a hunger for moral excellence, for courage, for friendship and for love. Whatever the speed of our feet or the power of our arms, each of us is capable of these highest virtues."

All of which is why President Ronald Reagan awarded Eunice Kennedy Shriver the Presidential Medal of Freedom, our nation's highest civilian honor, in 1984, and why Notre Dame soon followed suit with the Laetare Medal, its own highest honor, in 1988 (To Notre Dame's additional credit, it had hosted the Special Olympic of 1987, as Hesburgh entered retirement). In fact, far too numerous to mention are all the other honors, awards, and accolades that Eunice received throughout her wonderful life. However, this work would truly be remiss if it failed to fully air her ultimate tribute, the one which her family paid on her passing at Hyannis Port, August 11, 2009:

> *It's hard for us to believe: the amazing Eunice Kennedy Shriver went home to God this morning at 2 a.m.*

> *She was the light of our lives, a mother, wife, grandmother, sister, and aunt who taught us by example and with passion what it means to live a faith-driven life of love and service to others. For each of us, she often seemed to stop time itself - to run another Special Olympics games, to visit us in our homes, to attend to her own mother, her sisters and*

*brothers, and to sail, tell stories, and laugh and serve her friends. How did she do it all?*

*Inspired by her love of God, her devotion to her family, and her relentless belief in the dignity and worth of every human life, she worked without ceasing - searching, pushing, demanding, hoping for change. She was a living prayer, a living advocate, a living center of power. She set out to change the world and to change us, and she did that and more. She founded the movement that became Special Olympics, the largest movement for acceptance and inclusion for people with intellectual disabilities in the history of the world. Her work transformed the lives of hundreds of millions of people across the globe, and they in turn are her living legacy.*

*We have always been honored to share our mother with people of good will the world over who believe, as she did, that there is no limit to the human spirit. At this time of loss, we feel overwhelmed by the gifts of prayer and support poured out to us from so many who loved her. We are together in our belief that she is now in heaven, rejoicing with her family, enjoying the fruits of her faith, and still urging us onward to the challenges ahead. Her love will inspire us to faith and service always.*

*She was forever devoted to the Blessed Mother. May she be welcomed now by Mary to the joy and love of life everlasting, in the certain truth that her love and spirit will live forever.*

# 11

# Kennedy the Cowardly Lion

*"While the deep concern of a woman bearing an unwanted child merits consideration and sympathy, it is my personal feeling that the legalization of abortion on demand is not in accordance with the value which our civilization places on human life. Wanted or unwanted, I believe that human life, even at its earliest stages, has certain rights which must be recognized — the right to be born, the right to love, the right to grow old.*

*On the question of the individual's freedom of choice there are easily available birth control methods and information which women may employ to prevent or postpone pregnancy. But once life has begun, no matter at what stage of growth, it is my belief that termination should not be decided merely by desire.*

*When history looks back to this era it should recognize this generation as one which cared about human beings enough to halt the practice of war, to provide a decent living for every family, and to fulfill its responsibility to its children from the very moment of conception."*

**Excerpt of a letter from Senator Ted Kennedy to constituent Tom Dennelly, August 3, 1971, only eighteen months before publication of the opinion in *Roe v. Wade*.**

Ted Kennedy was, by most accounts, a largely kind and charismatic man, admired by his constituents and colleagues, and beloved by his close friends and family.  Likewise, the former Cardinal who prayed over his grave, Theodore McCarrick, would appear to have possessed these same endearing qualities.  But these two Irishmen, Ted and Ted, also had their less than admirable sides.

By some accounts, Ted Kennedy had acquired, over the course of his entire adult life, a consistent reputation for being a drunken, adulterous, misogynistic womanizer, but this deserved or undeserved image of the man pales in comparison to the fact that for the last three decades of his life, Ted Kennedy was an unrepentant advocate of abortion on demand, including the kind where the baby is nearly born, almost all the way out of the womb, so that a doctor can shove a scissors in her skull, and suck her brains out.  So dedicated was Ted to ignoring the unborn, he once took to the Senate floor and single-handedly savaged the personal and professional reputation of one of the most respected legal minds in the country - uniquely fit to sit on our nation's Supreme Court - for no other reason than the man's inclination to protect the innocent victims of abortion on demand.

But tisk-tisk-tisk to all of that, tinkered Teddy the former Cardinal McCarrick, as he stood there in Arlington Cemetery on August 29, 2009.  For in that burial casket next to him lay the unequaled Irish champion of secular social justice, and that was plenty good enough for the likes of the liberal McCarrick.  He was only too happy to heap on the praise, and endear himself to power in the process, while paying all faithfully practicing Catholics a little patronizing lip-service:

> *They called him 'the Lion of the Senate,' and*
> *indeed that is what he was. His roar, and his zeal for*

Given the glaring and unquestionably unchristian aspects of Kennedy's lifelong personal and professional history, and the fact that there have been nearly nineteen hundred senators in our nation's history, one cannot help but wonder what the former priest meant by "great." For even by the kindest measure of Christian forgiveness, to which we miserable sinners should certainly all aspire, it's hard to see why Ted Kennedy was so "great" compared to, say, any one of the other 1900 senators, from each side of the aisle, who were faithful to their wives, respectful of women, attentive to the needs of their constituents, and considerate of the culture of life.

Listening carefully to McCarrick, one can almost hear the echoes of his Irish prelate predecessors, praising the paternalistic instincts allegedly exhibited by southern slave owners, while keeping a lid on their growing threat to the Irish Catholic economy.

Alas, no struggling Catholic can look to either Kennedy or McCarrick for an un-muddled message of what their faith should

mean.  For that, one need look to others, and fortunately, there are
more than a few.  Here's one:

*I only met Edward Kennedy once.*

*I had been invited to visit then-senator Phil Gramm,
who was contemplating a run for the Republican
presidential nomination in 1996. Having read some of
my musings on the topic, Senator Gramm wanted to
brainstorm about some innovative welfare-reform
policies that would simultaneously make economic
sense and really help the poor.*

*After we had chatted for some time in his office, a bell
rang and Senator Gramm rose. "I need to take a vote.
Walk with me and let's continue this conversation," he
said.*

*As we walked down the corridor, I could spy familiar
names on the various Senate office doors. We came to
an elevator that would take us down to an
underground subway connecting the Senate offices to
the Senate chamber. It was a small elevator, no more
than a large closet. Senator Gramm, an aide, and I
tucked ourselves in and the door began to slide shut.*

*Just before closing, an arm came through to stop the
door's close. As it reopened, I found myself standing
face-to-face with the Lion of the Senate, arguably the
most prominent Catholic layman in the country, scion
of the most prominent Catholic family, perhaps, in U.S.
history. Kennedy immediately looked me up and down,*

and then quizzically glanced over to Senator Gramm trying to figure out why his colleague was hanging out with a priest.

As Senator Kennedy stepped into the elevator, Senator Gramm welcomed him with his Southern tones, "Come on in, Teddy. We've called you here to pray for you."

Without missing a beat, Senator Kennedy tossed a mischievous wink in my direction, nudging me with his elbow in Catholic camaraderie and replied in his Bostonian accent, "Uhh [there was that familiar pause of his], uhh, no Phil, Father and I have called you here to pray for you."

There was laughter as the elevator door slid closed. It was my turn to speak so I decided to enter the spirit of the moment.

I stood erect, place my hand on Senator Kennedy's broad shoulder and said, "Actually, senator, this is an exorcism."

The laughter in that elevator, which spilled out onto the train platform, was electric, causing the by-standing senators to look in our direction and wonder what in the world would have Senators Kennedy and Gramm in such uproarious laughter with a Catholic priest.

And so, I had mixed feelings on the news of Ted Kennedy's passing. A memory of a pleasant encounter, *but knowledge that despite our common baptism, Senator Kennedy and I differed in some very radical ways on issues of public policy, economics, heath care, marriage, and, most fundamentally, on matters related to life.*

*James Joyce once remarked that the Catholic Church was "Here comes everybody," and while I relish the experience of being part of a Church rather than a sect, a Church in which there are a host of matters on which faithful Catholics can disagree, I also recognize that there are some defining issues from which are derived the very sense of a shared identity. From my own life and in my pastoral work, I understand that not everyone lives up to the demands of the faith all the time. Graham Greene's famed "whiskey priest" in The Power and the Glory was the prototype of an essentially good, yet flawed man.*

*Yet there are some matters so grave that they go beyond mere flaws and work to diminish or even fracture an identity. I fear that this will be part of Ted Kennedy's legacy, notwithstanding his other personal weaknesses.*

*What might the face of the Democratic party, indeed American politics, today look like **if Ted Kennedy had, instead of reversing himself, maintained the unflinching stance of his late sister Eunice in her consistent defense of vulnerable human life** — whether that of a mentally handicapped child or sister or an infant in the womb? Instead, the senator* *took the dubious advice of certain Boston Jesuits to abandon that tradition and hence those most vulnerable.*

*Many will speak and write of the legacy of Ted Kennedy in the days ahead. For me, as an East Coast "ethnic" grandchild of immigrants, Kennedy's death symbolizes several cogent moments in Catholic America.*

*It marks the passing of a generation that thought that being Catholic, Democratic, and pro–New Deal were synonymous. We now live in an age where many Catholic Americans are very happy to be described as pro-market and are suspicious of New Deal–like solutions — as, of course, they are entitled to be in a way that they are not, for example, on life issues. Senator Kennedy had it exactly the wrong way around.*

*Kennedy's death also brings the Church face-to-face once again with the fact that there is a massive problem of basic Catholic education — catechesis — among the faithful. So many Catholics — even some clergy — make an absolute out of prudential issues such as economic policy, while relativizing absolutes, such as abortion, euthanasia, and marriage. This is done in the face of clear, binding teachings from John Paul the Great, who said that no other right is safe unless the right to life is protected, or, as Pope Benedict wrote recently in Caritas in Veritate, that life issues must be central to Catholic social teaching.*

*This also marks the passing of a certain type of cultural Catholicism — Northeast, Irish and increasingly Italian, concerned with obtaining political power while maintaining an identification with the Church, yet happy to relinquish the substance of the faith if it gets in the way. Indeed, today such cultural Catholics have dispensed even with the identity aspect and are often outright hostile to the Church of their baptism.*

*I would like to think that the letter, reported to have been ten pages, that Ted Kennedy wrote and asked President Obama to hand to Pope Benedict early in the summer renders an account of his life before God and the Church. I certainly pray he died at peace, reconciled with the Church of his fathers, and in God's merciful grace. And I shall pray for his eternal beatitude.*

"Kennedy The Catholic", Reverend Robert A. Sirico, Acton Institute.


The public has neither seen nor heard the entirety of Ted Kennedy's ten-page letter to Pope Benedict, and one suspects that it shouldn't. But it was treated to a self-promoting snippet, courtesy of the defrocked McCarrick, in which Kennedy was exceedingly kind to himself, and took the opportunity to tell Pope Benedict that Barack Obama, too, was a man of "deep faith," a myth that McCarrick corroborated by proclaiming it to all the world.  It was, in fact, a perversely premeditated, carefully orchestrated, sickeningly transparent display of partisan political gamesmanship from the grave, and McCarrick had apparently been happy to do his part.

As a result of Kennedy's failure to follow in the footsteps of his sister Eunice, and his scathing attack on Supreme Court nominee Robert Bork, the country wound up with another misguided Irishman on the Court - by the name of Kennedy no less - who betrayed four other justices prepared to put a fork in *Roe v. Wade,* and gave us the plurality opinion in *Planned Parenthood v. Casey,* 1992, perpetuating *Roe* to the present day.  Adding insult to injury, the defendant in that case was Robert Casey, the courageous pro-life Irish Catholic Democrat Governor of the State of Pennsylvania, sued by Planned Parenthood for placing legal restrictions on their big money abortion business (such as informed consent, a waiting period, and parental notification).  While the Court saw fit to uphold Casey's restrictions (without reversing *Roe v. Wade*), it was only two weeks after the issuance of its opinion on June 29, 1992 that the same Robert Casey, sitting Governor of the 5th largest state in the nation, would be banned by his own party from speaking at the Democratic National Convention that nominated Bill Clinton for President (Casey had also succeeded in stopping sex-selection abortions altogether, but this was because Planned Parenthood had determined to avoid the obvious double-edged dilemma of this particular women's issue by keeping it out of Court, just as they had determined to avoid  the double-edged dilemma of a powerful pro-life Democrat in their midst by keeping him out of the convention.)

If Kennedy had not torched Robert Bork, and had gone to bat for Bob Casey, it would have been a whole different story.  But he and all the other democrats of his ilk were tied to the gigantic purse strings of the monstrous Planned Parenthood. Thus, can it be said with great sadness and certainty that but for the betrayals of Edward Kennedy, the man whom defrocked McCarrick called "great", *Roe v.*

*Wade* would not likely have endured, nor abortion have continued as the law of the land.

Fitting that this chapter close, then, with the words of Justice Antonin Scalia, from his chilling dissent in the very same case of *Planned Parenthood vs. Casey*, in which he chides Anthony Kennedy, Sandra Day O'Connor (another Irish coward) and the others, for presuming to think that in reaffirming the insanity of *Roe v. Wade*, they were finally putting an end to the long raging controversy:

> *There is a poignant aspect to today's opinion. Its length, and what might be called its epic tone, suggest that its authors believe they are bringing to an end a troublesome era in the history of our Nation, and of our Court. "It is the dimension" of authority, they say, to "cal[l] the contending sides of national controversy to end their national division by accepting a common mandate rooted in the Constitution...*

> *There comes vividly to mind a portrait by Emanuel Leutze that hangs in the Harvard Law School: Roger Brooke Taney, painted in 1859, the 82nd year of his life, the 24th of his Chief Justiceship, the second after his opinion in Dred Scott. He is in black, sitting in a shadowed red armchair, left hand resting*

*upon a pad of paper in his lap, right hand hanging limply, almost lifelessly, beside the inner arm of the chair. He sits facing the viewer and staring straight out. There seems to be on his face, and in his deep-set eyes, an expression of profound sadness and disillusionment. Perhaps he always looked that way, even when dwelling upon the happiest of thoughts. But those of us who know how the lustre of his great Chief Justiceship came to be eclipsed by Dred Scott cannot help believing that he had that case - its already apparent consequences for the Court and its soon-to-be-played-out consequences for the Nation - burning on his mind. I expect that, two years earlier, he, too, had thought himself "call[ing] the contending sides of national controversy to end their national division by accepting a common mandate rooted in the Constitution."*

*It is no more realistic for us in this case than it was for him in that to think that an issue of the sort they both involved - an issue involving life and death, freedom and subjugation - can be "speedily and finally settled" by the Supreme Court, as President James Buchanan, in his inaugural address, said the issue of slavery in the territories would be. See Inaugural Addresses of the Presidents of the United States, S.Doc. No. 101-10, p. 126 (1989). Quite to the contrary, by foreclosing all democratic outlet for the deep passions this issue arouses, by banishing the issue from the political forum that gives all participants, even the losers, the satisfaction of a fair hearing and an honest fight, by continuing the imposition of a rigid national rule instead of allowing for regional differences, the Court merely prolongs and intensifies the anguish.*

*We should get out of this area, where we have no right to be, and where we do neither ourselves nor the country any good by remaining.*

# 12

# Cuomo Catholicism Comes to Campus

*All that is necessary for the triumph of evil is that good men do nothing.*

**Edmund Burke**


Justice Scalia instructs us, not only by what he said, but by what he didn't say.  He did not advocate in the Casey case, nor has he ever advocated in any case, that *Roe v. Wade* be replaced by another opinion in which nine men and women tell America that abortion is wrong.  Scalia was merely saying that *Roe* was wrong for telling America anything, because Americans are the ones with the right to decide what to do about the issue of abortion, and *Roe* took that right away from them.  As for what Americans should actually do about abortion, Scalia is conspicuously silent, leaving advocacy to the people, and to their preferred religious and political representatives. If for no other reason than this silence, all freedom loving Americans, no matter their views, ought to revere Justice Scalia.  For one suspects that as a practicing Catholic father of nine, and brilliant custodian of constitutional law, he had to resist the urge to otherwise advocate, as did Professor Byrn, the opinion that he likely harbors in his heart of hearts, but has kept moored there for the sake of liberty –

that life begins at the moment of conception, and that the framers of the fourteenth amendment assumed as much when they enshrined our right to life along with liberty.  Stated another way, Scalia's silence implicitly concedes that *Roe v. Wade* would have done equal violence to the tenets of liberty in a "pluralistic" society, and been the source of just as much divisiveness, had it adopted the opposite view, and taken voice away from the other half of the American people. Indeed, the same attributes that likely gave him his urge, and allowed him to resist it – his faith in both Catholicism and country – could only have helped him to appreciate, as he looked out at all that was happening to our culture, that the need for great political debate among the people, and for enlightened legislation from the will of "we the people," had grown ever more evident over the three decades from *Roe* to *Casey*.

In fact, thanks to John D. III and his pals at Planned Parenthood providing grade school sustenance to the Sanger-incited sexual revolution (through family unfriendly, culture-debasing, sex education programs), and despite their simultaneous, profit-motivated marketing of all sorts of artificial contraception (through federally assisted family planning programs to the tune of over $250 million dollars per year, and otherwise), out-of-wedlock births had increased six hundred (600%) percent from 1960 to 1990.  Such, that by 1991, as the case of *Planned Parenthood vs. Casey* made its way to our Supreme Court, over thirty (30%) percent of all U.S. births were without marriage (now 40%), including six out of every ten teenage pregnancies.  All of which, of course, proves Pope Paul VI to have been one of the greatest prophets in modern history.  And all of which, of course, led to a bloodbath of abortions in the wake of *Roe v. Wade*.  Indeed, a brand-new cottage industry for our growing economy.  Sadly, statistics state that the staggering rate has averaged about 1.3 million babies per year (or some 61 million since 1973). Nearly twenty (20%) percent of such procedures were initially funded by federal taxpayers at a cost of about $50 million dollars annually, until a courageous Irish Catholic statesman by the name of Henry Hyde put a plug in that (albeit a precarious one) by pushing his "Hyde Amendment" through Congress in 1976.

Hyde wasn't the only statesman to take a brave stand on the state of our nation after *Roe v. Wade* (1973), and on through the advent of *Planned Parenthood v. Casey* (1992). Others also appreciated their individual obligations and accepted them earnestly, such as Ronald Reagan, Robert Casey, and Teresa of Calcutta, while some accepted money from Planned Parenthood instead, paid a little lip service to the issue, and otherwise kept their mouths shut while the slaughter continued. Ted Kennedy springs to mind again here, together with Tip O'Neill, Daniel Patrick Moynihan, and John Kerry, just to fill out a foursome. Horsemen of the Apocalypse in progress, one might say, and fine fighting Irishmen at that. And then, there was Mario Cuomo.

While Governor of New York and a powerful figure in democratic party politics, Cuomo gave a "John A. O'Brien Lecture" to the University of Notre Dame Department of Theology about "Religious Belief and Public Morality" on September 13, 1984 (Rosemary Kennedy's 66th birthday, and this author's 31st), at the invitation of Notre Dame President Hesburgh.

Cuomo started his speech by explaining that as a good Catholic, he had come to bring his "honest - more intelligent" insights to bear on an issue that had been obfuscated by lesser men who, unlike him, had political demagoguery and motives in mind. Instead, he hoped that his own thoroughly selfless and apolitical approach would finally bring "clarification" and "relief to untold numbers of confused – even anguished – Catholics." In other words, he had come to the place where "the Church does its thinking" in order to tell Catholics what to think.

To accomplish this formidable task, Cuomo saw that he must first swipe the miters from the Bishops' heads, and the scepters from their hands, so to speak. He did this by improperly asserting, on several occasions interspersed throughout his speech, that the Church had given no preeminent weight to the issue of abortion, that it was merely one important part of the so-called "seamless garment" of social justice, that Catholics were free to join the secular consensus about what was right and wrong, and that the Bishops were really just a bunch of well-dressed bystanders, advisors whom we ought to respect on the one hand, but we were really quite free to ignore on the other.

Cuomo said all of this, of course, because he wanted it both ways. He wanted to give gravitas to Phyllis McGinley's nonsensical philosophy of "personally opposed but", and make it his own. He wanted, in essence, to embrace his Catholic faith, while supporting abortion on demand at the same time, which of course is utterly impossible because the two objectives are so inherently contradictory. No surprise, then, that in one and the same speech, he quoted John Paul II's call to arms against abortion and noted his own bishop's urgings that the Church so move its people, while Cuomo himself took exactly the opposite approach by resigning to the "reality" of *Roe v. Wade*, and therefore to abortion on demand. Indeed, he all but lamented the fact that the Bishops had braved the brink of tax-exemption (endorsing candidates was strictly out of bounds) to promote political efforts to ban abortion outright, and failing that, to return the issue to "we the people" for debate in Congress and the several States (The so-called Orrin "Hatch Amendment" to the Constitution). And he all but cheered because the bishop's efforts in this regard had failed. In short, the whole infernal purpose of his speech was to tell Catholics that they could vote for men like him with a clear conscience because abortion wasn't all *that* important, and even if it was, there just wasn't much that men like him could do about it (at least not without losing Planned Parenthood's patronage).

This, from a man who said, once again in the same speech, that he was "attached to the Church first by birth, then by choice, now by love," and therefore, in his own "lifelong struggle to understand [his faith] more fully and live it more truly," had personally come to "accept the church's teaching authority," which in fact has consistently and unequivocally asserted for two thousand years that life begins at the moment of conception, and that therefore every procured abortion and cooperation with abortion is gravely contrary to God's law. Furthermore, according to the Church's Catechism:

> *The inalienable rights of the person must be recognized and respected by civil society and the political authority.  These human rights . . . [do not] represent a concession made by society and the state . . .[but] are inherent in the person by virtue of the creative act from which the person took his origin. Among such fundamental rights. . . [are] life and physical integrity from the moment of conception until death.*
>
> *The moment a positive law deprives a category of human beings of the protection which civil legislation ought to accord them, the state is denying the equality of all before the law.  When the state does not place its power at the service of the rights of each citizen, and particular of the more vulnerable, the very foundations of a state based on law are undermined. . .*
>
> *As a consequence of the respect and protection which must be ensured to the unborn child from the moment of conception, the law must provide*

Thus, is the teaching authority of the Church, allegedly accepted by Cuomo, crystal clear on how a Catholic must view the impact of God's law upon the laws of man.  Cuomo's own words in fact echo as much, when he says he believes that "life or fetal life in the womb should be protected, even if five of nine Justices of the Supreme Court and my neighbor disagrees with me," and that regardless of what others might say, "the full potential of human life is indisputably there," which "by itself should demand respect, caution, indeed reverence."  And so, the first confounding question becomes, whether one is Catholic or Protestant, Jew or Muslim, Hindu or altogether agnostic, how does one believe, as Mario Cuomo believes, and not come to the immediate conclusion that the Justices were just plain wrong, that the life of the unborn child already has a fundamental 14th amendment constitutional right to protection, subordinate only to the life of its mother, and that *Roe v. Wade* should be reversed as soon as possible? In fact, to compound the confusion, Cuomo notes that the very 1st Amendment to the same Constitution –

*human desire for order, peace, justice, kindness, love,*
*any of the values most of us agree are desirable even*
*apart from their specific religious base or context.*

But then, rather than exercise that right to bravely and happily advance what he says is deeply imbedded in his conscience, he gives us this bit of drivel instead:

> *But if the breadth, intensity and sincerity of*
> *opposition to church teaching shouldn't be allowed to*
> *shape our Catholic morality, it can't help but*
> *determine our ability – our realistic, political ability –*
> *to translate our Catholic morality into civil law, a law*
> *not for the believers who don't need it but for the*
> *disbelievers who reject it.*
> *And it is, in our attempt to find a political*
> *answer to abortion – an answer beyond our private*
> *observance of Catholic morality – that we encounter*
> *controversy within and without the Church over how*
> *and in what degree to press the case that our morality*
> *should be everybody else's, and to what effect.*

What does this even mean, except that Cuomo himself is hopelessly conflicted because he's beholden to a political party whose official platform has embraced an absolute culture of death insofar as the unrestricted "right" to abortion on demand is concerned?  Truly, this is a man who has been hopelessly corrupted, or at the very least utterly confused, by the din of his shrill constituency.

Clearly, Cuomo was no Reagan.  For Reagan was a simple man (Cuomo and his kind would say he was a "simpleton"), and in the wisest sort of way.  For him, the answer was easy, because for him, there was never any question.  To make short work of it (a method one hopes he'd have admired), in his 1984 essay entitled *Abortion and the Conscience of the Nation*, Reagan essentially said that the nation indeed has a conscience, that its source is our Creator, and that abortion ought therefore be abhorrent to us. Reagan's essay was truly remarkable, not just for its plainspoken content, but owing to the fact that it had so easily issued, like a cowboy sliding off his saddle, from the pen of a sitting President on the eve of his re-election (an historic landslide in which Reagan carried 49 states, notably including Cuomo's own State of New York). And there it was, for all to see, even as Cuomo was addressing the Democratic National Convention with his same sorry sophistry not two months before his trip to Notre Dame, which alone spoke volumes about his allegedly "honest" motives. Cuomo just didn't get it, notwithstanding the claims of his own conscience. Nor, one supposes, had he taken the time to read Edward S. Corwin's classic *Harvard Law Review* article of 1928 entitled *The Higher Law Background of American Constitutional Law*, despite Cuomo having graduated 1st in his class from St. John's University Law School. To quote Corwin:

> *There are, it is predicated, certain principles of right and justice which are entitled to prevail of their own intrinsic excellence, altogether regardless of the attitude of those who wield the physical resources of the community. Such principles were made by no human hands; indeed, if they did not antedate deity itself, they still so express its nature as to bind and control it. They are external to all Will as such and interpenetrate all Reason as such. They are eternal and immutable. In relation to such principles, human laws are, when entitled to obedience save as to matters indifferent, merely a record or a transcript, and their*

*enactment an act not of will or power but of discovery*
*and declaration. . . They owe nothing to their*
*recognition in the Constitution – such recognition was*
*necessary if the Constitution was to be regarded as*
*complete.*

*Thus, the legality of the Constitution, its*
*supremacy, and its claim to be worshipped, alike find*
*common standing ground on the belief in a law*
*superior to the will of human governors.*

Had Cuomo bothered to inquire of Pope John Paul II about what to do before traveling to Notre Dame, he'd likely have heard words similar to the ones that the Holy Father spoke in his address to American Bishops on Freedom and the Moral Law exactly seventy years after Professor Corwin's classic law review article. Likely, because his words were undoubtedly the result of what men like Cuomo had done in the ensuing years since Corwin to take self-evident truths out of the public square. For here is what the Holy Father said:

*When the Church teaches, for example, that*
*abortion, sterilization or euthanasia are always*
*morally inadmissible, she is giving expression to the*
*universal moral law inscribed on the human heart,*
*and is therefore teaching something which is binding*
*on everyone's conscience. . . This and other such*
*instances are not, it must be emphasized, the*
*imposition of an external set of criteria in violation of*
*human freedom. Rather, the Church's teaching of*
*moral truth "brings to light the truths which*
*[conscience] ought already to possess", and it is these*

*truths which make us free in the deepest meaning of human freedom and give our humanity its genuine nobility. . .*

*In teaching the truth about conscience and its intrinsic relationship to moral truth, you will be challenging one of the great forces in the modern world. But at the same time, you will be doing the modern world a great service, for you will be reminding it of the only foundation capable of sustaining a culture of freedom – what the Founders of your nation called "self-evident" truths. . .*

*A society or culture which wishes to survive cannot declare the spiritual dimension of the human person to be irrelevant to public life. . . American Catholics, in common with other Christians and all believers, have a responsibility to ensure that the mystery of God and the truth about humanity that is revealed in the mystery of God are not banished from public life.*

*This is especially true of democratic societies, since one of the truths contained in the mystery of our creation by God is that the human person must be "the origin, the subject and purpose of all social institutions." Our intrinsic dignity and inalienable fundamental rights are not the result of social convention. They precede all social convention and provide the norms that determine their validity. The history of the twentieth century is a grim warning of the evils that result when human beings are reduced to the status of objects to be manipulated by the powerful for selfish gain or for ideological reasons. In proclaiming the truth that God has given men and*

*women rights from the moment of conception, you are
helping to rebuild the moral foundations of a genuine
culture of freedom, capable of sustaining institutions
of self-governance that serve the common good. . .*

*The future of democracy in fact depends on a
culture capable of forming men and women who are
prepared to defend certain truths.  It is imperiled when
politics and law are sundered from any connection to
the moral law written on the human heart.*

*If there is no objective standard to help
adjudicate between different conceptions of the
personal and common good, then democratic politics is
reduced to a raw contest for power.  If constitutional
and statutory law are not held accountable to the
objective moral law, the first casualties are justice and
equity, for they become matters of personal opinion.
Catholics in public life render a particularly important
service to society when they defend objective moral
norms as "the unshakable foundation and solid
guarantee of a just and peaceful human coexistence,
and hence of genuine democracy.*

But Cuomo made no such inquiries of the Pope, nor of New
York's John Cardinal O'Connor, who undoubtedly would have told
him the same thing.  Instead, Cuomo tried to justify his outright
abandonment of Church authority, and to encourage Hesburgh and
his friends to do the same (as if they needed any encouragement), by
jumping on the bandwagon of those 19th century Irish Bishops so
complicit in southern slavery that they helped pave the way to Civil
War.  For Cuomo said -

*Take, for example, the question of slavery.  It has been argued that the failure to endorse a legal ban on abortion is equivalent to refusing to support the cause of abolition before the Civil War. This analogy has been advanced by the bishops of my own state.*

*But the truth of the matter is, few if any Catholic bishops spoke for abolition in the years before the Civil War.  It wasn't, I believe, that the bishops endorsed the idea of some humans owning and exploiting other humans; Pope Gregory XVI, in 1840, had condemned the slave trade.  Instead, it was a practical political judgment that the bishops made. They weren't hypocrites; they were realists.  At the time, Catholics were a small minority, mostly immigrants, despised by much of the population, often vilified and the object of sporadic violence.  In the face of public controversy that aroused tremendous passions and threatened to break the country apart, the bishops made a pragmatic decision.  They believed their opinion would not change people's minds. Moreover, they knew that there were southern Catholics, even some priests, who owned slaves.  They concluded that under the circumstances arguing for a constitutional amendment against slavery would do more harm than good, so they were silent. . .*

*The decision they made to remain silent. . . on a constitutional amendment to abolish slavery. . . wasn't a mark of their moral indifference: it was a measure attempt to balance moral truths against political realities. As history reveals, Lincoln behaved with similar discretion.*

Apart from the fact that Cuomo clearly misrepresents history here, in that the bishops did in fact endorse domestic slavery and were by no means silent about their anti-abolitionist attitudes, and also in his outright libeling of Lincoln, the most incredible thing about this last appalling aspect of his speech is that he's actually defending the actions of those 19th century bishops, despite the light of history, in order to justify his own deer-in-the-headlights intransigence on abortion.  Ramesh Ponnuru, in his exquisitely insightful book entitled *The Party of Death* (Regnery Publishing, 2006), put it this way:

> *It is a mark of the strength of contemporary liberalism's commitment to abortion that one of its leading lights should have been willing to support temporizing on slavery in order to defend [abortion]. It is a further mark that liberals did not reject, or even take notice of, Cuomo's argument about slavery.*
>
> *Cuomo's parallel fails at every level. Lincoln never accepted the existence of a right to own slaves.  He never accepted that Dred Scott should remain the law of the land, or even that its principles should be binding on any branch of government.  His goal was not only to put slavery on a path to extinction in practice, but also to end it as a legal possibility. . . And he accepted an obligation to do what he could, under the political circumstances of the day, to advance his goals.  His parallel in the abortion debate is the pro-life incrementalist.  Cuomo's parallel in the slavery debate is not the bishop who failed to speak out for the abolition of slavery and of laws allowing it.  It is the man who <u>opposed</u> any move in that direction*

*[which was in fact what Archbishop Hughes and his fellow prelates had actually done.]*

Furthermore, Ponnuru quotes Robert P. George, Princeton philosopher and professor of political science:

> *Of course, it is possible for a person wielding public power to use that power to establish or preserve a legal right to abortion and even to provide public money for it while at the same time not wanting or willing anyone to exercise that right.  But this does not get Cuomo off the hook.  For someone who acts to protect legal abortion necessarily wills that abortion's unborn victims be denied the elementary legal protections against deliberate homicide that one favors for oneself and those whom one considers to be worthy of the law's protection.  Thus, one violates the most basic precept of normative social and political theory, the Golden Rule.  One divides humanity into two classes:  those whom one is willing to admit to the community of the commonly protected and those whom one wills to be excluded from it.  By exposing members of the disfavored class to lethal violence, one deeply implicates oneself in the injustice of killing them – even if one sincerely hopes that no woman will act on her right to choose abortion.  The goodness of what one hopes for does not redeem the evil of what one wills.*

Nevertheless, after allowing himself eighteen days to absorb Cuomo's nationally touted little lecture, the only word that Hesburgh could find to characterize it was "brilliant."  At the same time, Hesburgh apparently had nothing public to say about Congressman Henry Hyde (of no-abortion-money amendment fame) who had been quietly escorted onto campus a few days after Cuomo, and relegated to the student lounge in the basement of the law school to issue a counter-argument.  According to Notre Dame Law Professor Charlie Rice, who may have been the world's leading expert on Notre Dame's inconsistent attitude about abortion over the last 40 years, this was no accident.  As he explained in his ground-breaking book, *What Happened to Notre Dame?* ( St. Augustine's Press, 2009), it was as if Notre Dame were out to fulfill Cardinal Newman's prophecy that, after having cut itself off from Church authority in 1967, it would soon assume the role of Church rival on ecclesiastical matters; in this case, by extending its invitation to Cuomo in June of 1984, within two months of New York's Archbishop O'Connor having very publicly and unequivocally chastised New York Catholic vice-presidential candidate Geraldine Ferraro for incorrectly asserting that her pro-abortion position was compatible with Catholic teaching.  This was a high-profile controversy with substantial implications for the upcoming election.

Thus, by  scheduling New York Governor Cuomo's visit to campus for September of 1984, less than two months before the election, and using Notre Dame's good name to tell Catholics across the country that Ferraro was right and O'Connor was wrong, Hesburgh was effectively inviting heresy, and encouraging its use to influence the outcome of the election in favor of Mondale and Ferraro, and against one of the most popular sitting presidents in American history, who also happened to be proudly pro-life.

Thankfully, and notwithstanding all the choral support from the liberal mainstream media, the vast majority of Americans across the country, Catholics included, did not share Hesburgh's views on Cuomo, nor Cuomo's views on much of anything.  In fact, after the drubbing that his party took in 1984, despite his "wonderful" keynote convention speech and "brilliant" encore at Notre Dame, Cuomo slowly but steadily faded from the political scene, such that the once friendly media came to calling him "Hamlet on the Hudson," and allowed him to get his political ass kicked out of the Governor's office by George Pataki in 1994.

To be fair, in addition to praising Cuomo, Hesburgh had also wondered aloud about how Catholics might come to a workable consensus to alter the impact of *Roe v. Wade*, but his musings were mere directionless rhetoric.  In short, if Hesburgh had been trying to do the Church's thinking, he was doing a pretty lame job of it compared to Cardinal O'Connor.  Such, that a scene from *The Verdict* springs readily to mind.  In it, the Boston Irish attorney played by Paul Newman is examining his expert witness on the cause of his comatose client's condition, when the presiding judge, an evil Irishman on the take and in the tank for the doctor's defense, interrupts Newman and bullies his witness into making a clumsy and unintended admission.  Whereupon Newman looks up at the judge with contempt and cries: "If you're going to try my case for me, I wish you wouldn't lose it."

<h1 style="text-align:center">13</h1>

<h2 style="text-align:center">Casey the Champ</h2>

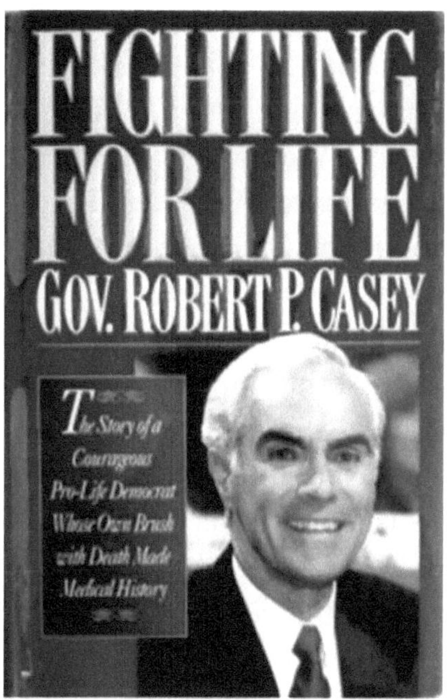

He died on May 30, 2000, at the age of 68, from assorted medical complications. But in both real and metaphorical ways, you could say that Robert Casey had been living with, and dying from, a Fighting Irishman's broken heart for over three decades. Real in the sense that he had finally been diagnosed, in April of 1991, with Appalachian Familial Amyloidosis, a disease found only in Americans of Irish ancestry, and one which had literally been breaking his heart long before that, and assaulting other organs as well.  Metaphorical in the way that he'd so loved life, and had so much to live for, that his fight for it kept him going, well beyond a weaker man's years, until he had given it his all, for a cause much greater than himself.  And therein lies the epitaph of this loyal son of Erin.

In 1851, Robert's paternal great grandfather, Edward, emigrated from Ireland at a tender age.  Away he went from Erin's fields, littered with black potatoes, and into the coal mines of Carbondale he crawled, to get at the hard-black anthracite.  There, Robert's grandfather, Thomas, together with his four brothers, would also work the mines, America's oldest.  Thomas had been a "fireman," stoking the furnaces that energized the mines. He died before reaching forty, likely of too much coal dust, but not before he and his wife, Sarah Haggerty, bred six more Casey kids.  Their second was Robert's father, Alphonsus Liguori Casey, named that at the urging of a parish nun from the Order of the Immaculate Heart of Mary.

Canonized a saint and declared a doctor of the Church by Pope Gregory XVI in 1839 (year of that infamous papal encyclical against slavery), the first Alphonsus Liguori was born in Naples, Italy, baptized in the Church of Our Lady the Virgin, and became a well-known attorney.  That is, until the day he abandoned that profession at the age of twenty-seven, telling his friend that "our profession is too full of difficulties and dangers; we lead an unhappy life and run risk of dying an unhappy death. For myself, I will quit this career, which does not suit me; for I wish to secure the salvation of my soul".  From there he turned to the priesthood, founding the Order of the Most Holy Redeemer, ministering to the poorest of the poor of Naples, and writing extensively on the glories of Mary at a time when the eighteenth-century age of Enlightenment was threatening to suffocate faith with reason (sound familiar?).  How fitting, then, may the reader find, that Robert's Irish father would receive this wonderful Neapolitan's good name.

Because his own father had died so young, Alphonsus (Casey, that is) began his work in the anthracite at the age of eleven in order to sustain his younger siblings, walking the mules and working their straps as they pulled their loads, car after car, from the very depths of darkness.  One day, he took a hoof square in the face from a mule who was "kicking the traces," that is, trying to get the straps off its back.  The kick crushed "Phonsi's" nose and gashed his face from forehead to chin, but work did not stop and no medics were called.  Instead, they wrapped his head in a bandage and sent him toward his mother, one boy replacing him to pull the next load, another escorting him on the long walk home.  While enroute, they lost their footing on a bridge, and fell into a river full of "slurry" (water thick with coal dust), which soaked right into Phonsi's head bandage.  After mom had a look at him, she called the doctor, who came and sewed him up, right there on the dining room table.  One imagines that he took the rest of the day off.  Maybe two.  But then, it was surely back to work, well into his twenties.  He had no choice.  His mother would soon follow his father to the grave, while Phonsi was still a teenager.

Safe to assume, then, that this experience lingered in his mind long afterward, enough to impact his decision, late in his thirties, to proceed in the opposite direction of his namesake, and become an attorney.  To hear his son Robert tell it:

> *As a lawyer, my father was always helping*
> *people down on their luck . . . Helping others just*
> *seemed his way, the natural reflex of someone who*
> *knew what it was like to need a break.  Faith for him*
> *was like the fresh air outside a coal mine - something*
> *he'd breathed in throughout his life and appreciated*
> *more than most men, without ever really thinking*
> *much about it.  He wasn't what you'd call a pious*
> *person.  But he had that quiet understanding about life*

Together with his wife, Marie Cummings, a kind and generous woman, such was the stock from which Robert Casey sprang. They were the source of his faith, wisdom, and strength, all of which he would need in the days that lay ahead. That, and an abundance of Irish luck, of which he suffered no shortage. The inspiring saga of his remarkable, love-filled life – one that produced eight children and twenty-plus grandchildren – laces its way between alternating chapters of his courageous political life, in an autobiographical account appropriately entitled *Fighting for Life* (Word Publishing, 1996). No summary can adequately capture its fighting spirit, but there is one abiding thread that must here be retold.

When Robert Casey ran for Governor of Pennsylvania for the fourth time, in 1986, his opponents took to calling him "the three-time loss from Holy Cross." This was quite simply because Casey had failed in his first three attempts, and because The College of the Holy Cross had been his alma mater. In fact, he had turned down an opportunity to play professional baseball for the Philadelphia Phillies in order to attend Holy Cross on a basketball scholarship, and had seen floor-time as a freshman while his senior teammate, the great Bob Cousy, was tearing up the boards en-route to NBA fame.  Each of Casey's political losses had their own set of various parochial explanations, but it was his first that had been the most foreboding, both for him and American Catholics of his time.

For the time, lo and behold, was 1966.  New York was in the process of adopting the abortion "reforms" so favored by Nelson Rockefeller and his friends, and thus abortion had become a key political topic on the lips of all the pundits in neighboring Pennsylvania.  Casey and his democratic primary opponent, Milton Shapp, were questioned about whether they too would favor such reforms for Pennsylvania.  Schapp played it politically safe and savvy, telling reporters that he would appoint a commission of women to study the issue, while Casey's response was unequivocal.  No, he would not support reform, and if it crossed his desk, he would veto it.  Looking back on it in his autobiography, he said:


> *I am fairly certain that my position hurt me, because in a Democratic primary where turnout was historically relatively low, liberal voters turned out in disproportionately large numbers and thus exercised a disproportionate influence on the outcome [against him].*
>
> *But I took the position instinctively. . . For me, the imperative of protecting unborn human life has always been a self-evident proposition.  I cannot recall the subject of abortion ever being mentioned, much less discussed in depth, in school or at home.  My position was simply a part of me from the very beginning.*

The problem, as Casey would plainly put it, was that "[t]he Catholic Church made it clear that it took no position in the primary, and many Catholics worked openly and actively for my opponent."  If Casey had been possessed of a little less gracious nature when he wrote his autobiography circa 1996, after running the gauntlet of grave health, and only four years away from his death, perhaps he would have put it a little more directly than that.  Perhaps he would have said that his Pennsylvania bishops had dropped the ball by failing to frankly admonish their flocks, early and often, against the looming dangers of abortion reform.  Truth be told, they may have miscalculated its inevitable coming, lurking just beneath the surface in the seeds of Sanger, and nourished by the foolishness of men like Shuster. Be that as it may, it would take twenty more years, and three more tries, before the people of Pennsylvania would finally figure out that Casey, who never once wavered from his original position, had been right from the very start.

In 1986, Robert Casey, running for the fourth time on a defiantly pro-life plank, this time with the aid of campaign managers James Carville and Paul Begala, soundly beat his pro-choice Republican opponent, William Scranton III, despite Scranton's powerful and deep-rooted Pennsylvania patriarch's pedigree.  So, Casey must certainly have held out faith that the people of Pennsylvania, particularly its Catholics, had finally awakened to the evils of abortion in the thirteen-year-long wake of *Roe v. Wade*.  If so, this faith was likely reinforced by the fact that he and his pro-life friends, in the pews of Pennsylvania's parishes and seats of its legislative assemblies, had succeeded in adopting the Abortion Control Act of 1989 ( the one which Planned Parenthood would take to the Supreme Court).  In doing so, Casey would later liken their actions to Lincoln, who had rejected *Dred Scott* from its outset, stubbornly refusing to surrender, to a morally sick Supreme Court, the right of the people "to be their own rulers."  And he would roundly criticize all the Cuomo-like, "personally opposed but" posturings of liberal party members as dishonest evasions made in weak-minded fear of secular militants, who were ever at the ready with fallacious accusations of religious arrogance.

But if Casey's faith in the face of opposition had in fact been invested with reason, one would never have known it from the pundits, whose predictions of a difficult 1990 re-election bid against another pro-choice Republican abounded.  Indeed, Democratic pollster Harrison Hickman, pointing to Casey's rigid pro-life position, predicted no better than a dead heat, while some piranha from the Pittsburgh chapter of the National Organization for Women predicted that "Casey will be dead by November."  This of course caused the chronically heartsick Casey to not so jokingly wonder whether the woman was referring to his physical or political health.  No matter.  Casey, once again with the aid of Carville and Begala, crushed pro-choice Republican Barbara Haffer in 66 out of 67 counties, amassing a landslide victory margin of over one million votes, or an unbelievable 68 to 32 percent, the largest winning percentage in Pennsylvania history.  So, it was score one for the pro-life Democrat Party of the pivotal, 5th largest electoral State in the Nation, or so Casey thought, until Carville and Begala turned traitor on him.

Now, Casey himself does not level this accusation at Carville and Begala, perhaps out of gratitude for victories past, or perhaps because the thought of two friends turning on him the way that they apparently did was just too painful.  But the facts make it exceedingly hard to infer otherwise.  For in 1992, Carville and Begala were running Bill Clinton's campaign to unseat the incumbent George H.W. Bush from his presidency, while having to deal with the wily, well-funded and worrisome Ross Perot.  Thus, it doesn't take an experienced political scientist to understand that in the minds of two very pragmatic campaign managers, internal dissension was one thing that their party ought avoid in order not to stifle the necessary turnout from its all-important liberal base.  And unfortunately, for the single state Catholic named Casey, this meant unity on abortion in a national party inundated with militantly pro-choice liberals in most of the other pivotal states.  Ergo, denying Casey face time at the 1992 convention was likely not a matter of much musing among Carville, Begala, and their boy Bill Clinton.  It was much more likely a virtual no-brainer, one that gave them about as much pause as ducking into the bathroom to take a quick piss on the way to the next campaign stop.

In the light of such hindsight, Casey would seem the silly old fool for having pressed to get speech time in the first place, and then a naïve one for having wondered very long about why he had been turned down.  And it is hard to argue against the accuracy of such caricatures.  Harder still, however, for lovers of the republic, is swallowing the sad reality from whence it all came.  Indeed, this is the deeper reality, the one beneath the surface, the one that was breaking Casey's heart.  Stated another way, it was not that Casey was a naïve old fool.  It was just that his foolishness was so innate - native to his heart and soul, native to his Christ and country, native to the air that his father once breathed every time he emerged from the Carbondale mines.  For Casey, the failure of his fellow Democrats to see the connection between abortion and social injustice would always remain a great mystery, deep and dark as the mines of his father's youth.  Not to see the connection, he would say, "requires a monumental act of denial."  Such that –

*As a cultural phenomenon, maybe it all has*
*something to do with the very innocence and*
*helplessness of children.  A child makes demands upon*
*us.  A child needs our constant attention.  A child calls*

*us beyond ourselves, beyond our wants and desires.  In this way children are the natural enemy of a culture inclined more and more to worship the Imperial Self – to hide, deny, or dispose of anything which interferes with our own wishes and whims.  This is especially true of the special-needs child, the child not up to our worldly standards of health, beauty, or general acceptability.*

*At some point my own party, once devoted to lifting up the powerless, bought into this idea.  We still hear the same noble-sounding phrases – "compassion," "social justice," "equal rights."  But they ring more and more hollow.  In the abortion debate, they are thin veils concealing visions of raw self-interest.  Whoever envisioned that the banner of "equal rights" would be unfurled over the abortion clinic?  Who expected that we would ever even <u>think</u> of a mother and a child as having separate interests, as rivals in a dispute over power, much less enshrine the idea into law?  Who ever imagined a political debate pitting mother against child, as if the child were some alien presence and not of her own flesh and blood?*

*Surely no two human beings could be more bound together, more natural allies in life and love than a mother and her baby.  So, infants were always viewed by humanity, especially by women themselves, at most times in most places – until our time, when suddenly we find them driven apart, when the maternal instinct to nurture and protect the child is turned on its head.*

*Everything depends on that tie of love.  Sever it, and you have not only set in motion countless little tragedies, you put society itself on a short route to chaos. The cause of this division is an ethic of pure selfishness which has seeped into our political lives, the "me-first" ethic my party has embraced and which will prove its own undoing. It is modern liberalism's new and improved version of the old "rugged individualism" of Republicans: "Forget the powerless, forget the needs of others. Me first!"*

*As night follows day, violence follows this attitude. Whatever the pretenses, it is a hard creed, foreign to everything my party once stood for. You can see this in the strange terminology used in its defense. Even as the unborn child is sacrificed, the deed is dressed up in the language of love and concern, touching solicitude for the child's own "quality of life." A child, if born, will face hardship: therefore, he or she is better off dead. A baby will only burden one's economic situation, or require public assistance, or cause inconvenience all around: therefore, do everyone the favor of aborting it. Just get rid of it, and all will be well. . .*

*A generation's worth of experience with the self-gratification gospel has left most of us feeling a void, a deep emptiness in our culture. A generation's climb into general affluence has left us feeling somehow poorer as a nation. At the heart of our political debate today is a fear for our whole culture, a fear that something has gone terribly wrong. And it has. Try as we might to put it all out of our minds, at the heart of that unease is abortion – the ultimate act of violence, the ultimate exploitation of the weak by the powerful. A society, least of all a society like ours, cannot turn its back on an entire class of human beings, wash its hands of so profound a problem, and still live at peace with itself...*

*Far from liberating women, abortion has become a lucrative industry, exploiting young women beyond anything ever imagined.*

*[T]oday's Democratic Party [has] traded our principles for power – the fleeting power offered by loud and well-financed factions like NARAL and Planned Parenthood...*

*It is a party that has lost its soul.*
Fight For Life, Word Publishing (1996)

When Casey learned that he would not be allowed to speak at the 1992 Democratic National Convention, he secured the signatures of 34 other accomplished and well-respected men and women from assorted and appropriate disciplines, on a full-page ad entitled *A New American Compact: Caring About Women, Caring for the Unborn*, which ran in the New York Times. Notably included among the signatures was Sargent and Eunice Kennedy Shriver, about whom enough cannot be said, and Mary Ann Glendon, on whom there will be more in a moment. An excerpt from that ad reads as follows:

*Over the next months and years, the American people will confront again the question that Lincoln posed at Gettysburg: Whether a nation conceived in liberty and dedicated to human equality can long endure. In this generation, the issue pressing that question on our consciences is the issue of abortion...*

*It is to be deeply regretted that the American people have been denied [by their Supreme Court] the deliberative role in shaping public policy on this issue*

213

*that has been played by the citizens of other developed democracies . . . .*

*For like the practice of slavery . . . the abortion issue raises the most fundamental questions of justice – questions that cannot be avoided, and that cannot be resolved by judicial fiat.*

*. . . Let there be no mistake about the impact of the Roe and Doe decisions: they did not "liberalize" abortion law; they abolished abortion law in all fifty states. Abortion on demand, throughout the full nine months of a pregnancy, for virtually any reason, became public policy in the United States of America. No other developed democracy had, or has, such a permissive abortion regime. . . [and a] vast abortion industry, generating some half a billion dollars annually, sprang into existence in the wake of Roe and Doe. . .*

*That is not the kind of America that expresses the abiding decency and compassion of our people. . .*

*Advocates of unrestricted abortion do not want the public to focus on [the] undeniable facts of fetal development, but the facts cannot be ignored. They make plain that abortion is a violent act, not against "potential life," but against a living, growing human being – a life with potential. . .*

*The advocates of abortion on demand falsely assume two things: that women must suffer if the lives of unborn children are legally protected; and that women can only attain equality by having the legal option of destroying their innocent offspring in the womb. The cynicism of these assumptions reflects a terrible failure of moral imagination and social*

*responsibility and an appalling lack of respect for*
*women. . .*

> *Our moral, religious, and political traditions*
*are united in their respect for the dignity of human life.*
*. .*

Ironically enough, about three months after the convention, at the annual Al Smith Dinner in New York, Casey got his chance to speak because the presidential candidates who would normally have monopolized that important political platform had agreed to participate in a nationally televised debate that same night.  Casey would have this to say to those in attendance:

> *. . .[T]his dinner is all about. . .the*
*defining legacy of Al Smith.*
> *To this day, he remains a powerful*
*summons to a great and continuing challenge – to*
*advance the tolerance which his life embodied, his*
*presidential nomination vindicated, and his shameful*
*defeat denied.*
> *I believe tolerance is once again at risk –*
*in a different way than it was then, but one that goes*
*to the heart and summit of our public life.*
> *The immediate cause is the issue of*
*abortion – and this time the danger comes from a*
*political tradition from which I myself come.  There is*
*a new liberal intolerance which will not abide doubt or*
*dissent – which claims it stands for freedom of choice,*
*but stifles freedom of speech.  And so a movement that*
*began by saying let every person decide, has ended up*
*by trying to silence anyone who disagrees. . .*

*This absolutism, the imposed conformity
which treats the right to life as an idea beyond even the
pale of discussion, has peer and precedent in our
national history. In 1860, at Cooper Union [about 3
miles south of the Al Smith - Waldorf Astoria dinner
site], Lincoln warned of an established opinion which
would tolerate nothing short of saying slavery is right
– which "will grant a hearing to pirates or to
murderers" but not to opponents of slavery. . .*

*There is an indefensible contradiction
between liberal principles as I once learned them and
the new liberal intolerance. There are also disturbing
signs that the intolerance has reached beyond the issue
of abortion to religious belief itself – bringing us in a
sad full circle back to the 1928 of Al Smith. . .*

*Anti-Catholicism has become a
fashionable, barely disguised prejudice. A cancer in
our national life every bit as malignant as racism or
anti-Semitism. The legacy of the man whose memory
we revere tonight would be dishonored if we were to
fail to condemn all such forms of bigotry and hatred.
And to tear them out by the roots, wherever we find
them in our society. . .*

Casey knew from whence he spoke about anti-Catholic bigotry.
At the convention three months earlier, militant "pro-choice"
delegates wore lapel buttons depicting Casey dressed up as the Pope.
Fortunately, the following spring of 1993, when he went to the
commencement of his youngest son, Matthew Alphonsus Casey, from
the University of Notre Dame, no one was seen wearing those lapel
buttons, and to its credit, the administration awarded Governor
Casey an honorary degree. They would have done far better,

however, had they asked him (no offense to Tom Brokaw) to deliver the actual Commencement address, in which case the students (not to mention the faculty and administration) would undoubtedly have been treated to something along the lines of what he said at Franciscan University the following year (May of 1994):

> *It's probably fair to say that America is slowly arriving at a rough consensus. We are at last beginning to realize that there are problems beyond the power of politics or science or wealth to repair. More and more we sense an absence. A void. We seem to agree that something crucial is missing from what, by all material calculations, should be the picture of perfect national contentment. . .*
>
> *In some respects, our culture resembles a place foreseen by the Scottish author John Buchan... [who] described "the coming of a too garish age, when life would be lived in the glare of neon lamps and the spirit would have no solitude. . . [and where] everyone would have leisure. But everyone would be restless, for there would be no spiritual discipline in life . . . It would be a feverish, bustling world, self-satisfied and yet malcontent, and under the mask of a riotous life there would be death at the heart. In the perpetual hurry of life there would be no quiet for the soul. [In such a world] life would be rationalized and padded with every material comfort, [but] there would be little satisfaction for the immortal part of man."*
>
> *. . .[W]hatever explanations [for this] we favor, I am absolutely sure of one thing. And I offer it as my contribution to the national debate. There is*

*nothing at all vague about our problems. They are not of some mysterious origin. . .*

*All of these trends, these disturbing, violent, garish trends, come together in the issue of abortion. Whatever fine gloss we put on it, here is the ultimate act of unreason, of aggression, of exploitation of the weak by the strong. Because abortion is the ultimate violence. The abortion movement isn't just another cause; it is the telltale passion of a deeply disturbed society. . .*

*But today I want to offer a much more encouraging report . . . The abortion movement is doomed to fail; it is a crusade without a cross. Quietly, slowly, painfully, America is facing up to these questions. Is this really what we want? Is <u>this</u> the endpoint of progress? Is this the sort of culture we want our own children to live in? Must we really destroy what we lack the courage to love? And America's answer, the more we are pressed with the issue, is No.*

*If anyone doubts this, here's a question for you: Remember the Freedom of Choice Act? I seem to recall that this legislation was going to enshrine, once and for all, the holdings of Roe v. Wade. It was to be the culmination of the whole abortion movement.*

*But when last seen, it was being quietly tabled for later consideration. In other words, it failed. It didn't have the votes. Here we have a president, a House, and a Senate controlled by a party formally committed to unrestricted abortion. We have in such groups as NARAL and Planned Parenthood perhaps the most ferocious, relentless lobby in Washington. And yet, in the end, they were afraid even to bring their bill to the floor. After all the big talk and bold promises, they couldn't pull it off. Neither, it turns out, could they repeal the Hyde Amendment. . .*

*And finally, consider the remarkable sight we witnessed on television after Mother Teresa's recent appearance in Washington. She was there to speak at a prayer breakfast [and railed against abortion with words of wisdom appearing in the next chapter]. To her right sat [President and Mrs. Clinton]. To her left, [Vice-President and Mrs. Gore].*

*Well, if every age is remembered by a snapshot image, one picture captures something essential about the times, here was a new one for the gallery. Saying these words, Mother Teresa was almost drowned out in applause. Everybody applauded, except four people. And as one who has spent a lot of energy pursuing political power myself, I had to wonder: What power is really worth the price of having to sit in the presence of someone like that, and hear her message in awkward silence? What have we come to when the leaders of the free world are not even free to applaud words of such obvious wisdom and power? . . .*

*The world will try again and again, in a thousand different forms, to sell you power, popularity, acceptance. But look very closely because usually the price is a high one. The price is to surrender the greatest power and freedom any man or woman could ever have – your conscience. . .*

> *This is the message I leave with you:*
> *Never forget that beneath all the slogans and fierce*
> *arguments is the fate of innocent children.  They need*
> *your love; their mothers need your courage.  Do not be*
> *discouraged in the face of scorn: Press on!*
> *Try, as St. Francis and all the really*
> *great ones have done, to have compassion for those*
> *who offer only anger and bitterness.  In the long term,*
> *you possess no greater weapon: Press on!*
> *And finally, give your country not what it*
> *wants or will reward, but what it needs.  Lend it in*
> *your own lives that goodness without which it cannot*
> *be great, and the grace without which it cannot be*
> *saved:  Press on!*

To be fair, Casey was invited to Notre Dame the next year, and spoke on the very same topic, but to members of the Center for Ethics and Culture, not to members of the class of 1995.  To type his words now, some 25 years later, is both depressing and encouraging.

They are depressing in the sense that *Roe v. Wade* is still the law of the land, thanks largely to President Clinton, who replaced Byron White with Ruth Bader Ginsburg in his first year in office, and Harry Blackmun with Stephen Bryer in his second year.  White had been a strong dissenter from the decision in Roe v. Wade, castigating the Court for valuing "the convenience, whim or caprice of the putative mother more than the life or potential life of the fetus." Ginsburg, on the other hand, in an interview for the July 12, 2009 edition of the *New York Times Sunday Magazine*, lamented that the Hyde Amendment had been upheld by the Court in 1980 when she rather casually admitted that - "Yes, the ruling about that surprised me. Frankly, I had thought that at the time <u>Roe</u> was decided, there was concern about population growth and particularly growth in

populations ***that we don't want to have too many of.*** So that
*Roe* was going to be then set up for Medicaid funding for abortion."
(and this Malthusian eugenicist racism from the mouth of a Jewish
woman no less.)  Breyer, meanwhile, mostly sides with Ginsburg as a
reliable member of the Court's liberal wing.

But Casey's words are also encouraging, in the sense that
Obama, yet another President from the Democratic Party, who ran on
the promise of passing FOCA, and who had an even greater
Congressional majority from his party than did Clinton, had to table
the FOCA bill once again. Thanks to the organized protest efforts of
Catholic bishops and their faithfully practicing parish constituents all
across the country, many of whom were moved to anger by what had
happened at Notre Dame (See Chapter 17), advocates of abortion on
demand did not have enough support to legislate *Roe v. Wade.*
(Thanks to President Obama, however, they succeeded in securing
federal funding for abortion despite vocal opposition from the vast
majority of the American people.)

In 1996, Casey would seriously explore a challenge to
President Clinton's incumbency, but grew ill on the eve of the
scheduled announcement of his candidacy on *60 Minutes,* and
cancelled that appearance.  The heart and liver transplants he
underwent in 1991 had bought him only so much time, and it was
slowly running out.  He passed from this vale of tears to meet his
Maker, but not before making a lasting impact on the minds of many,
particularly Irish Catholics who had been on the fence.

May he always walk in sunshine.  May he never want for more.
May Irish angels rest their wings right beside his door.

# 14

# Teresa the Teacher

Her homely and misshapen four-foot eight frame held less than one hundred pounds, which survived, for most of her last seventy years, on biscuits soaked in tea, hours spent in prayer, and the body and blood of Christ.  And yet, before she died in 1997 at the age of eighty-seven, she and her Missionaries of Charity had ministered to millions of the most destitute people, in almost every slum in the world.  All on account of a single call that came from Christ himself, on a train ride from Calcutta to Darjeeling on "Inspiration Day," September 10, 1946, when He told her, in a small voice deep inside the stillness of her soul, that "I want you to serve Me among the poorest of the poor."

Up until that time, Agnes Bojaxhiu of Skoplje, Yugoslavia, had been going about her business as little Teresa (of Lisieux), a nun from the Order of Loreto out of Dublin (Ireland indeed), and headmistress to the middle-class Bengali girls attending St. Mary's High School in Calcutta.  Little did she know it at the time, but the students from this school would become the source of many the young woman who would join her ranks as her missions continued to grow.  Today, since the day she started with a single helper vowing "wholehearted free service to the poorest of the poor" over 70 years ago, there are over 5000 sisters serving the poor at over 750 centers of charity in 120 countries, with a list full of local bishops waiting, hoping and praying for more.

Thus, it is utterly impossible, in this single chapter, to do justice to this great Saint about whom volumes have been written.  On the first page of her book, *Something Beautiful for God*, appears a picture of the sign above the entrance to the first of those 750 missionary centers: *"Corporation of Calcutta – Home for Dying Destitutes."*  Holder of the Nobel Peace Prize, the Presidential Medal of Freedom, and dozens of other international awards, she's been hailed by hundreds from every walk of life – from every religion and none at all - as one of the greatest champions of social justice ever to grace this world.  And yet, when she received that Nobel Peace Prize, and was asked what the rest of us could do to help promote world peace, she simply and easily replied - "Go home and love your family."  Faithful to that very same theme, here then is what she said at that National Prayer Breakfast on February 3, 1994, exactly six months after the U.S. Senate confirmed Clinton's Justice Ginsburg to replace Byron White (the same breakfast referenced by Robert Casey a few months later in his aforementioned Commencement speech to the students of Franciscan University):

> *And God loved the world so much that He gave His son – it was a giving. God gave his son to the Virgin Mary, and what did she do with Him? As soon as Jesus came into Mary's life, she went in haste to give that good news. And as she came into the house of her cousin, Elizabeth, Scripture tells us that the unborn child – the child in the womb of Elizabeth – leapt with joy. While still in the womb of Mary, Jesus brought peace to John the Baptist who leapt for joy in the womb of Elizabeth. The unborn was the first one to proclaim the coming of Christ.*
>
> *. . .*
>
> *I was surprised in the West to see so many young boys and girls given to drugs. And I tried to find out why. Why is it like that, when those in the West have so many more things than those in the East? And the answer was: 'Because there is no one in the family to receive them.' Our children depend on us for everything – their health, their nutrition, their security, their coming to know and love God. For all of this, they look to us with trust, hope and expectation. But often father and mother are so busy they have no time for their children, or perhaps they are not even married or have given up on their marriage. So, their children go to the streets and get involved in drugs or*

*other things.  We are talking of love of the child, which is where love and peace must begin.  These are the things that break peace.*

*But I feel that the greatest destroyer of peace today is abortion, because it is a war against the child, a direct killing of the innocent child, murder by the mother herself.  And if we accept that a mother can kill even her own child, how can we tell other people not to kill one another?  How do we persuade a woman not to have an abortion?  As always, we must persuade her with love and we remind ourselves that love means to be willing to give until it hurts.  Jesus gave even His life to love us.  So, the mother who is thinking of abortion, should be helped to love, that is, to give until it hurts her plans, or her free time, to respect the life of her child.  The father of that child, whoever he is, must also give until it hurts.*

*By abortion, the mother does not learn to love, but kills even her own child to solve her problems.  And by abortion, that father is told that he does not have to take any responsibility at all for the child he has brought into the world.  The father is likely to put other women into the same trouble.  So, abortion just leads to more abortion.  Any country that accepts abortion is not teaching its people to love, but to use any violence to get what they want.  This is why the greatest destroyer of love and peace is abortion.*

*Many people are very, very concerned with the children of India, with the children of Africa where quite a few die of hunger, and so on.  Many people are also concerned about all the violence in this great country of the United States.  These concerns are very*

At about the same time that Teresa the Teacher delivered this lecture to our executive and legislative representatives present at the prayer breakfast, she also addressed our judiciary down the street, as *amicus curiae* ("friend of the court") in a case that came out of this author's home State of New Jersey, originating in the Morristown Municipal Court.  There, Alexander Loce had been charged with criminal trespass for blocking the entrance to the operating room of the local abortion clinic where his fiancé had gone to terminate her pregnancy, and his fatherhood.  After the trial, Judge Michael J. Noonan found, as a matter of incontrovertible scientific fact, that the fetus is a complete human being from the moment of conception.  He made this finding based upon testimony from the world's foremost authorities on fetal development, including: Dr. Bernard Nathanson, the repentant former co-founder of NARAL who had supervised the abortions of over 75,000 children before converting and producing *The Silent Scream* when an ultrasound machine perfected in the 70's portrayed an unborn child recoiling from an abortion doctor's instrument of death;  Dr. Jerome Lejeune, the "Father of Modern Genetics" and discoverer of the cause of Down's Syndrome; Dr. Hymie Gordon, the Chairman of the Department of Genetics at the Mayo clinic, who stated unequivocally that "[b]y all the criteria of modern molecular biology, life is present from the moment of conception; and Sir William Liley, pioneer of fetal therapy and author of *The Fetus as a Personality*, wherein he asserted that the fetus is not a lump of tissue, but a full and vigorous human partner in his mother's pregnancy. However, Judge Noonan also felt compelled to find, based upon the binding "higher" authority of *Roe v. Wade*, that the mother's termination of her baby's life was legal, and that Loce was therefore guilty of trespassing.  But this legal finding was also a good thing, because it allowed Loce's lawyers to appeal, which they did, all the way through the New Jersey Court system and up to the U.S. Supreme Court, where they filed what is known as a Petition for Certiorari, urging the Justices to take and hear the case (which they were not bound by law to do).  It was at this stage that (Saint) Teresa, in collaboration with New Jersey pro-life attorney Harold Cassidy, entered the fray with her letter to the Court, the entire text of which reads as follows:

I hope you will count it no presumption that I seek your leave to address you on behalf of the unborn child. Like that child I can be considered an outsider. I am not an American citizen.

*My parents were Albanian. I was born before the First World War in a part of what was not yet, and is no longer, Yugoslavia.*

*In many senses I know what it is like to be without a country.*

*I also know what is like to feel an adopted citizen of other lands. When I was still a young girl I traveled to India.*

*I found my work among the poor and the sick of that nation, and I have lived there ever since.*

*Since 1950 I have worked with my many sisters from around the world as one of the Missionaries of Charity. Our congregation now has over four hundred foundations in more then one hundred countries, including the United States of America.*

*We have almost five thousand sisters.*

*We care for those who are often treated as outsiders in their own communities by their own neighbors — the starving, the crippled, the impoverished, and the diseased, from the old woman with a brain tumor in Calcutta to the young man with AIDS in New York City.*

*A special focus of our care are mothers and their children.*

*This includes mothers who feel pressured to sacrifice their unborn children by want, neglect, despair, and philosophies and government policies that promote the dehumanization of inconvenient human life. And it includes the children themselves, innocent and utterly defenseless, who are at the mercy of those who would deny their humanity.*

*So, in a sense, my sisters and those we serve are all outsiders together. At the same time, we are supremely conscious of the common bonds of humanity that unite us and transcend national boundaries.*

*In another sense, no one in the world who prizes liberty and human rights can feel anything but a strong kinship with America. Yours is the one great nation in all of history that was founded on the precept of equal rights and respect for all humankind, for the poorest and weakest of us as well as the richest and strongest.*

*As your Declaration of Independence put it, in words that have never lost their power to stir the heart: "We hold these truths to be self-evident: that all men are created equal; that they are endowed by their creator with certain inalienable rights; that among these are life, liberty, and the pursuit of happiness..." A nation founded on these principles holds a sacred trust: to stand as an example to the rest of the world, to climb ever higher in its practical realization of the ideals of human dignity, brotherhood, and mutual respect.*

*Your constant efforts in fulfillment of that mission, far more than your size or your wealth or your military might, have made America an inspiration to all mankind.*

*It must be recognized that your model was never one of realized perfection, but of ceaseless aspiration. From the outset, for example, America denied the African slave his freedom and human dignity. But in time you righted that wrong, albeit at an incalculable cost in human suffering and loss of life.*

*Your impetus has almost always been toward a fuller, more all-embracing conception and assurance of the rights that your founding fathers recognized as inherent and God-given.*

*Yours has ever been an inclusive, not an exclusive, society.*

*And your steps, though they may have paused or faltered now and then, have been pointed in the right direction and have trod the right path.*

*The task has not always been an easy one, and each new generation has faced its own challenges and temptations. But in a uniquely courageous and inspiring way, America has kept faith.*

*Yet there has been one infinitely tragic and destructive departure from those American ideals in recent memory. It was this Court's own decision in Roe v. Wade (1973) to exclude the unborn child from the human family. You ruled that a mother, in consultation with her doctor, has broad discretion, guaranteed against infringement by the United States Constitution, to choose to destroy her unborn child.*

*Your opinion stated that you did not need to "resolve the difficult question of when life begins." That question is inescapable. If the right to life is an inherent and inalienable right, it must surely exist wherever life exists.*

*No one can deny that the unborn child is a distinct being, that it is human, and that it is alive. It is unjust, therefore, to deprive the unborn child of its fundamental right to life on the basis of its age, size, or condition of dependency.*

*It was a sad infidelity to America's highest ideals when this Court said that it did not matter, or could not be determined, when the inalienable right to life began for a child in its mother's womb.*

*America needs no words from me to see how your decision in Roe v. Wade has deformed a great nation. The so-called right to abortion has pitted mothers against their children and women against men. It has sown violence and discord at the heart of the most intimate human relationships.*

*It has aggravated the derogation of the father's role in an increasingly fatherless society.*

*It has portrayed the greatest of gifts — a child — as a competitor, an intrusion, and an inconvenience. It has nominally accorded mothers unfettered domination over the independent lives of their physically dependent sons and daughters.*

*And, in granting this unconscionable power, it has exposed many women to unjust and selfish demands from their husbands or other sexual partners.*

*Human rights are not a privilege conferred by government. They are every human being's entitlement by virtue of his humanity. The right to life does not depend, and must not be declared to be contingent, on the pleasure of anyone else, not even a parent or a sovereign.*

*The Constitutional Court of the Federal Republic of Germany recently ruled that "the unborn child is entitled to its rights to life independently of acceptance by its mother; this is an elementary and inalienable right that emanates from the dignity of the human being." Americans may feel justly proud that Germany in 1993 [once home to the Holocaust that American blood helped to extinguish] was able to recognize the sanctity of human life.*

*You must weep that your own government, at present, seems blind to this truth.*

*I have no new teaching for America. I seek only to recall you to faithfulness to what you once taught the world.*

*Your nation was founded on the proposition — very old as a moral precept, but startling and innovative as a political insight — that human life is a gift of immeasurable worth, and that it deserves, always and everywhere, to be treated with the utmost dignity and respect.*

In her stirring words, one can clearly see that (Saint) Teresa's mind was utterly without the muddle caused by false definitions of freedom, and wholly free of worries over false accusations of inappropriate intrusion into the sacred realm of pluralism.  In short, she was "filled with a noble spirit that stirred her womanly heart with manly courage" (2 *Maccabees* 7:1,20-31), the same kind of courage that was present in the hearts of Eunice Kennedy and Robert Casey, but conspicuously absent from the hearts of Edward Kennedy and Mario Cuomo, at least when it came to abortion and the unborn child.

"We did not come to be social workers," she once said, "but to belong to Jesus. . . Our life has no other reason or motivation.  This is a point many people do not understand."  When taken in the context of everything else she said, this seems Teresa the Teacher's way of telling us, in a very profound way, that social justice is **not** a seamless garment, but one with a conspicuous beginning and end in the eternal life of Christ, which cannot exist when we tolerate abortion.

Tragically, the Court, whose scales of justice had just been tipped further to the left with the addition of Justice Ginsburg, refused to talk and listen to Loca's case. Meanwhile, (Saint) Teresa shuffled humbly away, always in search of something more to do. *Something beautiful for God.*

# 15

# John Paul The Great

Since the end of the Civil War and the advent of Margaret Sanger, church leaders have lamented the declining influence of Christianity in America, and the resulting rise of a moral relativism that would eventually sanction abortion to suit mere convenience.

In 1874, John Cardinal Newman warned that America's conscience was at risk of being "superceded by a counterfeit" where men "in no sense [recognize] the rights of the Creator, nor the duty to Him, in thought and deed . . . but the right of thinking, speaking, writing, and acting, according to their judgment or their humor, without any thought of God at all."

In 1899, Pope Leo XIII called it "Americanism" in his apostolic letter to Baltimore's James Cardinal Gibbons entitled *Testem Benevolentiae Nostrae* (or "Witness to our Good Will"), in which he warned against American civil liberties were turning truth into a relative term, and conscience into a construct of man, as opposed to the place where man encounters God.

In 1907, Pope Pius X renamed it "modernism" in his encyclical entitled *Pascendi Dominici Gregis* (or "Feeding the Lord's Flock"), proclaiming that it was "the synthesis of all heresies," and lamenting that it was being spread from within the Church by prominent religious and laity who "seize upon chairs in the seminaries and universities" to scatter their seeds of weeds among the wheat.

No need here to reiterate what has already been said about events since then, except to state that modernism remained the name for it all until, as mentioned earlier, Pope John Paul II took to using the word "consumerism" as a means of pointing to man's essential motive – material comfort and wealth - for bathing himself in the blood of a culture of death.  Such, that according to a survey conducted by *U.S. News and World Report* in 1992 (let's call it the year of Robert Casey's cries in the wilderness), 60% of the freshmen at 19 Jesuit-run schools favored legalized abortion. Which is precisely why John Paul The Great, now a Saint, on three very special and specific occasions in the last ten years of the 20th Century, urged his American Bishops to reassert their authority *From the Heart of the Church*, to revel in *The Splendor of Truth*, and to seize upon *The Springtime of Evangelization.*

First, in *Ex Corde Ecclesia*, or "*From the Heart of the Church*", he declared from the Chair of Saint Peter in Rome on August 15, 1990, the Solemnity of the Assumption of the Blessed Virgin Mary into Heaven, that:

*It is the honor and responsibility of a Catholic university to consecrate itself without reserve to the cause of truth.  This is its way of serving at one and the same time both the dignity of man and the good of the Church. . .*

*For, what is at stake is . . .the very meaning of the human person. . .*

*Every Catholic University, as Catholic, must have . . .fidelity to the Christian message as it comes to us through the Church. . .*

*In a Catholic University, therefore, Catholic ideals, attitudes and principles penetrate and inform university activities . . .*

*Every Catholic University . . . has a relationship to the Church that is essential to its institutional identity. . .*

*One consequence of its essential relationship to the Church is that the institutional fidelity of the University to the Christian message includes the recognition of and adherence to the teaching authority of the Church in matters of faith and morals. . .*

*Bishops have a particular responsibility to promote Catholic Universities, and especially to promote and assist in the preservation and strengthening of their Catholic identity, including the protection of their Catholic identity in relation to civil authorities.  This will be achieved more effectively if close personal and pastoral relationships exist between University and Church authorities, characterized by mutual trust, close and consistent cooperation and continuing dialogue.  Even when they do not enter directly into the internal governance of the University, Bishops should be seen not as external agents but as participants in the life of the Catholic University...*

***If need be, a Catholic University must have the courage to speak uncomfortable truths which do not please public opinion, but which are necessary to safeguard the authentic good of society...***

*By its very nature, each Catholic University makes an important contribution to the Church's work of evangelization.  It is a living institutional witness to Christ and his message, so vitally important in cultures marked by secularism...*

*Any official action or commitment of the University is to be in accord with its Catholic identity...*

*Every Catholic University is to maintain communion with the universal Church and the Holy See; it is to be in close communion with the local Church and in particular with the diocesan Bishops of the region or nation in which it is located...*

*Each Bishop has a responsibility to promote the welfare of the Catholic Universities in his diocese and has the right and duty to watch over the preservation and strengthening of their Catholic character...*

*The mission that the Church, with great hope, entrusts to Catholic Universities holds a cultural and religious meaning of vital importance because it concerns the very future of humanity.  The renewal requested of Catholic Universities will make them better able to respond to the task of bringing the*

*message of Christ to man, to society, to the various*
*cultures.*

But Notre Dame President Emeritus Hesburgh, for one, did
not appreciate the efforts that some would undertake in response to
*Ex Corde Ecclesia*, commenting in a 1991 issue of Fordham Magazine
that "the people who have produced these documents have never
created anything in Catholic higher education themselves . . .
American Catholic higher education is a success story.  We don't need
to be reformed."  Of course, Hesburgh was overlooking the fact that
*Ex Corde Ecclesia* itself was authored by a former Catholic university
professor who held doctorates in both sacred theology and
philosophy, and was fluent in no less than nine languages.  Not to
mention the fact that Blessed Basil Moreau, the founder of the
religious congregation to which Hesburgh belonged, had not "created
anything in Catholic higher education" either when he said quite
simply "that the mind could not be cultivated at the expense of the
heart."  Nor had Hesburgh's first predecessor, Edward Sorin, the
founder of Notre Dame, yet created anything in Catholic higher
education when he dedicated the university first and foremost to the
Immaculate Mother of God and told Blessed Basil that he thereby
hoped to establish "one of the most powerful means for good in this
country."  In short, the words of two men on their way to sainthood,
and another who did nothing if not to please Mary, were mere thorns
in the side of academic freedom, in the opinion of Father Hesburgh
and his ilk.  And so, from that same Chair of Saint Peter, on August 6,
1993, the Feast of the Transfiguration of the Lord, John Paul the
Great revealed once again *Veritatis Splendor* - "The Splendor of
Truth" - when he said:

*Today . . . it seems necessary to reflect on the*
*whole of the Church's moral teaching, with the precise*

*goal of recalling certain fundamental truths of Catholic doctrine which, in the present circumstances, risk being distorted or denied [by] . . . the spread of numerous doubts and objections . . . with regard to the Church's moral teachings. It is no longer a matter of limited and occasional dissent, but of an overall and systematic calling into question of traditional moral doctrine . . . At the root . . . is the more or less obvious influence of currents of thought which end by detaching human freedom from its . . . relationship to truth.  Thus, the traditional doctrine regarding the natural law, and the universality and the permanent validity of its precepts, is rejected; certain of the Church's moral teachings are found simply unacceptable; and the Magisterium itself is considered capable of intervening in matters of morality only in order to "exhort consciences" and to "propose values," in the light of which each individual will independently make his or her decisions and life choices. . .*

*Revelation teaches that the power to decide what is good and what is evil does not belong to man, but to God alone. The man is certainly free, inasmuch as he can understand and accept God's commands. And he possesses an extremely far-reaching freedom, since he can eat "of every tree of the garden." But his freedom is not unlimited: it must halt before the "tree of the knowledge of good and evil," for it is called to accept the moral law given by God. In fact, human freedom finds its authentic and complete fulfillment precisely in the acceptance of that law. God, who alone is good, knows perfectly what is good for man, and by*

*virtue of His very love proposes this good to man in the
commandments. . .*

*Moral theologians, who have accepted the
charge of teaching the Church's doctrine, thus have a
grave duty to train the faithful to make this moral
discernment, to be committed to the true good and to
have confident recourse to God's grace. . .*

*Opposition to the teaching of the Church's
Pastors cannot be seen as a legitimate expression
either of Christian freedom or of the diversity of the
Spirit's gifts. When this happens, the Church's Pastors
have the duty to act in conformity with their apostolic
mission, insisting that the right of the faithful to
receive Catholic doctrine in its purity and integrity
must always be respected.*

Nevertheless, in February of 1994 (let's call it the month that
Mother Teresa took the nation to task), Father Edward Malloy,
President of the University of Notre Dame since Hesburgh's
retirement in 1987, went so far as to say, while presiding over the
steady decline in Notre Dame's Catholic faculty, that recent Church
mandates intended to turn back the tide of infidelity were offensive to
the American Catholic theological community – a community in
mutiny, according to Michael J. Mazza in *Heart Attack: Catholic
Academe Meets Ex Corde Ecclesiae* (Fidelity Magazine, February
1995):

*The mutiny of the Catholic academics is one of
the most serious problems afflicting the Catholic
Church in the United States today.  The institutions
that should be educating Catholics to critically*

*examine the categories of the dominant culture have
instead become the main vehicle by which Catholics
are indoctrinated into the sexual values of the liberal
regime.*


Therefore, John Paul "pressed on," as his good friend Robert
Casey would say, again urging his U.S. Bishops to enter the fray, and
put the work of Lucifer at bay. He did this in a series of addresses to
them on the occasion of their visits to him *ad limina*, that is to say,
"at the threshold" of St. Peter's Chair in Rome, in fulfillment of their
obligations, as his surrogate vicars of Christ, to periodically report to
him on the state of each Bishop's diocese. This occurred in 1998, the
addresses then compiled into a text appropriately entitled the
*Springtime of Evangelization*, (Rev. Thomas Williams, L.C., Editor;
Basilica Press, San Diego, 1999). Already mentioned, in relation to
Mr. Cuomo, was some of what John Paul said to them about freedom
and the moral law in the context of American politics. Here's a little
more of what he said about that and some other vital things. Many of
the specific quotations and other enunciations were taken from John
Paul's 1995 encyclical entitled *Evangelium Vitae*, "The Gospel of
Life," and some from Vatican II's Pastoral Constitution on the Church
in the Modern World entitled *Gaudium et Spes*, "Joy & Hope:"


> *A new phase in the history of freedom is
> opening up, and in these circumstances it is necessary
> that the Church, especially through her Pastors, teach
> and evince that "the liberating capacities of science,
> technology, work, economics and political activity will
> only produce results if they find their inspiration and
> measure in the truth and love which are stronger than*

*suffering – the truth and love revealed to men by Jesus Christ."*

*. . . For if freedom is not linked to truth and ordered to goodness, "the ground is laid for society to be at the mercy of the unrestrained will of individuals or the oppressive totalitarianism of public authority."*
*. . . In a cultural climate in which moral norms are often thought to be matters of personal preference, Catholic schools have a critical role to play in leading the younger generation to realize that freedom consists above all in being able to respond to the demands of the truth . . .*

*If Catholic universities are to become leaders in the renewal of higher education, they must first have a strong sense of their own Catholic identity. This identity . . . comes from its living within the Church today and always, speaking from the heart of the Church (ex corde Ecclesiae) to the contemporary world . . . as a true center of learning, where the truth of the created order is fully respected, but also ultimately illuminated by the light of the new creation in Christ.*

***The Catholic identity of a university necessarily includes the university's relationship to the local Church and its Bishop. It is sometimes said that a university that acknowledges a responsibility to any community or authority outside the relevant academic professional associations has lost both its independence and its integrity. But this is to detach freedom from its object, which is truth. Catholic universities understand that there is no contradiction between the free and***

**vigorous pursuit of the truth and a
"recognition of and an adherence to the
teaching authority of the Church in matters of
faith and morals."** . . .

The false promises of the "sexual revolution" are now
painfully obvious in the human suffering caused by
unprecedented rates of divorce, by the scourge of
abortion and its lasting effects on those involved . . .

We are coming to the end of a century which
began with confidence in humanity's prospects of
almost unlimited progress, but which is now ending in
widespread fear and moral confusion. If we want a
spring-time of the human spirit, we must rediscover
the foundations of hope. Above all, society must learn
to embrace once more the great gift of life, to cherish it,
to protect it, and to defend it against the culture of
death, itself an expression of the great fear that stalks
our times. One of your most noble tasks as Bishops is
to stand firmly on the side of life, encouraging those
who defend it and building with them a genuine
culture of life. . .

Thirty years after Humanae Vitae, we see that
mistaken ideas about the individual's moral autonomy
continue to inflict wounds on the consciences of many
people and on the life of society. Paul VI pointed out
some of the consequences of separating the unitive
aspect of conjugal love from its procreative dimension:
a gradual weakening of moral discipline; a
trivialization of human sexuality; the demeaning of
women; marital infidelity, often leading to broken
families; state-sponsored programs of population
control based on imposed contraception and

*sterilization. The introduction of legalized abortion and euthanasia, ever increasing recourse to in vitro fertilization, and certain forms of genetic manipulation and embryo experimentation are also closely related in law and public policy, as well as in contemporary culture, to the idea of unlimited dominion over one's body and life. . .*

*Reflection on a very different anniversary serves to heighten the sense of the urgency of the pro-life task. In the twenty-five years which have passed since the judicial decision legalizing abortion in your country there has been a widespread mobilization of consciences in support of life. The pro-life movement is one of the most positive aspects of American public life, and the support given it by the Bishops is a tribute to your pastoral leadership. Despite the generous efforts of so many, however, the idea that elective abortion is a "right" continues to be asserted. Moreover, there are signs of an almost unimaginable insensitivity to the reality of what actually happens during an abortion, as evidenced by recent events surrounding so-called "partial-birth" abortion. This is a cause for deep concern. A society with a diminished sense of the value of human life at its earliest stages has already opened the door to a culture of death. As Pastors, you must make every effort to ensure that there is no dulling of consciences regarding the seriousness of the crime of abortion, a crime which cannot be morally justified by any circumstance, purpose or law . . .*

*An essential feature of support for the inalienable right to life, from conception to natural death, is the effort to provide legal protection for the unborn, the handicapped, the elderly, and those suffering from terminal illness.  As Bishops, you must continue to draw attention to the relationship of the moral law to constitutional and positive law in your society: "Laws which legitimize the direct killing of innocent human beings . . . are in complete opposition to the inviolable right to life proper to every individual; they thus deny the equality of everyone before the law."*

*What is at stake here is nothing less than the indivisible truth about the human person on which the Founding Fathers staked your nation's claim to independence.  The life of a country is much more than its material development and its power in the world.  A nation needs a "soul."  It needs the wisdom and courage to overcome the moral ills and spiritual temptations inherent in its march through history.  In union with all those who favor a "culture of life" over a "culture of death," Catholics, and especially Catholic legislators, must continue to make their voices heard in the formulation of cultural, economic, political and legislative projects which, "with respect for all and in keeping with democratic principles, will contribute to the building of a society in which the dignity of each person is recognized and the lives of all are defended and enhanced."  Democracy stands or falls with the values which it embodies and promotes.  In defending life, you are defending an original and vital part of the vision on which your country was built.  America must become, again, a hospitable society, in which every unborn child and every handicapped and terminally ill person is cherished and enjoys the protection of the law.*

After absorbing his thirteen addresses, which were delivered to thirteen different geographical groups of Bishops, they all got together and issued their own encyclical of sorts entitled *Living the Gospel of Life*, extensively referenced in Archbishop Charles J. Chaput's insightful work entitled *Render Unto Caesar: Serving the Nation by Living Our Catholic Beliefs in Political Life* (Doubleday, 2008).  From Chaput, one learns that at the heart of his fellow Bishops' work is paragraph 23, which reads:

> *Adopting a consistent ethic of life, the Catholic Church promotes a broad spectrum of issues . . . Opposition to abortion and euthanasia does not excuse indifference to those who suffer from poverty, violence and injustice.  Any politics of human life must work to resist the violence of war and scandal of capital punishment.  Any politics of human dignity must seriously address issues of racism, poverty, hunger, employment, education, housing and health care. Therefore, Catholics should eagerly involve themselves as advocates for the weak and marginalized in all those areas.  Catholic public officials are obliged to address each of these issues as they seek to build consistent policies which promote respect for the human person at all stages.  But being "right" in such matters can never excuse a wrong choice regarding direct attacks on innocent human life. Indeed, the failure to protect and defend life in its most vulnerable stages renders suspect any claims to the "rightness" of*

*positions in other matters affecting the poorest and least powerful of the human community. If we understand the human person as "the temple of the Holy Spirit" – the living house of God – then these latter issues fall logically into place as the crossbeams and walls of that house. All direct attacks on innocent human life, such as abortion and euthanasia, strike at the house's foundation. These directly and immediately violate the human person's most fundamental right – the right to life. Neglect of these issues is the equivalent of building our house on sand. Such attacks cannot help but lull the social conscience in ways ultimately destructive of other human rights.*

To top it off, Chaput points out that "the late Cardinal Joseph Bernardin warned against the misuse of his 'seamless garment' imagery to falsely invest different social issues with the same moral gravity." This observation is a critical one, because its misuse has been widespread and rampant. It began with men like Kennedy, Cuomo, and McCarrick, was perpetuated by men like Moynihan, Clinton, and Kerry, and has continued all the way through to Jenkins and Obama, when they spewed that very same heresy from the stage to the students at Notre Dame, and all over the national news wires, as discussed in Chapter 17 of this book.

# 16

# Benediction



*Faith by nature is blind, but it sees what
reason can't find.*
**Patrick X. Amoresano, Advent , 2009**

In 1966, German Archbishop Joseph Ratzinger, still a decade away from his red hat, and four from the start of his papacy as Benedict XVI, had this to say about the modernizing schemes of the Second Vatican Council:

> *I think it is important to note that with all our satisfaction over the work of the council's renewal . . . . The faith of those who are simple of heart is the most precious treasure of the Church. [See Timothy Dolan, infra]. To serve and to live this faith is the noblest vocation in the renewal of the Church.*

Such a profoundly simple message, from a scholar among scholars in the heady days of the sixties; speaking of which, the German scholar George Shuster springs readily to mind again.

Nearly forty years before Shuster took Pope Paul VI to task on *Humanae Vitae*, "many [Bishops had already] warned that it would be impossible to restrict [contraception] to married couples." In other words, for all of Shuster's 1960's musings about how artificial contraception could aid in the continuum of marriage, he and his intellectual friends had missed the forest for the trees.  The trees not lost on the simple-hearted faith and prayerful contemplations of Pope Paul VI, when he envisioned what birth control would do to fuel sex outside of marriage, and open the doors to degradation and abortion. The Washington Post, of all papers, put it this way, as far back as 1931: *"The suggestion that the use of legalized contraception would be 'careful and restrained' is preposterous."* The point of this little chronological retreat is not to rehash Shuster, but to give Paul VI and John Paul II and Benedict XVI their due.

It follows that once he was made Cardinal and Prefect of the Congregation for the Doctrine of the Faith in 2002, Joseph Ratzinger would write a book entitled *God and the World*, wherein he likened man's movement toward genetic manipulation - such as seen in embryonic stem cell research and associated therapeutic cloning - to the picking of forbidden fruit from Eden's Tree of Life, and warned that *"we can be certain of this: God will take action to counter an ultimate crime . . . of self-destruction . . . by the production of slave-beings. . . far beyond the original sin and the first fall and all of its negative consequences."*

Then in 2004, a year before the beginning of his papacy, he reminded America's bishops, as they assembled in annual conference (called the USCCB), of what John Paul II had already told them, and what they had already said in their own *Living the Gospel of Life*, namely, that *"[n]ot all moral issues have the same weight as abortion and euthanasia. . . There may be a legitimate diversity of opinion even among Catholics about [other important issues of social justice], but not however with regard to abortion and euthanasia."*

This statement by Cardinal Ratzinger, while redundant of the man he was about to succeed as well as of the Bishops themselves, is nonetheless noteworthy for helping to produce a pivotal reciprocal pronouncement by the Bishops conference, wherein they set eminently appropriate standards, and made perfectly reasonable requests, to educators and others in the Catholic community:

> *We need . . . to teach clearly and help other Catholic leaders to teach clearly on our unequivocal commitment to the legal protection of human life from the moment of conception until natural death. . .*
>
> *Catholics need to act in support of these principles and policies in public life. . .*
>
> **The Catholic community and Catholic institutions should not honor those who act in defiance of our fundamental moral principles. They should not be given awards, honors or platforms which suggest support for their actions.**

Lastly, in his formal *Address to Catholic Educators* as their Pontiff on April 17, 2008, about a year before Notre Dame announced that it would honor Barack Obama, and thereby openly defy the Bishops, Benedict XVI said:

> *In regard to faculty members at Catholic colleges and universities, I wish to reaffirm the value of academic freedom. In virtue of this freedom you are called to search for the truth wherever careful analysis of evidence leads you. Yet it is also the case that any appeal to the principle of academic freedom in order to*

*justify positions that contradict the faith and the
teaching of the Church would obstruct or even betray
the university's identity and mission; a mission at the
heart of the Church's munus docendi and not somehow
autonomous or independent of it.*

    *Teachers and administrators, whether in
universities or schools, have the duty and privilege to
ensure that students receive instruction in Catholic
doctrine and practice. This requires that public
witness to the way of Christ, as found in the Gospel
and upheld by the Church's Magisterium, shapes all
aspects of an institution's life, both inside and outside
the classroom. Divergence from this vision weakens
Catholic identity and, far from advancing freedom,
inevitably leads to confusion, whether moral,
intellectual or spiritual.*

Benedict could hardly have been clearer, but his words would fall on long-deaf ears at dear old Notre Dame.

# 17

# "Big Mistake"

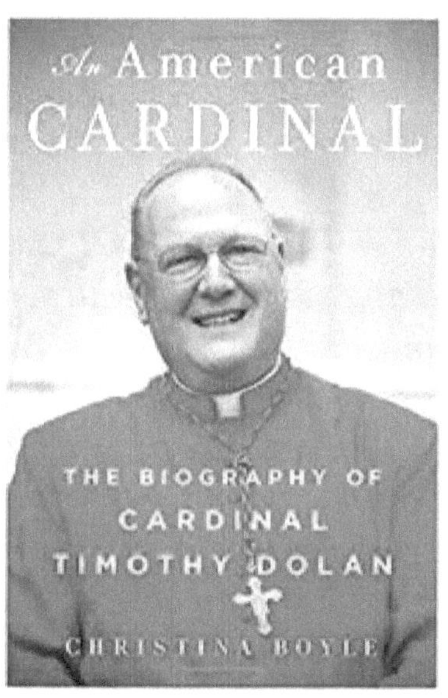

In February of 2009, a month before Notre Dame announced that it would honor Barack Obama as a Doctor of Law, the Vatican announced that it would honor Timothy Michael Dolan as the 10th Archbishop of New York, some 145 years after his predecessor, the infamous Archbishop Hughes, had stood on his balcony, just before his death, and begged his fellow Irishmen to end the bloodshed which had stemmed from his muddled statements on slavery.

When news of Dolan's transfer from Milwaukee to New York first reached the folks Midwest, one of Milwaukee's leading journalists, Patrick McIlheran, reacted this way in a piece to the *New York Post*:

> *People like Dolan. They think they could offer*
> *him a beer at a church festival and that he'd enjoy it. . .*
> *When it was definite we'd lose him, people were*
> *calling radio shows, recounting how the Archbishop*
> *was phoning their homes to check up on some relative*
> *on whose behalf they'd asked him to pray months*
> *before.  He showed up at people's houses to bless the*
> *sick. . .*
> *Watch him say Mass and you sense him feeling*
> *each word, speaking ritual as if he urgently wanted to*
> *tell you something. . .*
> *The first chapter of his book is a rundown of*
> *specific ways to have a more prayerful, holy life.  It's a*
> *how-to for people who want to respond to the shocking*
> *realization that God is personally in love with them.*
> *News like that could brighten your whole day or year*
> *or life.  That his job involves spreading that news*
> *probably explains Dolan's ebullience as much as does*
> *his inborn makeup.*

Then, when Dolan was installed at St. Patrick's Cathedral on April 15, 2009, he began the process of affirming everything that McIlheran had said about him by delivering a first homily that included the following:

> *You are all so very welcome here, in this*
> *"cathedral of suitable magnificence," - as Archbishop*

*John Hughes, whose cross I wear today, termed it -
that has been such a warm, embracing spiritual home
for untold millions. . .all of God's people, children of
our one Father and brothers and sisters in the Lord.*

*I hope you can understand, as grateful as I am
to all of you, there is another claim on my gratitude
that towers above all the rest.  Above all, I give praise
to God, our Father, for raising His Son Jesus Christ
from the dead!  For 'Christ is risen.' He is truly risen!
'Give thanks to the Lord for He is good!  His mercy
endures forever!'*

*For us as Catholics, Christ and His Church are
one.  The triumph, the life, the light, the mercy, the
raising up, the salvation which exploded Easter
morning as Jesus rose from the dead continues in His
Church, an extraordinary spiritual family that gathers
men and women of every nation, race, language, and
background into a breathing tapestry of faith. . .*

*God's love for us is so personal, so passionate,
so intense, that He gave his only begotten Son for our
salvation.  And when God the Father raised His Son
from the dead, He put His divine seal of approval upon
His work of art, the human project, on women and
men made in his own image and likeness, washed
clean by the blood of His Son on Good Friday, destined
to spend eternity at His side. . .*

*The Resurrection of Jesus goes on in our
apostolate for the struggling, searching, and
marginalized, as thousands of those closest to Christ's
Sacred Heart – the hungry, homeless, sick, troubled,
and immigrants – find solace and help in our Catholic
charities and healthcare. . .and . . .* **the Resurrection**

*goes on, as His Church continues to embrace
and protect the dignity of every human person,
the sanctity of human life, from the tiny baby
in the womb to the last moment of natural
passing into eternal life.  As the Servant of God
Terrance Cardinal Cooke wrote, "Human life is
no less sacred or worthy of respect because it is
tiny, pre-born, poor, sick, fragile, or
handicapped."  Yes, the Church is a loving
mother who has a zest for life and serves life
everywhere, but she can become a protective
"mamma bear" when the life of her innocent,
helpless cubs is threatened.*

And so, of the eighty-something outspoken U.S. Bishops who
unanimously objected to Notre Dame's decision to honor Barack
Obama, perhaps it was St. Patrick's endearing new Archbishop who,
far from the cluttered balcony of Archbishop Hughes, spoke the
wholehearted words from a loving Holy Spirit of Almighty God
himself when he said, plain and simple, that - "They made a big
mistake."  He said this, because on March 20, 2009, when the
trustees of the University of Notre Dame announced that it would
give Barack Obama the coveted platform of its Commencement
Address, and award him an honorary Doctor of Laws degree, they did
so -

    with full knowledge that he was one of the most ardent legal
champions of unrestricted access to abortion on demand in U.S.
political history; and

    in spite of the fact that the United States Conference of
Catholic Bishops had explicitly urged them to refrain, in no uncertain
terms, from awarding such platforms and honors to public enemies
of core Church teachings, such as the sacredness of human life; and

without even so much as exercising the simple Christian courtesy, let alone obligation, of letting John D'Arcy, their own local Bishop, know about the invitation to Obama in the first place.

In other words, "the place where the Church does its thinking" – a common refrain from Father Hesburgh, and one often echoed by Father John Jenkins, ND's current president - was telling the world that worshiping the American Idol of the moment meant much more to them than respect for the Magisterium, for Notre Dame's sacred name and Catholic identity, or for the dignity of defenseless human life.  Here's something of what they knew, or should have known, about the legal record of the man around whose neck they were about to drape Our Lady's *Salve Regina* ("Our life, Our sweetness, and Our hope"), and on whom they were about to confer the Blessed Mother's Honorary Doctor of Laws degree.

In 2001, when Barack Obama was a state senator, he was all but single-handedly responsible for killing an Illinois legal bill known as the "Born Alive Act," the sole purpose of which was to protect newborn babies who'd survived botched abortions from murder by abandonment.  In other words, arguably worse than partial-birth abortion - if that's inhumanly possible - Illinois babies who'd escaped from wombs induced to violence by the drugs of an abortionist, and found to be breathing on their own atop the birthing table, were being abandoned, literally set aside to suffer and die, usually from insufficient oxygen to their lungs.  Sometimes this took only a few minutes.  Other times, it took hours (Presumably, it was precisely this sort of unsightly little nuisance that first led doctors to murder by partial-birth abortion instead.  No slipping out of the womb, as it were).

In one case, a nurse (at Chicago's United Church of Christ Hospital, no less) was instructed to take the breathing baby and deposit him in a soiled utility closet.  Thanks to Jill Stanek - one of the nurses at the hospital and now a nationally renowned pro-life speaker - this case caused enough commotion to capture the attention of none other than Patrick O'Malley. An Illinois State Senator, O'Malley sponsored a "Born Alive" bill intended to stop the insanity after James Ryan, the Irish Republican Illinois Attorney General, regrettably concluded that *Roe v. Wade* protected such abominable conduct.  At first, the bill had some alleged flaws that arguably ran afoul of *Roe v. Wade*.  But *after* these issues had been resolved by an amendment that satisfied absolutely everyone on the legislative committee considering the bill, including Barack Obama, the bill was kept from ever reaching the Senate floor by a vote of 6 to 4, thanks to the "No" vote of the committee's chairman, Senator Barack Obama.

Now, before explaining what happened next, it needs to be underscored that the *amended* Illinois State bill which Barack Obama killed in 2001, was *identical* in every material respect to the Federal Born-Alive Infants Protection Act, *unanimously* adopted by the United States Senate (of which Obama was not yet a member) one year later (before Obama joined their ranks), by a vote of 98-0.  This fact is vitally important, not only for what it says about where Obama stood, but because it proves, as a matter of public record, that during his presidential election campaign, when he pleaded to the friendly mainstream media that the bill he killed was unconstitutional, he was telling a bold-faced lie.  The mainstream media essentially let him slide, when it should have been wondering why on earth wasn't Barack Obama, a Harvard Law School graduate, going out of his way to make certain that a bill against infanticide before his committee withstood all constitutional scrutiny and became law?  Why wasn't he fighting for it, instead of working against it?  98 U.S. Senators, including Hillary Clinton and all of her most liberal colleagues, had supported the law.  But not Barack Obama, now the 44th President of the United States of America, and recipient of Notre Dame's Honorary Doctor of Laws degree.

Given this, it would seem superfluous to talk at any length about Obama's support for partial-birth abortion; or his promise to resurrect Clinton's unlimited abortion-fest, cravenly named the "Freedom of Choice" Act; or his immediate reversal of the Mexico City policy that had kept our tax dollars from funding foreign abortions; or his advocacy of "therapeutic" cloning, that is, the creation of human life for the sole purpose of ending it to harvest embryonic stem cells, and so on, in order to sustain Archbishop Dolan's pithy observation that Notre Dame had indeed made a very "big mistake."  But who at Notre Dame?  Who would invite such a man to be honored by an institution dedicated by its founder to Mary The Immaculate Conception, and to the blessed fruit of her womb. The same Mary who hastened over the hills to her cousin Elizabeth, and witnessed John the Baptist leap in Elizabeth's womb at the sound of Mary's voice as she herself carried the unborn Christ in her own. Who?  Alas, the answer is almost as calculating and cold as the heart of the man who killed that bill, and mocked the Special Olympics.

According to an article by author Frank Walker from the publication *Pewsitter*, The Board of Trustees which administers the University of Notre Dame was apparently dominated by those from the wealthiest and most influential class in the country, many of whom helped make up the very "Chicago power structure" which fed and nurtured the political fortunes of none other than Barack Obama:

First, there was the ND Fellow and Chairman of the Board of Trustees, Richard Notebaert (Qwest Communications), whose wife Peggy's Notebaert Nature Museum was the fortunate recipient of federal funding earmarked by then U.S. Senator Obama. In fact, Frank Clark, a member of Notebaert's Museum board, was a "key Obama campaign fundraiser."  This was the same Richard Notebaert who could be seen and heard saying, on Notre Dame's video website (*video.nd.edu*, more on this later), that nothing is more important than ethics, and that over time, the truth comes out about whether someone is "walking the talk," or only in it for themselves.  This was also the same Richard Notebaert who said, in his Obama-ND commencement address post-mortem entitled *The Church and the University* (*America Magazine*, August 31, 2009), that "We must work hard at the relationship between our faith and our culture.  We cannot take a position that lets the ground lie fallow *because we are unwilling to be teachers.*"  This was a man who, after he and his cohorts at Notre Dame were heard saying and seen doing absolutely *nothing* about FOCA in the aftermath of the Commencement (while faithful Catholics across the country petitioned the Congress at the urgings of their bishops, much like they did in sterilization days), actually wanted credit for increasing *"the possibility of meaningful dialogue"* about abortion;

Next, there was Arthur Velasquez (Aztec Foods), a former ND Fellow and then current Trustee who contributed to Obama's political campaigns and also saw his pet Chicago Museum of Science and Industry receive federal earmarks at Obama's behest;

Next, the Honorable Ann Claire Williams, an ND Trustee who was an assistant U.S. Attorney out of Chicago, then appointed by Clinton to sit on the 7th U.S. Circuit Court of Appeals Judge, and was apparently on Obama's list of potential Supreme Court nominees;

Next, Chicago businessman Philip Rooney (Waste Management), whose 2002 indictment by the SEC for fraud resulted in his removal from the boards of all publicly traded companies, but not in his removal from the Board of Trustees of the University of Notre Dame;

Next, Chicago-connected, Chinese Communist-sympathizing Douglas Tong Hsu (billionaire Chairman of The Far Eastern Group), whose 2006 indictment for forgery and breach of trust did not affect his 2009 trusteeship on Notre Dame's Board.

Other Notre Dame Trustees, not necessarily connected to Chicago, nonetheless have issues to give one pause.  For example:

Investment bankers Robert Conway (Goldman Sachs/AIG), Philip Purcell (Morgan Stanley and Dean Witter), and Enrique Hernandez (Wells Fargo Bank), each of whom, from a financial sector then in severe crisis, certainly had self-evident business reasons for befriending Barack Obama;

Dr. Mary Anne Fox, chancellor of UC San Diego and Vice-Chair of the National Science Board, an unapologetic proponent of embryonic stem cell research; and finally,

Raymond G. Chambers, co-founder of the anti-poverty but pro-abortion Millenium Promise project, of which Notre Dame had been an official partner, and on whose board Father Jenkins had served despite its objective "to expand access to safe abortions."  This is especially noteworthy, inasmuch as it casts a disturbing shadow over the wonderful work that the Congregation of Holy Cross has been doing in Uganda for so many years, and unfortunately suggests to the world that Notre Dame may be guilty of more than mere sins of omission when it comes to abortion (more on this sad notion near the end of the book).  Jenkins recently resigned from the Millenium Board, but only after publication of an eye-opening letter from William H. Dempsey, Notre Dame Class of 1952 Valedictorian and President of the *Sycamore Trust* project, an exceptional organization devoted to restoring Notre Dame's Catholic character:

> *We are frank to say that we do not understand how advising the Millenium Promise board that you would not participate in matters relating to abortion or artificial contraception solves, or even mitigates, the problem.  The organization's fund-raising projects surely do not mention your disclaimer, and accordingly your membership amounts to a Notre*

*Dame stamp of approval for the organization's fund-*
*raising efforts.  The abortion and contraception*
*programs are among the beneficiaries.  Thus, the*
*Board has the advantages of your membership*
*without the disadvantage of your unsympathetic*
*participation in matters relating to abortion and*
*contraception. . .*

*Moreover, now that Millenium Promise's*
*abortion and contraception policies are becoming well*
*known in connection with your board membership,*
*especially in the pro-life Catholic community, Notre*
*Dame's reputation on life issues specifically, and as a*
*robustly Catholic institution more generally, is*
*suffering.*

Along this same line, in his ground-breaking book, What
Happened to Notre Dame (St. Augustine Press, 2009, the late great
ND Professor Charlie Rice explains what Pope Benedict's recent
encyclical, *Caritas in Veritate*, had said on the subject of
organizations such as Millenium Project:

*A disturbing reality, as noted in [Caritas in*
*Veritate], is the imposition on developing countries of*
*anti-life policies that impede development.  "Not only*
*does. . .poverty still provoke high rates of infant*
*mortality in many regions, but some parts of the world*
*. . . experience . . . demographic control, on the part of*
*government that. . . promote contraception and even . .*
*. impose abortion. . .*

*"Some non-governmental Organizations work*
*actively to spread abortion, promoting . . . sterilization*
*in poor countries, in some cases not even informing the*

*women concerned.  Development aid is sometimes
linked to . . . strong birth control measures.  Further
grounds for concern are laws permitting euthanasia
as well as pressure . . . nationally and internationally,
in favor of its juridical recognition.*

*"Openness to life is at the center of true
development.  When a society moves towards the
denial or suppression of life, it ends up no longer
finding the . . . motivation and energy to strive for
man's true good."*

Thus, the tragically sad but true reality is that South Bend's shamefully disrespected Bishop D'Arcy was only half right when he said that Notre Dame had "chosen prestige over truth," because he left out the part about influence and power, the same sort of influence and power which the Rockefellers wielded toward Hesburgh, Shuster, and the United States Supreme Court.  But what's in a name? Prestige, influence, power.  They all share a common refrain in their disdain for higher authority.  For twenty-four years, Bishop D'Arcy had come to campus to tell Notre Dame's next graduating class how he'd received no honors when he was in their shoes, for which he would receive warm rounds of applause from all the unremarkable students.  Little did he know that come 2009, Notre Dame would choose to dishonor him so, treating him like some senile uncle, kept completely in the dark about Notre Dame's plans to honor Obama. What's a lonely old man to do for under such tragic circumstances, but surround himself with smiling youth who'd assembled at Notre Dame's Grotto, praying to Notre Dame Our Mother for the reparation of souls?  So that is exactly what Bishop D'Arcy did, though most of the world would not know it, nor the South Quad Mass that preceded it. This is because the media's coverage was carefully choreographed by Notre Dame, streams of colorful pomp and circumstance contrasted with staccato-like stillborn images held by a handful of the in-your-face folks.  One supposes that to have shown the South Quad Mass, of the recitation of the Rosary at the Grotto, would have been unconducive to "the possibility of meaningful dialogue" in the opinion of Notebaert *et al.*  Little would the world know that nearly 3000 men and women had assembled on the South Quad that day, some from as far away as Mexico and Florida, to celebrate Mass with ND Response, a coalition of ten separate student groups engaged in peaceful protest.  Their statement told the whole tragic tale:

> *. . . Our objection is not a matter of political partisanship, but of President Obama's hostility to the Catholic Church's teachings on the sanctity of human life at its earliest stages.  His recent dedication of federal funds to overseas abortions and to embryonic stem cell research will directly result in the deaths of thousands of innocent human beings.  We cannot sit idly by while the University honors someone who believes that an entire class of human beings is undeserving of the most basic of all legal rights, the right to live. . .*
>
> *President Obama's actions have consistently shown contempt for this principle . . . Leadership that puts the lives of the most innocent at risk is leadership we must disdain.  In the face of President Obama's actions, Father Jenkin's words [asserting that Notre Dame intends to honor his leadership rather than his view on abortion] ring hollow.*
>
> *It is a great [tragic would have been a better word] irony that the University has chosen to award President Obama an honorary law degree.  As the*

Nor would the world learn that ND Response was joined by 40 graduates, processing to the Grotto, where over 800 hundred people huddled together to give them their own special prayer-filled Commencement. Four years living with, and working with, and loving their fellow classmates, and forty skipped their own graduation to be at the Grotto with the Blessed Mother, in search of that Spirit of Notre Dame, the one that would "light up the universe," if only those in charge of Notre Dame would let it. One wonders how many others, together with their parents, have since harbored unspoken misgivings, deep inside their hearts. And why? Why did Notre Dame's administrators have to do it? Why couldn't they have chosen someone else?  Even if they thought Obama would be a real reformer – one who might be open to restricting abortions – why couldn't they just wait and see what kind of president this untested man might be?  This man with precious little record, the one from whom Arizona State withheld its honors, precisely because he was so young, and so very inexperienced.  How sad that Notre Dame would allow itself to be outclassed in this way.

Unfortunately, the conduct of Father Jenkins suggested, as did the profiles of his buddies on the board, that they were all adept at unseemly political gamesmanship for gain.

For example, at the same time ten dedicated young Holy Cross priests were trying to describe and publicize their heartfelt objections to Father Jenkin's actions on behalf of their alma mater, Jenkins was busy dissembling those actions, while dissing other equally crestfallen protestors in the process - protestors on campus, among the alumni, and all across the country.  Here is some of what those ten priests had to say, in their April 8, 2009 letter to the editor of the *Notre Dame Observer:*

> *We write as priests of the Congregation of Holy Cross and as proud graduates of the University of Notre Dame to voice our objection to the University's decision to honor President Obama by inviting him to deliver this year's Commencement address and by conferring on him an honorary Doctor of Laws degree.*
>
> *We wish to associate ourselves with and encourage those courageous students and treasured alumni who, while deeply loving Notre Dame, vigorously oppose this sad and regrettable decision of the University administration.*
>
> *It is our deep conviction that Notre Dame should lead by word and deed in upholding the*

*Church's fundamental teaching that human life must
be respected and protected from the moment of
conception...*

*We especially regret the fissure that the
invitation of President Obama has opened between
Notre Dame and its local ordinary and many of his
fellow bishops. We express our deep gratitude to
Bishop John D'Arcy for his leadership and moral
clarity...*

*The University pursues a dangerous course
when it allows itself to decide for and by itself what
part of being a Catholic institution it will choose to
embrace...*

*...Notre Dame's decision has caused moral
confusion and given many reason to believe that the
University's stance against the terrible evil of abortion
is weak and easily trumped by other considerations.*

*We prayerfully request that Father Jenkins and
the Fellows of the University, who are entrusted with
responsibility for maintaining its essential character
as a Catholic institution of higher learning, "revisit this
matter" immediately ...*

But Father Jenkins did not revisit the matter, at least not in
the manner envisioned by his fellow priests. Instead, he engaged in
exactly the kind of demagoguery that one would expect from
someone who speaks from a place that pretends to do the Church's
thinking for it, and in the process, insulted about 400,000 people in
close communion with his fellow priests. He did this, in a very public
way, by telling the Wall Street Journal that "[t]he [Cardinal] Newman
Society has no ecclesiastical standing [not that this would have
mattered much to him] and no academic standing [not that this has

any relevance whatsoever to the issue]. For me, it resembles nothing more than a political action committee." The reader is invited to visit the Cardinal Newman Society website, which garnered over 350,000 signatures from church-going grassroots Catholics all across the country on a protest position, to assess its motives and tactics, which speak for themselves. In addition, the reader may wish to visit the website of that other "political action committee" called the Project Sycamore Trust, which garnered thousands of signatures of its own, mostly from alumni, and has been actively engaged in attempting to stop the steady erosion of Notre Dame's Catholic character for the last several years.

Father Jenkins, who steadily banged the drum of "meaningful dialogue" with President Obama throughout the controversy, right up to and including his introductory remarks at the Commencement ceremony, dissed the protesting Notre Dame students under his own charge. Already referenced above are the heartfelt remarks of those students. After they took Father Jenkins up on his ostensible invitation to speak with them about their concerns, they learned that in light of their desire to exchange mutual gestures of good will with the administration, and to hold their meeting in an open and suitably sized forum, Jenkins would renege. He would tell them that "conditions for constructive dialogue simply do not exist," which was his way of saying that meeting with a handful of students behind closed doors would be fine, but encountering them in an open, free-flowing forum, where he could not control the message which might be sent to the media, was entirely out of the question.

Next came the dissembling. Something had to be done about the bishops' statement, the written one that was therefore undeniable, and too troublesome to ignore. The one that nearly five years earlier had said, in effect, that – "if you're thinking of doing this, don't," recited here to be crystal clear:

*The Catholic community and Catholic institutions should not honor those who act in defiance of our fundamental moral principles. They should not be given awards, honors, or platforms which would suggest support for their actions.*

In response to this statement, which kept popping up in letters and news articles and such, Father Jenkins rather eagerly took some really bad (and anonymous) legal advice, and told everyone – wait for it – that the statement only applied to Catholic politicians, and not to non-Catholic ones. In other words, it wasn't ok to honor pro-abortion Catholics politicians, just non-Catholic ones. Here is what Canon attorney Ed Peters had to say on his web blog, aptly named *In the Light of the Law*, about Father Jenkins' dissembling:

*Notre Dame President Fr. John Jenkins continues to flail about for an adequate response (though short of resigning, there <u>isn't</u> an adequate response) to his monumental gaff of bestowing an honorary doctor of laws degree on a president who has spent his entire political career seeing to it that millions of human beings are excluded from the protection of law. Jenkin's latest lunge is for the life [preserver] stamped "canon lawyers we consulted." Figures.*

*It is paradigmatic of the theological Left to ignore canon law when it poses the slightest inconvenience for its plans, but to hide behind canons (or at least behind canonists, even anonymous ones) when they afford some cover (however thin) for obvious blunders or malfeasance...*

*Does Jenkins really think that Catholic bishops
would countenance a Catholic institution honoring a
philanthropic murderer, or a free-speech crusading
pornographer, or a right-to-privacy pimp, provided
merely that the awardee was not a Catholic?  Really,
that's too bizarre for words . . .*

*Seriously, what I wonder is, why, amid the
canon lawyers Jenkins claims to have consulted, not
one, it seems, pointed out the most obvious solution to
their client's problem:*

*The USCCB's statement applies only to "Catholic
institutions", right?  Well, all Jenkins and the ND
board need to do is declare that Notre Dame is not a
Catholic institution, and poof!, all these problems
disappear.  Notre Dame could confer honorary
doctorates in law on anybody it wants after that, even
on people who have built a career out of denying
unborn babies the protection of law, and nary a bishop
would say a word about it.*

South Bend's Bishop D'Arcy, on the other hand, despite the
shameful way in which he was publicly insulted by Jenkins, was
considerably more temperate in his constructive criticism of the man:

*Recently, Father Jenkins . . . indicated that it
was his conviction that the [USCCB] statement did not
apply in this matter . . .*

*. . . Since the matter is now public, it is my duty
as the bishop of this diocese to respond and correct.  I
take up this responsibility with some sadness, but also
with the conviction that if I did not do so, I would be
remiss in my pastoral responsibility.  Rather than*

*share my full letter, which I have shared with Church leadership, I prefer to present some key points:*

*The meaning of the sentence in the USCCB document relative to Catholic institutions is clear. . .*

*When there is a doubt concerning the meaning of a [USCCB] document . . . authentic interpretation . . . is found in the local bishop, who is the teacher and law giver in his diocese . . .*

*I informed Father Jenkins that if there was any genuine questions or doubt about the meaning of the relevant sentence in the [USCCB] document, any <u>competent</u> Canonist with knowledge of the tradition and love for Christ's Church had the responsibility to inform Father Jenkins of the fundamental principle that the diocesan bishop alone bears the responsibility to provide an authoritative interpretation. . .*

*Father Jenkins . . . consulted presidents of other Catholic universities, and at least indirectly, consulted other bishops . . . [but] he chose not to consult with his own bishop who, as I made clear, is the teacher and law-giver in his own diocese. I reminded Father Jenkins that I was not informed of the invitation until after it was accepted by the President. . .*

*Father Jenkins declared [that] the invitation to President Obama does not "suggest support" for his actions, because [Father Jenkins] has expressed and continues to express disagreement with him on issues surrounding protection of life. I wrote that the outpouring of hundreds of thousands who are shocked by the invitation clearly demonstrates that this invitation has, in fact, scandalized many Catholics and other people of goodwill. In my office alone, there*

*have been over 3,300 messages [as of April 22, 2009]
of shock, dismay, and outrage, and they are still
coming in . . .*


A few days later, Father Jenkins would receive this letter from
Mary Ann Glendon, Harvard Law Professor and U.S. Ambassador to
the Vatican:

*Dear Father Jenkins,*
*When you informed me in December 2008 that I had
been selected to receive Notre Dame's Laetare Medal, I
was profoundly moved. I treasure the memory of
receiving an honorary degree from Notre Dame in
1996, and I have always felt honored that the
commencement speech I gave that year was included
in the anthology of Notre Dame's most
memorable commencement speeches. So, I
immediately began working on an acceptance speech
that I hoped would be worthy of the occasion, of the
honor of the medal, and of your students and faculty.*

*Last month, when you called to tell me that the
commencement speech was to be given by President
Obama, I mentioned to you that I would have to
rewrite my speech. Over the ensuing weeks, the task
that once
seemed so delightful has been complicated by a
number of factors.*

*First, as a longtime consultant to the U.S. Conference*

*of Catholic, Bishops, I could not help but be dismayed by the news that Notre Dame also planned to award the president an honorary degree. This, as you must know, was in disregard of the U.S. bishops' express request of 2004 that Catholic institutions "should not honor those who act in defiance of our fundamental moral principles" and that such persons "should not be given awards, honors or platforms which would suggest   support for their actions."* ***That request, which in no way seeks to control or interfere with an institution's freedom to invite and engage in serious debate with whomever it wishes, seems to me so reasonable that I am at a loss to understand why a Catholic university should disrespect it.***

*Then I learned that "talking points" issued by Notre Dame in response to widespread criticism of its decision included two statements implying that my acceptance speech would somehow balance the event:*

*• "President Obama won't be doing all the talking. Mary Ann Glendon, the former U.S. ambassador to the Vatican, will be speaking as the recipient of the Laetare Medal."*

*• "We think having the president come to Notre Dame, see our graduates, meet our leaders, and hear a talk from Mary Ann Glendon is a good thing for the president and for the causes we care about."*

*A commencement, however, is supposed to be a joyous*

*day for the graduates and their families. It is not the
right place, nor is a brief acceptance speech the right
vehicle, for engagement with the very serious
problems raised by Notre Dame's decision — in
disregard of the settled position of the U.S. bishops —
to honor a prominent and uncompromising opponent
of the Church's position on issues
involving fundamental principles of justice.*

*Finally, with recent news reports that other Catholic
schools are similarly choosing to disregard the
bishops' guidelines, I am concerned that Notre Dame's
example could have an unfortunate ripple effect.*

*It is with great sadness, therefore, that I have
concluded that I cannot accept the Laetare Medal or
participate in the May 17 graduation ceremony.
In order to avoid the inevitable speculation about the
reasons for my decision, I will release this letter to the
press, but I do not plan  to make any further comment
on the matter at this time.*

*Yours Very Truly,
Mary Ann Glendon*


When the news of Professor Glendon's letter circulated among
all of the Cardinal Newman Society and Sycamore Trust petition
signers, and all those in quiet communion with them, the anecdotal
evidence is that there were a dozen stadiums full of re-spirited
Catholics, standing up and cheering "GO IRISH!"

And then there was Kansas City Archbishop Joseph Naumann, who summed it up so well when he said:

> *In reality, Notre Dame's invitation signals to President Obama that there is no need for dialogue. Why should the president feel a need to dialogue when he is honored by our nation's most prestigious Catholic university no matter how extreme his policies and actions supporting legalized abortion?*

All of this, of course, fell on deaf ears, and needless to say, Jenkins and Obama were at their resplendent, dissembling best, when it came time for Commencement.  Here is a selected sampling of what some noteworthy fellows had to say about those speeches. First, from William McGurn, Wall Street Journal contributor from Notre Dame's Class of 1980:

> *Seldom does dawn rise on an America where the morning's New York Times displays a more intuitive grasp of a story than the New York Post. The coverage of Barack Obama's commencement address at Notre Dame, however, was such a day. Where the Post headlined an inside spread with "Obama In the Lions' Den," the Times front page was dominated by a color photograph of a beaming president, resplendent in his blue-and-gold Notre Dame academic gown, reaching out to graduates eager to shake his hand or just touch his robe.*

*It was precisely the message President Obama wanted to send: How bad can he be on abortion if Notre Dame is willing to honor him?*

*We cannot blame the president for this one. During his campaign for president, Mr. Obama spoke honestly about the aggressive pro-choice agenda he intended to pursue -- as he assured Planned Parenthood, he was "about playing offense," not defense -- and his actions have been consistent with that pledge. If only our nation's premier Catholic university were as forthright in advancing its principles as Mr. Obama has been for his.*

*In a letter to Notre Dame's Class of 2009, the university's president, the Rev. John Jenkins, stated that the honors for Mr. Obama do not indicate any "ambiguity" about Notre Dame's commitment to Catholic teaching on the sanctity of human life. The reality is that it was this ambiguity that the White House was counting on; this ambiguity that was furthered by the adoring reaction to Mr. Obama's visit; and this ambiguity that disheartens those working for an America that respects the dignity of life inside the womb.*

*We've been here before. In his response to an inquiry from this reporter, Dennis Brown, the university's spokesman, wisely ignored a question asking whether "ambiguity" would be the word to describe a similar decision in 1984 to give Mario Cuomo, then governor of New York, the Notre Dame platform he so famously used to advance his personally-opposed-but argument. Or the decision a few years later to bestow its highest Catholic award on Sen. Daniel Patrick Moynihan, another supporter of legal abortion. It seems that whenever Democratic leaders find themselves in trouble over their party's abortion record, some Notre Dame honor or platform will be forthcoming to provide the needed cover.*

*Probably Notre Dame is rich enough that it can safely thumb its institutional nose at the [80 or so] bishops who publicly challenged the university for flouting their guidelines on such invitations. Nor can we expect much from Notre Dame's trustees. At a time when Americans all across this country have declared themselves "yea" or "nay" on the Obama invite, the reaction of Notre Dame's board is less the roar of the lion than the silence of the lambs.*

*Pro-lifers are used to this. They know their stand makes them unglamorous. They find themselves a stumbling block to Democratic progressives -- and unwelcome at the Republican country club. And they are especially desperate for the support of institutions willing to engage in the clear, thoughtful and unembarrassed way that even Mr. Obama says we should.*

*With its billions in endowment and its prestigious name, Notre Dame ought to be in the lead here. But when asked for examples illuminating the university's unambiguous support for unborn life, Mr.*

*Brown could provide only four: help for pregnant students who want to carry their babies to term, student volunteer work for pregnant women at local shelters, prayer mentions at campus Masses, and lectures such as a seminar on life issues.*

*These are all well and good, but they also highlight the poverty of Notre Dame's institutional witness. At Notre Dame today, there is no pro-life organization -- in size, in funding, in prestige -- that compares with the many centers, institutes and so forth dedicated to other important issues ranging from peace and justice to protecting the environment. Perhaps this explains why a number of pro-life professors tell me they must not be quoted by name, lest they face career retaliation.*

*The one institute that does put the culture of life at the heart of its work, moreover -- the Center for Ethics and Culture -- doesn't even merit a link under the "Faith and Service" section on the university's Web site. The point is this: When Notre Dame doesn't dress for the game, the field is left to those like Randall Terry, who create a spectacle and declare their contempt for civil and respectful witness.*

*In the National Portrait Gallery of the Smithsonian, there is a wonderful photograph of Father Ted Hesburgh -- then Notre Dame president -- linking hands with Martin Luther King Jr. at a 1964 civil-rights rally at Chicago's Soldier Field. Today, nearly four decades and 50 million abortions after Roe*

v. Wade, *there is no photograph of similar prominence of any Notre Dame president taking a lead at any of the annual marches for life.  Father Jenkins is right: That's not ambiguity. That's a statement.*

Then, there were these wonderfully insightful observations from John Henry Westen, Editor of LifeSiteNews:

> *. . . Obama told the students [that] "the ultimate irony of faith is that it necessarily admits doubt [and therefore] should compel us to remain open and curious and eager to continue the spiritual and moral debate."*
>
> *The Christian view of faith, however, excludes doubt about the articles of faith and does not admit it as Obama suggests that it "necessarily" does. . .*
>
> *The Catechism of the Catholic Church notes specifically: "Faith is certain.  It is more certain than all human knowledge because it is founded on the very word of God who cannot lie.  To be sure, revealed truths can seem obscure to human reason and experience, but the certainty that the divine light gives is greater than that which the light of natural reason gives."*
>
> *My name sake, John Henry Newman [of Jenkins "political action committee" fame], wrote on*

*the subject.  While admitting intellectual difficulties with the Christian Creed, he never doubted the doctrines attached to them.  He said famously: "Ten thousand difficulties do not make one doubt."*

*In [fact, as far back as] the 12th century, St. Bernard of Clairvaux wrote [that a] "faith that lacks certainty is not really faith but rather opinion."*

*. . .Christians need never doubt the evil of abortion . . .absolute unchangeable truth taught by faith but also knowable by human reason – and therefore doubly certain. . .*

*The President then [ironically asserted that] "if there is one law that we can be most certain of, it is the . . .Golden Rule – the call to treat one another as we wish to be treated."*

Except for unborn children apparently, as noted in Princeton political science Professor Robert George's previously cited criticism of Obama's fellow dissembler, Mario Cuomo; speaking of whom, there was this from the "Mile High" city's Archbishop Charles Chaput:

*The [commencement] events do have some fitting irony, though.  Almost exactly 25 years ago, Notre Dame provided the forum for Gov. Mario Cuomo to outline the "Catholic" case for "pro-choice" public service.  At the time, Cuomo's speech was hailed*

*in the media as a masterpiece of American Catholic
legal and moral reasoning.  In retrospect, it's clearly
adroit.  It's also, just as clearly, an illogical and
intellectually shabby exercise in the manufacture of
excuses.  Father Jenkins' explanations, and President
Obama's honorary degree, are a fitting national
bookend to a quarter century of softening Catholic
witness in Catholic higher education.  Together,
they've given the next generation of Catholic
leadership all the excuses they need to baptize their
personal conveniences and ignore what it really
demands to be "Catholic" in the public square.*

Clearly, it's an understatement to say that Chaput - whose
*Render Unto Caeser* gives witness to the *Springtime of
Evangelization* – is a tough act to follow, but there are three who give
it a pretty good try.  First, from Bevil Bramwell of the Order of the
Oblates of Mary Immaculate, with a Ph.D from Boston College:

> *Notre Dame has done a great service to the
> Catholic Church. . . For the first time in a long while, a
> noted "Catholic" institution has given clear public
> witness to its "Catholicism" in a way that cannot be
> fudged or swept under the rug. It is not every day that
> you can enlist the President of the United States, and a
> non-Catholic at that, to help you in making such an
> unequivocal assertion of your deepest understanding
> of what it means to be Catholic.*

*. . . Catholic institutions are Catholic if they teach all of the interrelated truths completely and in harmony with one another – and then live out those teachings in communion with the whole Church. Then they give honorary doctorates, not as you would a box of DVDs to say "thank you for coming," but to acknowledge that a specific person has promoted and served the cause of the truth in some highly significant way. That is to say: all of the truths together, since mankind is one and there is one truth about mankind – expressed in Jesus Christ . . .*

*Facilitating the killing of babies or earmarking more money for killing babies, not only here but around the world, are actions that cannot be put in the balance with anything else (and by the way, say something about your view of justice and peace). . . Honoring the man means participating in the trade-off of a specific human life – tragically and often enough a poor, black life as well – for something of far lesser value. It says: We have found something (his presence on our campus, his aspirations towards some aspects of social justice) that all but eliminates what should be our repugnance towards the wholesale taking of innocent human life. This is seriously flawed thinking, and in a civilized society, . . . unconscionable.*

Next, George Weigel, world-renowed author, professor, and expert in Catholic theology:

*Obama [inserted himself into the debate about American Catholicism] by suggesting, not altogether subtly, who the real Catholics in America are. The real Catholics, you see, are those like the late Cardinal Joseph Bernardin, who . . . was best known publicly for his advocacy of a "consistent ethic of life," in which the abortion issue was linked to the abolition of capital punishment and nuclear arms control. . . the "seamless garment" approach. . . [T]he net effect . . . was to validate politically the intellectual mischief of Mario Cuomo's notorious 1984 Notre Dame speech and to give two generations of Catholic politicians a virtual pass on the abortion question by allowing them to argue that, hey, I'm batting .667 on the consistent ethic of life.*

*The U.S. bishops abandoned the "seamless garment" metaphor in 1998, substituting the image of the "foundations of the house of freedom" to explain the priority to be given the life issues in the Church's address to public policy — and in the consciences of Catholic politicians. The foundations of the house of freedom, the bishops argued, are the moral truths about the human person that we can know by reason. Those truths are embodied in law in what we call civil rights. Thus, the life issues are the great civil-rights issues of the moment. This powerful argument did not, however, sit well with Catholics comfortable with the Cuomo Compromise ("I'm personally opposed, but I can't impose my views on a pluralistic society"), for these good liberals and progressives had long prided*

*themselves on being — like Father Hesburgh —
champions of civil rights.*

*So the "seamless garment" went underground
for a decade, [until] Obama-supporters on the Notre
Dame board saw their chances and took 'em,
arranging for the president to come to Notre Dame to
complete the seamless garment's dust-off and give it a
new lease on life by presenting the late Cardinal
Bernardin — "a kind and good man . . . a saintly man"
(who expressly disavowed what had been done to twist
his ethic before his death) — as the very model of a real
Catholic in America. Not the kind of Catholic who
would ever criticize Notre Dame for bestowing an
honorary doctorate of laws on a man determined to
enshrine in law what the Catholic Church regards as a
fundamental injustice. Not the kind of man who would
suggest that, with the life issues, we're living through
the moral equivalent of the Lincoln/Douglas debates,
with Barack Obama unhappily choosing to play the
role of Stephen A. Douglas. Not a man, in other words,
like Cardinal Francis George of Chicago, Cardinal
Bernardin's successor, the president of the United
States Conference of Catholic Bishops, and one of the
most articulate critics of Notre Dame's decision to
honor a president who manifestly does not share what
Notre Dame claims is its institutional commitment to
the Church's defense of life. Whether or not President
Obama knew precisely what he was doing — and I'm
inclined to think that this politically savvy White
House and its allies among Catholic progressive
intellectuals knew exactly what they were doing — is*

*irrelevant. In order to secure the political advantage
Obama had gained among Catholic voters last
November, the president of the United States decided
that he would define what it means to be a real
Catholic in 21st-century America — not the bishop of
Fort Wayne–South Bend, who in sorrow declined to
attend Notre Dame's commencement; not the 80-some
bishops who publicly criticized Notre Dame's decision
to invite the president to receive an honorary degree;
not the U.S. Conference of Catholic Bishops, which
explicitly and unambiguously instructed Catholic
institutions not to do what Notre Dame did. He,
President Obama, would settle the decades-long intra-
Catholic culture war in favor of one faction — the
faction that had supported his candidacy and that had
spent the first months of his administration defending
his policies.*

Finally, and most profoundly, there is Francis J. Beckwith, Senior Visiting Fellow in the Notre Dame Center for Ethics & Culture at the University of Notre Dame, and protestant professor of philosophy and church-state studies at Baylor University:

> *. . .According to Catholic moral theology, a
> regime whose laws sequester a group of human beings
> from its protections for reasons that are capricious
> and gravely immoral is a regime whose laws on this
> matter are not really laws at all. In fact, we need not
> even consult a Catholic theologian, philosopher, or
> legal scholar to receive clarity on this question. We can*

*cite the words of a Baptist minister, who made generous use of St. Augustine and St. Thomas Aquinas in what has become one of the most important epistles in American political discourse. On April 16, 1963, in his "A Letter from a Birmingham Jail," Dr. Martin Luther King Jr. penned these words:*

*"I would agree with St. Augustine that "an unjust law is no law at all." Now, what is the difference between the two? How does one determine whether a law is just or unjust? A just law is a man-made code that squares with the moral law or the law of God. An unjust law is a code that is out of harmony with the moral law. To put it in the terms of St. Thomas Aquinas: An unjust law is a human law that is not rooted in eternal law and natural law. Any law that uplifts human personality is just. Any law that degrades human personality is unjust."*

*According to Catholic moral theology, the unborn human being, from the moment of conception, is a full-fledged member of the human community. That means that the unborn's personhood is not like a matter of taste, preference, or a "deep concern" of "personal belief." It is a fact that pro-lifers are convinced they know is true, just like such other facts as that Julius Caesar crossed the Rubicon, that it's wrong to torture children for fun, that Mother Teresa was morally better than Adolf Hitler, and that the Earth is the third planet from the Sun . . .*

*During his presidential campaign, Senator Obama affirmed his support for the right to abortion by explaining that he did not want his daughters to be "punished with a baby" if they made a mistake. He made no secret of his desire to repeal the Hyde Amendment, which prohibits federal tax dollars from being used to pay for abortions except those intended to save the life of the mother or for women who had become pregnant as a result of rape or incest. He also declared during his campaign that he would sign into law the Freedom of Choice Act (FOCA), a piece of federal legislation that would eliminate restrictions on state and federal funding of abortion as well as virtually all state and federal restrictions on abortion, including the federal and state partial-birth abortion bans and parental notification and consent statutes. It would also eliminate conscience clauses that presently allow pro-life health care workers to opt out of performing or participating in abortions or referring patients to abortion providers . . .*

*And earlier this month, the president lifted the ban on federal funding of embryo-destruction research.*

*This executive order also permitted human cloning as well as funding for it, with the caveat that no human clone may be implanted in a womb and brought to term. A human clone, according to the president's order, may only be used for research purposes. So, for the first time in American history, a president has by executive order mandated that some human beings, merely because of the means by which they came into being, must be destroyed as a matter of federal law. And finally, the president rescinded the Mexico City policy that prohibited U.S. funds to be used for the procuring of abortions internationally.*

*So, this is the man on whom the University of Notre Dame wants to bestow an honorary doctorate of laws? But, as we have clearly seen, Obama, in spite of all his personal talents and accomplishments, explicitly and unapologetically rejects the intrinsic dignity of the human person, the proper subject of the natural and canonical laws on which the university's jurisprudential patrimony rests. It is a jurisprudential patrimony that the university not only claims to believe, it claims both to believe that it is true and that it knows that it is true. . .*

*We should defer again to the words of Martin Luther King Jr.:*

*"There was a time when the church was very powerful—in the time when the early Christians rejoiced at being deemed worthy to suffer for what they believed. In those days the church was not merely a thermometer that recorded the ideas and principles of popular opinion; it was a thermostat that transformed the mores of society. Whenever the early Christians entered a town, the people in power became disturbed and immediately sought to convict the Christians for being "disturbers of the peace" and "outside agitators." But the Christians pressed on, in*

*the conviction that they were "a colony of heaven," called to obey God rather than man. Small in number, they were big in commitment. They were too God-intoxicated to be "astronomically intimidated."* ***By their effort and example they brought an end to such ancient evils as infanticide*** *and gladiatorial contests. Things are different now. So often the contemporary church is a weak, ineffectual voice with an uncertain sound. So often it is an arch-defender of the status quo. Far from being disturbed by the presence of the church, the power structure of the average community is consoled by the church's silent—and often even vocal—sanction of things as they are.*

*But the judgment of God is upon the church as never before. If today's church does not recapture the sacrificial spirit of the early church, it will lose its authenticity, forfeit the loyalty of millions, and be dismissed as an irrelevant social club with no meaning for the twentieth [and twenty-first] century."*

How incredibly ironic and altogether tragic that the Christian institution influenced by Reverend Hesburgh for the last sixty years - the same Reverend Hesburgh that once walked arm-in-arm with the same Reverend King - would turn its back on King's profound teachings at a pivotal moment of truth, to honor such a deeply misguided African-American man as symbolic of our supposed progress in the struggle for social justice and civil rights.

***President Barack Obama wearing Notre Dame's traditional doctoral robe inscribed with prayer to Virgin Mary, May 17, 2009. (AP Photos)***

*From CNSNews.com - While receiving an honorary doctorate in law from the University of Notre Dame yesterday, President Barack Obama wore the school's traditional doctoral robe that is inscribed with a prayer to the Virgin Mary as a reminder that all of the school's activities are dedicated to the Mother of God.*

*The robe is inscribed with two copies—one on each breast--of Notre Dame's coat of arms, which includes the words "Vita, Dulcedo, Spes," which are part of the traditional Roman Catholic prayer the Salve Regina— or Hail Holy Queen.*

*"The phrase 'Vita, Dulcedo, Spes,' taken from the
ancient prayer to the Virgin, the 'Salve Regina,' means
'our life, our sweetness, our hope' and the combination
of these phrases with the symbol for the university
indicates the dedication of all Notre Dame's activities,
intellectual, spiritual, athletic, and so on, to Our Lady,"
explained the February 1931 issue of the Notre Dame
Alumnus magazine.*

## <u>SALVE REGINA</u>

*Hail Holy Queen, Mother of Mercy,
our life, our sweetness, and our hope.
To thee do we cry, poor banished children of Eve.
To thee do we send up our sighs,
mourning and weeping in this valley of tears.
Turn then, thy most gracious advocate,
thine eyes of mercy towards us.
And after this our exile,
show unto us the blessed fruit of thy womb,
Jesus.
O clement, O loving, O sweet Virgin Mary!
Pray for us, O Holy Mother of God,
that we may be made worthy of the promises of Christ.*

# 18

# Where Are The Fighting Irish?

The irony of ignoring King in order to honor Obama did not end with Notre Dame's May '09 Commencement, but lingered on. While Jenkins was preparing to wow his captive audience, Notre Dame campus security personnel were rounding up 88 peaceful protestors on other parts of the campus. These protestors, according to Thomas Breicha, had been there "to bear peaceful, prayerful witness to the sanctity of human life. . . praying the rosary and singing religious hymns," only to be "arrested, handcuffed, and hauled off to jail where they spent the night and sometimes longer." But this was not enough to satisfy the insult to Notre Dame's institutional integrity.  Notre Dame would not ask that the charges be dropped. The charges would be pressed, the trespassers prosecuted, or asked to play their get out of jail free cards, and pay diversionary fines and fees.

Breicha, a Notre Dame alumnus, would know.  As chief counsel at the Chicago-based civil rights law firm known as The Thomas More Society, he was the lead lawyer in the defense of this All-American legion of "88" subway Irish. Breicha's firm was first founded for the express purpose of defending a similar case in which he successfully cited that very same letter from Martin Luther King's Birmingham jail cell to show that his pro-life clients had legally engaged in "peacable, non-violent direct action." The name of the case was the *National Organization for Women (NOW) v. Scheidler*, and the fight would last a full twenty years.  In the end, justice would prevail, the United States Supreme Court siding with defendants in each of two successive landmark cases.

Among the many notable defendants in the Notre Dame case were Norma McCorvey, the reformed "Jane Roe" from *Roe v. Wade*, and Jane Brennan (*Motherhood Interrupted*), who preaches in Archbishop Chaput's Denver diocese "about hope and healing after abortion."  However, the most compelling witness to life among them was Father Norman Weslin.  Breschia was his attorney too, but in an earlier case, another attorney by the name of Charlie Rice (*What Happened to Notre Dame?, St. Augustine Press, 2009)* had gotten to know the man.  Here is how Notre Dame's Emeritus Law Professor Rice, now deceased, described the case in general, and his former client in particular, in an open letter to Father Jenkins dated September 21, 2009:

> *Those 88 defendants were on the other side of the campus, far removed from the site of the Commencement. They are subjected by Notre Dame to the criminal process because they came, as individuals, to Notre Dame to pray, peacefully and non-obstructively, on this ordinarily open campus, in petition and reparation, as a response to what they rightly saw as a facilitation by Notre Dame of various objectively evil policies and programs of Notre Dame's honoree, President Obama. Those persons, whom Notre Dame has subjected to legal process as criminals, are neither statistics nor abstractions. Let me tell you about a few of them.*
>
> *Fr. Norman Weslin, O.S., 79 years old and in very poor health, was handcuffed by Notre Dame Security Police as he sang "Immaculate Mary" on the campus sidewalk near the entrance. He asked them, "Why would you arrest a Catholic priest for trying to stop the killing of a baby?" The NSDP officers put him on a pallet and dragged him away to jail. St. Joseph County Police were also there. I urge you to watch the readily available videos of Fr. Weslin's arrest [on Youtube and other internet sites]. If you do, I will be surprised and disappointed if you are not personally and deeply ashamed.*
>
> *Such treatment of such a priest may be the lowest point in the entire history of Notre Dame. You would profit from knowing Fr. Weslin. Notre Dame should give Fr. Weslin the Laetare Medal rather than*

*throw him in jail. Norman Weslin, born to poor Finnish immigrants in upper Michigan, finished high school at age 17 and joined the Army. He converted from the Lutheran to the Catholic faith and married shortly after earning his commission. He became a paratrooper and rose to the rank of Lieutenant Colonel in the 82nd Airborne Division, obtaining his college degree enroute. After a distinguished career, he retired in 1968. As the legalization of abortion intensified, he and his wife, Mary Lou, became active pro-lifers in Colorado. In 1980, Mary Lou was killed by a drunk driver. Norman personally forgave the young driver. Norman Weslin was later ordained as a Catholic priest, worked with Mother Teresa in New York and devoted himself to the rescue of unborn children through nonviolent, prayerful direct action at abortuaries. In 1990 at Christmastime, I was privileged to defend Fr. Weslin and his Lambs of Christ when they were arrested at the abortuary in South Bend. One does not have to agree with the tactic of direct, non-violent action at abortuaries to have the utmost admiration, as I have, for Fr. Weslin and his associates. At Notre Dame, Fr. Weslin engaged in no obstruction or disruption. He merely sought to pray for the unborn on the ordinarily open campus of a professedly Catholic university. The theme of Notre Dame's honoring of Obama was "dialogue." It would have been better for you and the complicit Fellows and Trustees to dialogue with Fr. Weslin rather than lock him up as a criminal. You all could have learned something from him. His actions in defense of innocent life and the Faith have been and are heroic.*

It would take 2 years of relentless pressure from Rice and other influential figures before Notre Dame was finally persuaded to drop all charges against the "88" in May of 2011. Unfortunately, this is not the only way in which Notre Dame has persistently exhibited an unwillingness to publicly associate its once sacred and glorious name with a fundamental Catholic doctrine which finds origin and expression in Our Lady herself; Mary the Immaculate Conception; Mary the Mother of God. Case in point:

During the nationally televised broadcasts of Notre Dame football games over the last 12 years (2007 – 2018), millions of viewers have been treated to compelling clips of Notre Dame engaging in a variety of unquestionably worthwhile social justice endeavors all over the world.  These clips (Ironically 88 of them at last count – February 14, 2019) are thematically connected in that they all come to the same stirring end - with the bold assertion, echoed by each of three proud participants, that "we are. . .we are. . .we are . . . *The Fighting Irish!*"  In addition to television, each of these clips can be viewed on the internet at Notre Dame's website (fightingfor.nd.edu), or on its associated Youtube channel.

This author's personal favorite video by far is the "Bengal Bouts."  It explains that for the last 80 years, going all the way back to the Rockne era, Notre Dame students have trained for and participated in exhibition boxing matches to raise money for the Holy Cross missions in Bangladesh, not far from Mother Teresa's Calcutta.  The inspirational motto of the Bengal Bouts is "strong bodies fight, that weak bodies may be nourished."  Mike Weber, 2008-09 Captain of the Notre Dame Men's Boxing Team, puts it this way: "We're not only fighting for ourselves.  We're not only fighting so that we can grow.  We're fighting so others can grow.  That mentality is so essential to what the Notre Dame experience is."  Fighting so others can grow.  That could be the motto of another video, one showing Notre Dame at battle for the millions of unborn.  If only it were so, Saint Teresa would say.

Another video which begs the question is "Fighting for a Voice", wherein international students from oppressive regimes make lasting impressions on U.S. students about the value that democracy lends their voices, and the solemn obligations that go with it.  So, where is the video of those fighting for the silenced voices of the most vulnerable, inside their mothers' womb, or even for the voice of democracy itself, smothered by *Roe v. Wade*?

Then there is the heart-rending footage about "Fighting for the Lives of Children," in which viewers learn that three of Coach Ara Parsegian's grandchildren, that is, three of Cindy and Mike

Parsegian's four children, lost their lives at a tender age due to an incurable genetic disorder.  What an extraordinary testimony to Mr. & Mrs. Parsegian's incredible courage. The courage to say yes to new life, even in the face of death, knowing how those deaths would tear at their hearts.  The Parsegian's were proving the sanctity of life by portraying a level of parental love that knows no limits to sacrifice. Why didn't Notre Dame come right out and say so?  Why not say that we should all "Fight for Life" - no matter what?  What viewer would react to this in any other way than to stand up and cheer, and wipe away tears?  Surely, no one worthy of "dialogue."

Getting closer to the issue is the footage of "Fighting to Restore Vision", where Notre Dame scientists use only adult stem cells to experiment with zebra fish, which apparently have the capacity to regenerate tissue and organs, and may hold the key to curing blindness, as well as Alzheimer's and Parkinson's disease.  With this, the camera pans across the candles in the Grotto, while the narrator says: "As a Catholic university, Notre Dame is committed to cutting edge research, respects the dignity of human life from conception to death, and does <u>not</u> engage in human embryonic stem cell research." Here Notre Dame is getting somewhere, but why still so squeamish about discussing abortion, the single most important social justice issue since slavery?

Father Hesburgh, in "Fighting for Democracy," a segment about changing the lives of oppressed Chileans, said this: "Movements are successful if they have great leadership, and . . . Our task is **to go where human dignity is being violated**, and . . . **get in there and change the tide**. . ."  How about going wherever it takes to relentlessly defend the womb - home to the very origins of human dignity and site of the ultimate violence against it - and changing the blood-tide of abortions performed by profiteers like Planned Parenthood?  How about "Fighting for Rachel's Children?"

Just one video, perhaps of high-tech sonogram footage, images of infants "Fighting For Their Precious Lives."

After all, there are already multiple separate videos on fighting for our precious environment, notably including "The Catholic University and Sustaining the Environment," which teaches that "the primary argument is a theological one.  If we understand humanity as created in the image of God and part of God's creation, [but] live in ways that are unsustainable, we are really severing our relationship with God."  But what could be more unsustainable to our eternal souls than the elimination of 60 million of God's greatest creations in the United States alone.  Where is there just one video on that?

In sum, while "We are the Fighting Irish" is the obvious common theme of Notre Dame's national public relations campaign, there is another theme that 'silently screams' from behind the scenes. It is one, this author is deeply sad to say, which tells us that the Fighting Irish have been part-time cowards, conspicuously absent from the democratic "dialogue" (which <u>Roe</u> stole from us) when it comes to any organized efforts to bring legalized abortion on demand (the sin that <u>Roe</u> has visited on us) to some merciful end.  Never mind education, encouragement, and adoption for a moment (although there are no videos on these either).  These are all well and good, and who besides the bean counters at Planned Parenthood cannot agree on these.  No. We are talking here about openly, regularly, and fearlessly advocating that *Roe v Wade* be overturned so that so that the people in our "pluralistic society", the people in each and every state, can have a "meaningful dialogue" about it again. States in a nation whose people have been telling us, in poll after poll, that they don't agree, and in fact have never knowingly agreed, with the real ruling and the actual consequences of *Roe v. Wade*.  This would not require Notre Dame to embrace the bombing of abortion clinics, or bloody fetuses flying overhead.  All it would require is a little resolve, an ounce of that which Christ showed us when He got up off his knees at Gethsemane, and went to pick up His Cross. Apparently, as the polls point out, not to mention other indicators, there is evidence of a *Springtime of Evangelization* blooming in many places, but not yet at Notre Dame, where wintertime's "lake effect" has been lingering far too long.

If history is any indication, fear is the primary factor. Fear of intimidation.  Fear of ridicule.  Fear of false accusations of intolerance by the intolerant.  Fear of some fleeting loss of inflated academic freedom. Fear that has taught Notre Dame how to comfortably sit complicit with eugenicists, so long as it suffers no unseemly associations with the likes of Father Weslin.  Better that he be hauled away to jail than be seen and heard on campus, carrying his cross, and singing *Immaculate Mary*.

# 19

# Will Notre Dame Reclaim
# The Glory of Her Name?

As explained by the legal team of the United States Conference of Catholic Bishops, and acknowledged by many others on both sides of the issue, the Obamacare bill adopted by the Senate about a year after Notre Dame's invitation to Obama, and with Obama's explicit encouragement to the Senate – (1) earmarked $11 billion dollars directly to Community Health Centers for services that will certainly include abortion absent clear and specific additional legislative action; (2) established certain insurance plans which mandate the payment of premiums for contraception and abortion services; and (3) was absent necessary conscience protections for medical professionals and faith-based institutions.

For these reasons, and despite President Obama's support, Congressman Bart Stupak had led a small coalition of Democrats in the House of Representatives (including a certain congressman from South Bend, Indiana) against the approval of the Senate bill, and in favor of the so-called "Stupak Amendment" which would have solved most of the abortion-funding and conscience protection problems created by the Senate Bill.

Once again, Obama interceded on the side of the Senate bill, and in a despicably dishonest way. He did this by offering Stupak and his pals phony political cover in the form of an essentially meaningless and ineffective presidential Executive Order. While this Order purported to express an intention on the part of the president that his healthcare legislation not do what it clearly did about abortion-funding and conscience protection, it is meaningless because the courts have made it clear that presidential executive orders cannot and do not trump legal statutes adopted by Congress. If they did, the system of checks and balances established by the founding fathers would be easily destroyed, and the president would have essentially absolute power. In other words, we'd be back to the system over which we'd fought the Revolutionary War.

And so, either Obama knew this when he signed the Order, and did it anyway as a cheap parlor trick, or he didn't know it, in which case serious questions would have to be raised about his basic legal competency (notwithstanding his Harvard Law Degree), and that of his administration. In any event, his ramming of this abortion-friendly legislation through Congress, over the objections of the American public and with absolutely no bipartisan support whatsoever, spoke volumes about the Trustees of Notre Dame, and their naive quest for "meaningful dialogue."

Would that this were the worst of it. Alas, according to at least one wire service, on Sunday, March 21, 2010, almost one year to the day from when Notre Dame announced that it would honor President Obama –

> *In the tense hours Sunday leading up to the House vote on a historic health care bill, House Speaker Nancy Pelosi, D-Calif., took time to call the former president of Notre Dame, the Reverend Theodore Hesburgh.*
>
> *[Pelosi] was not seeking spiritual guidance. What she wanted was Hesburgh to help lock up the vote of Representative Joe Donnelly, a Democrat from South Bend, Indiana, who was wavering over the abortion issue. Donnelly ultimately pressed the yes button late Sunday night [and ultimately lost his Senate seat in November 2018 on the heels of his failure to support the confirmation of Justice Bret Kavanaugh to the Supreme Court seat vacated by Justice Kennedy.]*

According to the Sycamore Trust, watchdog to Notre Dame and witness to its steadily eroding Catholic character, Congressman Donnelly confirmed that Father Hesburgh did in fact call him on Pelosi's behalf, but did not tell him how to vote. Nevertheless, after Hesburgh's call, Donnelly voted with Pelosi and helped pass Obama's pro-abortion health care bill. Now there's some "meaningful dialogue."

Within weeks of the passage of the bill, Planned Parenthood announced plans to open two new "community health centers" in Detroit, Michigan and St. Paul, Minnesota, in order to deal with the expected "onslaught" of women seeking abortions in the wake of the bill and the $11 billion dollars in funding expected to flow from it.

Then, in August of 2011, the Obama administration formally announced plans to mandate coverage for contraception and abortion-inducing drugs.  This exposed Obama's Executive Order as a sham, and unleashed a firestorm of criticism from the U.S. Conference of Catholic Bishops and like-minded Christians across the country.  It also exposed Notre Dame's efforts at dialogue –which it continued for the next two years - to be so much folly; until its Trustees were left with no choice but to deal with the ever-growing scandal and implicitly concede their "big mistake".

They did this by suing the Obama administration in May of 2013 for a conscience clause to exempt Notre Dame and other faith-based institutions from obeying the mandate.  In short, Notre Dame was reduced to filing a lawsuit against the very man upon whom they'd conferred an honorary doctor of laws degree.  Coincidentally, or perhaps providentially, another pivotal event occurred at Notre Dame in May of 2013.  May 19th, to be specific, Pentecost Sunday. That is the day when Timothy Cardinal Dolan - the very man who'd told Notre Dame they'd made a "big mistake" honoring Obama in 2009 – gave the Commencement address to Notre Dame's 2013 graduating class, and was awarded an Honorary Doctor of Laws Degree. Now, Dolan is not a lawyer, except in the ecclesiastical sense, but that's a different degree. So, draw your own conclusions.  Here is what the good Cardinal said:


*Thank you, Notre Dame, for the joy of your*
*company, the gracious invitation, the warm welcome,*

*and the high honor of this degree. It was so obvious I almost missed it . . .*

*See, ever since, almost a year ago, Father Jenkins, with characteristic thoughtfulness, invited me to deliver this commencement address, I've been mulling over just what to say to you, class of 2013. Only Friday a week ago I still had not yet completed this talk, and I got on the train in New York City to travel to D.C. In Philadelphia, a distinguished looking man boarded the train and sat next to me.*

*He turned out to be a fanatical, in-your-face, obnoxious Notre Dame alumnus! You ever met one? Nice to meet you! Now I guess I am proudly one, after the privilege of this honorary degree which I so appreciate and cherish!*

*He begins to speak with obviously radiant pride and gratitude about Notre Dame, telling me his faithful Jewish parents wanted him to attend a Catholic college - - because, in their words. "The Church founded the universities, and educate better than anybody else" - - and reporting to me that, even as a faithful Jew, he considers his four years here at this Catholic university a gift beyond measure. When I told him I'd be here for graduation, he beamed.*

*"Father," he went on, holding my arm and looking me in the eye, "let me tell you the secret of Notre Dame. It's*

*not the library, as first-rate as it is; it's not the
professors and courses, as stellar as they are; it's not
the campus, as enchanting as it is, or even the football
team, as legendary as it is. No, the secret of Notre
Dame is really a person, whom we Jews call 'Miriam,'
and you Christians call 'Mary.' She's there . . . she looks
down from the 'golden dome'; and, if you really want
to discover the secret of Notre Dame, visit that grotto
you Catholics call "Lourdes." There's something there .
. . no, there's someone there . . . we call her Notre
Dame, and she's the secret of her university."*

*Thank you, Howard. Hope you're listening to
me now, as you promised me on that train you would.
Because with those words you solved the riddle about
what I should say in these few moments. That was
Mother's Day weekend; it was May, the month
dedicated to her; and I had just returned, with fifty
sick and disabled people, from a pilgrimage to the
"real" Lourdes in France. So obvious I had almost
missed it . . . I'm going to speak of Notre Dame . . .
Notre Dame . . . our Lady . . . Mary, the mother of
Jesus. One can make the point that she's perhaps the
most important human person ever.*

*Even history itself is divided "before" and "after" the
birth she gave to her firstborn. She was there at
Christmas at His birth; at Cana, His first miracle; at
the foot of the cross; at Pentecost, the feast we
celebrate today.*

*"But when the appointed time came, God sent His own Son, born of a woman . . ." St. Paul writes the Galatians;*

*"And while there in Bethlehem, Mary gave birth to her firstborn . . ." records St. Luke;*
*"Mary said to the servants at Cana. 'Do whatever He tells you . . .'" reports St. John;*

*"Near the cross of Jesus stood His mother . . ." recalls the Beloved Disciple;*

*"The apostles were in continuous prayer, together with Mary, the mother of Jesus . . ." writes St. Luke in the Acts of the Apostles, in the account of Pentecost.*

*Notre Dame . . . Our Lady . . .*

*John Ruskin held that "every brightest and loftiest achievement of the arts, dreams, advancement, and progress of humanity has been but the fulfillment of that poor Israelite woman's prayer, 'He who is mighty has magnified me!' . . ."*

*While Wordsworth extolled her as "our tainted nature's solitary boast."*

*"All things rising, all things sizing, Mary sees sympathizing . . ." . . . claims Gerard Manley Hopkins, as you, the class of 2013, have sensed her maternal*

*presence "rising, sizing, and sympathizing" these blessed years on a campus wrapped in her mantle, and praise God that Father Sorin and that pioneer band of priests and brothers of the Congregation of the Holy Cross placed this most noble endeavor under her patronage from day one 171 years ago.*

*Might I propose to you, my new classmates, class of 2013, that she's not just our patroness, but our model. It all comes down to this: she - - Miriam, Mary, Notre Dame, our Lady - - humbly, selflessly, generously, with trust, placed her life in God's hands, allowing her life to unfold according to His plan. She gave God's son a human nature; she gave the Eternal Word - - God the Son, the second Person of the Blessed Trinity - - flesh. That's called the Incarnation. God became one of us.*

*"And the Word became flesh, and dwelt among us." The Incarnation . . .*

*Now, as you complete years at this acclaimed university dedicated to her, you are asked the same pivotal question the Archangel Gabriel once posed to her: will you let God take flesh in you? Will you give God a human nature? Will He be reborn in you? Will the Incarnation continue in and through you?*

*I dare say you gratefully claim that God's Word has certainly taken flesh on this campus in your years here: in your classes and professors, in your friends and service projects, in the prayer and sacraments, in the "all-nighters" and exams, in the memories and promises.*

*And now it's your turn to let God take flesh in your lives.*

*You can answer the way Mary did, "Let it be done to me according Thy will" - - Fiat . . . or, you can reply with a term New Yorkers use, "forgetaboutit!"*

*Notre Dame challenges us to reply, Fiat! Yes! For, at her best, this university has the heart of Mary, meaning this university gives us Jesus and His Church, and clings to them both with love, loyalty, and service.*

*Here at Notre Dame we do not strive to be like Harvard or Oxford, but like Bethlehem, Nazareth, Cana, Calvary, and the Upper Room at Pentecost . . .with Mary, as the "Word becomes flesh" in the one who called Himself "the Way, the Truth and the Life."*

*Here our goal is not just a career, but a call; not just a degree, but discipleship; not just what we've gotten but what we're giving; not just the now but eternity; not just the "I" but the "we"; not just the grades but the gospel.*

*My friend on that train ride ten days ago, now my fellow alumnus of this university, will be glad to know that I took him up on it. Last night I snuck down to discover the secret of Notre Dame. Kind of a cool breeze off the lake; the voices of visiting families and friends, the songs, and laughter subsided as I got close; there were the candles, hundreds of them, with wax droppings to remind us of prayers of past generations; there many of you were, kneeling, standing, sitting on the ground; there was quiet, there was a welcome; there was light; there was peace; there was warmth; there was Notre Dame, Mary, our Lady.*

*There was Bethlehem, as I saw moms, dads and grandparents beaming over their babies of twenty-two years ago, now graduates;*

*There was Nazareth, as families were united in prayers of thanksgiving; There was Cana, as students remembered miracles;*

*There was Calvary, as one or two of you had tears in your eyes, perhaps recalling a past or present cross or crown of Thorns, made a bit more bearable by the one also called the Pieta.*

*There was Pentecost, as this class whispered that favorite prayer of Father Hesburgh, united with Our Lady and the apostles in that Upper Room, Come, Holy Spirit!*

*There, I joined my prayers with yours, with hers, and entrusted her university, with her call, her mission, her Catholic identity, her excellence, yoked to the truth of the Gospel;*

*There I prayed for this class of 2013, their folks and families;*

*There I prayed for Bishop Rhoades, and for our much-missed Bishop D'Arcy, for Father Jenkins, the board, the alumni, the benefactors, the faculty, staff, for Father Dick Warner and Congregation of the Holy Cross.*

*There I prayed for you, Howard . . . because, on that train ride, you were right: at this grotto there's a touch of the transcendent, a hint of the beyond, a whisper of the sacred, that reminds us that we're not just minds and bodies, but hearts and immortal souls, called not to a "crap shoot" called life but an adventure in fidelity that beckons us to cast out to the deep, and, yes, even walk on water toward Him, the Son of God, the Son of Mary; she'd remind us that He has a plan for us, that these years of college have been a part of it, and that we're happiest when our plans are consonant with His.*

*There indeed was the secret of Notre Dame, not something but someone: our Lady, who gave the Divine a human nature, and invites us, equipped, please God, with what she's given us here, to do the same!*

*Congratulations Class of 2013. May Jesus Christ be praised!*

*May Notre Dame, our Lady, reign in our hearts! Tell the world our secret!*

Then in 2014, about a year after Cardinal Dolan's deeply moving Commencement Speech, Notre Dame's Center for Ethics and Culture invited staunchly pro-life New Jersey Congressman Chris Smith to receive its annual *Evangelium Vitae* Medal, an award which was inspired by St. John Paul II the Great's aforementioned encyclical of the same name – The Gospel of Life.  The medal was given to Congressman Smith during a celebratory dinner, which was followed by Mass at Notre Dame's Basilica of the Sacred Heart. During his acceptance speech, Smith quoted St. Patrick, who'd suffered through huge obstacles thrown at him by Ireland's secular rulers: "I cannot keep silent" said Patrick . . . "[E]xalt Him and confess His wonders before every nation under heaven."

That same year, however, Notre had to start providing contraception and abortion insurance coverage after the Federal Seventh Circuit Court of Appeals ruled in favor of the Obama administration in the lawsuit that Notre Dame had filed against it.

Then in October 2017, with Obama gone, HHS, the federal agency responsible for enforcing the contraception and abortion mandates, announced that it would not do so with respect to faith-based institutions.  Initially, Notre Dame fully embraced this decision and announced that it would discontinue the coverage.  Of course, this prompted high praise from one side of the cultural aisle, and scathing criticisms from the other.  So, in February of 2018, Notre Dame announced a modification of its original decision to discontinue coverage completely.  In short, coverage for "simple contraceptives" would be resumed, but coverage for "abortion-inducing" drugs would remain unavailable.  Here is the full text of Father Jenkins' letter explaining Notre Dame's decision:

*Dear Faculty and Staff,*

*In recent weeks I have received a number of emails and letters about the University's policy on access to contraceptive coverage, and I have spoken personally to faculty, staff and students about this matter. I addressed the topic initially in my Address to the Faculty in November, and have had the chance to give it further thought with the benefit of additional information. I write to announce steps based on Catholic principles that nevertheless provide access to some of the coverage that members of our community seek.*

*As I stated in my Faculty Address on November 7, 2017, the University joined a lawsuit against the U.S. Department of Health and Human Services and other federal agencies to challenge a mandate requiring employers to provide a range of what were called "contraceptive drugs and services." As I said then, the mandate was not part of the Affordable Care Act legislation passed by Congress, but was an administrative decree that was part of the implementation of the Act.  It departed from a long tradition in federal law by distinguishing between religious institutions that were exempt, such as parishes, and those that were not, such as universities and hospitals, and it created a precedent for further constraints on the latter's religious freedom. The University of Notre Dame joined other plaintiffs in challenging this mandate to protect its ability to act in accord with its religious mission.*

*A federal court decision compelled the University to provide the challenged drugs and services through its third-party insurance administrator and funded by the government. Consequently, those enrolled in our health plans have had access to these drugs and services since January 2014. In October 2017, however, the case was settled favorably, giving the University, its insurers and third-party administrators the option of an exemption from providing these drugs and services.*

*The use of artificial contraceptives to prevent conception is contrary to Catholic teaching, though many conscientiously disagree with this particular teaching. When I delivered my Faculty Address in November, I thought it best, having established our right to decide, to allow the government-funded provision of these drugs and services to continue so that our employees could have access without University funding or immediate and direct involvement in their provision. The government-funded program, however, also includes abortifacients, which, because they involve the destruction of innocent human life, are most gravely objectionable in the Catholic tradition. With further thought, wider consultation and more information, I concluded that it was best to reconsider this decision.*

*We must be unwavering in our fidelity to our Catholic mission at Notre Dame, while we recognize that among the values in our Catholic tradition is a respect for other religious traditions and the conscientious decisions of members of our community. Our health plans cover over 17,000 people—a group consisting of employees, students not covered by their parents' plan (who are primarily graduate students) and their respective family members. A tension exists between establishing policies in accord with Catholic teaching and respecting the religious traditions and decisions of the many members of our community. That tension is particularly pronounced in the area of health care, where the University recognizes its responsibility, grounded in its Catholic mission, to provide health insurance to employees, their families and many students, and most of those covered have no financially feasible alternative but to rely on the University for such coverage. The various parties are constrained in such a way that the decisions of the University inevitably affect those who rely on it for insurance.*

*The situation is one that demands discernment— something to which Pope Francis has called the Church in his various writings and addresses. Discernment, which has a long history in the Catholic spiritual tradition, is, of course, a process of weighing thoughtfully considerations for and against various courses of action. Yet it also demands prayerful attention to God's guidance through the prompting of the Holy Spirit.*

*As noted above, allowing the government-funded provision of drugs and services to continue through a third-party administrator would provide access to contraceptives without University funding or immediate involvement. The government-funded program, however, includes the provision of abortion-inducing drugs, which are far more gravely objectionable in Catholic teaching. Stopping any access to contraceptives through our health care plan would allow the University to be free of involvement with drugs that are morally objectionable in Catholic teaching, but it would burden those who have made conscientious decisions about the use of such drugs and rely on the University for health care benefits.*

*I have reached the conclusion that it is best that the University stop the government-funded provision of the range of drugs and services through our third-party administrator. Instead, the University will provide coverage in the University's own insurance plans for simple contraceptives (i.e., drugs designed to prevent conception). The University will also provide in its plans funding for natural family planning options—options that do not use artificial contraceptives but employ natural methods for preventing conception. The University's insurance*

*plans (as opposed to the government-funded program)
have never covered, and will not cover, abortion-
inducing drugs.*

*Sterilization procedures for the purpose of preventing
conception (as opposed to those intended to treat an
illness) have never been covered and will not be
covered in the University's insurance plans. Although
contraceptive in nature, permanent sterilization
through surgical intervention in a healthy bodily
organ is viewed as more gravely objectionable than
contraceptive drugs in Catholic teaching.*

*The University will provide to all who sign up for
health care benefits a statement of the Catholic
teaching on contraceptives, so that the Church's
teaching is clearly presented. Although Pope Paul VI's
Encyclical letter, Humanae vitae, written nearly fifty
years ago now, has been controversial within and
without Catholic circles since its publication, its
prophetic quality is clear. It remains an important and
thoughtful challenge to tendencies in our culture, even
more pronounced today, toward the sexual
objectification of women, the decline of committed and
faithful marriages and family life, the threat of
government intervention in human procreation, the
lack of a healthy respect for the natural processes of
our bodies and the threats of manipulation of our
bodies and our environment through technology. I
hope the University statement will invite reflection on
the important moral questions at stake.*

*Some will ask why the University sued the government over the provision of "contraceptive drugs and services" only now to provide contraceptives in its plan. What we sincerely and firmly fought for in court was the ability, as a Catholic institution, to make decisions about the provision of health care consistent with Catholic principles. Until the federal mandate was imposed on us, we were among relatively few Catholic universities that excluded from our health plans contraceptives, except when prescribed to treat a medical condition. Having been required to provide access to contraceptives for several years, we now take account of the fact that some of those enrolled in our health plans — an increasingly diverse group — have come to rely on access to contraceptives through enrollment in our plans. While some may criticize the approach above as overly restrictive and others as not restrictive enough, it is our best effort to respect the many considerations at stake in a manner consistent with Catholic principles. The purpose of our lawsuit was to win the right to make that effort.*

*In order to provide time for all to prepare for this change, we will implement it in the middle of the plan year for employees on July 1, 2018. The Office of Human Resources will communicate to you more information about this change in March. The change to the student health plan will begin with its new plan year in August 2018.*

*I conclude by thanking all those who have offered their thoughts on this matter. I thank every member of this*

What a remarkable letter; an open window where the fresh air of authentic faith can be tasted; the warm sunshine of hope seen seeping through some parting clouds; a window into the heart and mind of a very fine man and priest, trying mightily to reconcile academic freedom in an increasingly secular progressive society with the immutable truths and teachings of the Magisterium of the Catholic Church, to which Notre Dame owes its faithful allegiance, its Catholic identity, and indeed its very name, as so poignantly explained by Cardinal Dolan.

That said, two additional observations are in order.

First, Father Jenkins' contention that the contraception and abortion mandates were only in the administrative regulations and directives which implemented the Obamacare Act, and not in the text of the Act itself, is pure legal sophistry unfit for inclusion in an otherwise wonderful letter. Perhaps Father Jenkins added it defend Father Hesburgh's telephone call to Congressman Donnelly, but everyone familiar with what was actually happening, including Father Hesburg's phone pal, Nancy Pelosi (who famously said Obamacare would have to be enacted before anyone knew what was really in it), knew full well the inevitable consequences of Obamacare when it came to contraception and abortion.  The problem for Father Jenkins here is that in defending Father Hesburgh and whoever else among the ND Trustees may have been supportive of Obamacare, he indicts Obama himself by suggesting that things were just fine with Obamacare until his administration gave the green light to implementing contraception and abortion mandates; which brings us to the second, even more startling and disturbing observation concerning events described in Father Jenkins' letter.

If Notre Dame had never provided contraception coverage before Obama's mandate, but has now decided to continue providing it because the Notre Dame family has become accustomed to it since implementation of the Obama mandate, then Notre Dame has in effect allowed itself to become the instrument by which Obama has perpetuated fulfillment of the elegant prophecy in the *Humanae Vitae* encyclical of Paul Paul VI (see Chapter 8), ironically referenced in Jenkins' letter.  Surely, this observation is not lost on Jenkins, a man of considerable scholarship.  One has to wonder whether he's looked back and winced when he realized where the once ostracized George Shuster and his friends had led Father Jenkins' late great predecessor, Father Ted.

Alas, much like the majority members of the Supreme Court in *Dredd Scott, Rove v. Wade, and Planned Parenthood v. Casey*, who all hoped they were helping to put a divisive social justice issue to rest, Father Jenkins now finds Notre Dame a defendant in a lawsuit, started by Notre Dame's own students in June of 2018, to get their abortion pills back; likewise do the Sisters of the Poor, in litigation instigated in January of 2019 by pro-choice activists in 13 states to prevent the current administration from enforcing the exemptions it has given to the Sisters, to Notre Dame, and to other faith-based organizations. Meanwhile, professors from Notre Dame's Gender Studies Department are busy defending abortion rights by mouthing the latest pro-choice talking point – that the pro-life movement is nothing but a bunch of white supremacists.

As this book prepares to go to print, Notre Dame's 2008 Commencement Speaker and Honorary Doctor of Laws Degree recipient, former Cardinal Theodore McCarrick, has been permanently ejected from the priesthood by Pope Francis for decades of sexually predatory behavior toward minors and young adult seminarians; tried and found guilty of several crimes, including "solicitation in the Sacrament of Confession, and sins against the Sixth Commandment with minors and adults, with the aggravating factor of the abuse of power," pronounced the Vatican on February 16, 2019, according to the New York Times. Upon receiving the news, Notre Dame formally rescinded McCarrick's 2008 honorary degree after resisting months of pressure to act earlier.  Poor Father Jenkins must wish his dear friend Father Ted was still around to toss back some beers together, or maybe something a wee bit stronger.

But it's wonderful beyond words, for the author of this book now a decade in the making, that he's able to complete it with news which could not be more encouraging to all those who've been grieving for the last 10 years; From the Reverend John L. Jenkins, C.S.C., President of the University of Notre Dame, February 7, 2019:

*In recent weeks, New York state legislators passed and its governor signed into law a bill sweeping away protections for unborn — and some born — children. New York law now allows abortions any time up until delivery for vaguely defined reasons of "health," including social well-being. The legislators removed from law provisions that require the mother's consent, that allow manslaughter charges against an abortionist who causes the woman's death during an abortion, that discourage self-induced abortions and — shockingly — that require care for a child born alive during an attempted late-term abortion. [House Minority Whip Steve Scalise (R-La.) and Rep. Ann Wagner (R-Mo.) introduced a resolution on Wednesday (Feb. 6) that would require babies who survive attempted abortions to receive medical care; Sen. Ben Sasse (R-Neb.) also tried to seek unanimous consent for a similar law, but was defeated by the objections of Sen. Patty Murray (D-Wash.).] The New York law has been described by abortion rights advocates as an "inflection point" that will add momentum for expanded access to abortion in states such as Connecticut, Colorado, Delaware, Massachusetts, New Jersey, New Mexico and Wisconsin.*

*Signed on Jan. 22, the anniversary of Roe v. Wade, the law is seen as a reaction to a potential threat to that decision in the Supreme Court as currently composed. As such, the legislative initiative follows a pattern, adopted by both left and right, that makes our political life today so toxic: When your position is challenged, adopt an even more extreme, inflexible version of it, thereby eliminating any possibility of any reasonable compromise. We see that pattern in debates about immigration, a border wall and international agreements. It recently shut down our government for 35 days.*

*The new legislation will no doubt deepen the wound on the body politic that is the abortion controversy. In addition to aggravating the denial of equal justice under law for the unborn, it will steal away the time, energy and goodwill we need to work together as a society to require that men support the children they father and the women who are their partners, and to strengthen families. It will distract us from efforts to provide financial, medical and emotional support for expectant mothers, and daycare, access to good schools for their children, health care and economic opportunities for them when a child is born.*

*The laws that have, throughout human history, protected unborn and new life did not arise from some obscure ecclesiastical doctrine or particular ideology, but from a moral instinct we all share to care for innocent human life.* **As the late Pennsylvania Gov. Robert Casey said on a visit to Notre Dame, "A pro-life consensus ... grows every time someone looks at a sonogram."** *Such a sensibility is fundamental to human civilization. It is behind not only laws that protect the unborn or infants, but the protection for all innocent and vulnerable life. The great threat of the New York law is not only that it will remove protections for children in or recently out of the womb as well as for the mothers' lives, but that it will also further numb this moral instinct so central to our common life. History, sadly, is full of examples where the lives of one or another group is deemed not worthy of protection — whether it is the physically disabled, the cognitively impaired, certain ethnic groups or the old and infirm. As we contemplate the effects of this law and the lives it will take, we can only ask, with fear and trembling, "Who is next?"*

Thank you, Father Jenkins.

May Notre Dame at last reclaim the Glory of Her Sacred Name.

***GO IRISH!!!***

# Author's Note

If you believe others would benefit from reading this book, please consider sharing your sentiments by alerting your family and Facebook friends, and by posting a review on Amazon. Just go to Amazon.com/author/patrickxavier and click through to the page where the book is being offered for sale. Thank you.

# About the Author

Patrick X. Amoresano was born in Paterson, New Jersey, on September 13, 1953, and grew up in nearby Glen Rock, where he lived with his wife Carolyn until they moved to Belmar in 2014. Pat has 6 kids (Luke, Mary, Mike, Elaine, Joe, and Frank), and 2 grand kids (Josh and Matt), each one of them a miracle and a blessing. Pat himself was the 3rd of Winnie and Floyd's 5 kids. Winnie Richmond's blood line traces back to Donegal, Ireland, and Kilwinning, Scotland. Floyd's blood line traces back to the Salerno and Calabria regions of Italy, and then further back to Spain, some believe. Amoresano means "love and health" in Italian, and "perfect love" in Spanish. Pat loves his last name, and revered his late father, but uses Xavier as a pen name because it fits better on book covers. Plus, it's a pretty neat name for an author, no? 'Twas an Irish priest persuaded his mom to name him Patrick Xavier. Anyway, Pat eventually followed in his father's footsteps and became a lawyer after attending St. Catharine School (now the Academy of Our Lady) in Glen Rock; St. Joseph Regional High School in Montvale; Fordham University in the Bronx; and Seton Hall Law School in Newark.

Pat's been a trial lawyer in New Jersey since 1980, prosecuting mainly medical malpractice and other serious personal injury matters. For a profile of his law practice, or to send him an email, you can visit his website at www.doingjustice.com.

Pat's first book, *From Which We Stem*, is a fast-paced work of legal suspense with a pro-life theme.

Pat is also a Sacristan and Lector at St. Rose of Lima Parish in Belmar; a St. Vincent DePaul Society member; and a volunteer National Disaster Action Team member and Emergency Response Vehicle operator for the American Red Cross.  In his spare time, he's a pretty bad golfer, but a pretty good sous chef for his wife, who's a whiz in the kitchen.  He's been a life-long lover of the Fighting Irish of Notre Dame, where 2 of his kids were attending college when Barack Obama came to campus to receive his Honorary Doctor of Laws degree.  Today, they're both proud members of Notre Dame's outstanding alumni, forever grateful (as am I) for their exceptional education, and the precious time they were privileged to spend there.

# Acknowledgements

To my wonderful Irish mother-in-law, Marion Greehey Casey, who convalesced and passed from this life to the next in my Glen Rock home - in the sun room adjacent to my home office - as I was frantically researching and writing the beginnings of this book in the latter half of 2009; and to my wife, who cared so lovingly for her mom, and put up with me, during that difficult time.

To my fine Irish friend, Sheila O'Halloran Kenny, who read every page of the brutally long and tedious first draft, and offered me invaluable insights.

To my dear and brilliant brother Guy, who read the second draft, and called me with words of encouragement so special they've stayed with me for nearly ten years now, as this finished work prepares for publication.

To the folks at Amazon, Google, and Facebook, without whom the publication and dissemination of this book would simply not have been possible.

To the Good Lord, who never gives up on me, no matter what.

# End Notes

<u>**Prologue**</u>

King, Martin Luther Jr., *A Letter from a Birmingham Jail.* Birmingham, 1963.

<u>**Chapter 1: The Immaculate Conception of Notre Dame**</u>

Holweck, Frederick. "Immaculate Conception." The Catholic Encyclopedia. Vol. 7 New York: Robert Appleton Company, 1910. 18 Feb. 2019<http://www.newadvent.org/cathen/07674d.htm>.

Minges, Parthenius. "Blessed John Duns Scotus." The Catholic Encyclopedia. Vol. 5. New York: Robert Appleton Company, 1909. 18 Feb. 2019<http://www.newadvent.org/cathen/05194a.htm>

O'Connell, Marvin R. *Edward Sorin.* Notre Dame: University of Notre Dame Press, 2001.

Saint Luke *Holy Bible, New Testamant, Gospel of Luke, 1:41-55*

Sorin, Edward *The Chronicles of Notre Dame du Lac.* Notre Dame: University of Notre Dame Press, 1992.

<u>**Chapter 2: Here Come the Irish**</u>

Burton, Edwin, Edward D'Alton, and Jarvis Kelley. "Penal Laws." The Catholic Encyclopedia. Vol. 11. New York: Robert Appleton

Company, 1911. 18 Feb.
2019 <http://www.newadvent.org/cathen/11611c.htm>.

Capt, E. Raymond *Jacob's Pillar-Stone of Destiny*. Muskogee:
Artisan Publishers, 2005.

Carew, Mairead *Tara and the Ark of the Covenant*. Dublin: Royal
Irish Academy, 2003.

Corson, Dorothy V. *The Spirit of Notre Dame: Notre Dame Legends
and Lore*. University of Notre Dame Archives, 1953
<https://www3.nd.edu/~wcawley/corson/whyfightingirish.htm>

Costin, M. Georgia *Priceless Spirit-A History of the Sisters of the
Holy Cross, 1841-1893*. Notre Dame: University of Notre Dame Press,
1994.

D'Alton, Edward. "Daniel O'Connell." <u>The Catholic Encyclopedia.</u> Vol.
11. New York: Robert Appleton Company, 1911. 18 Feb.
2019 <http://www.newadvent.org/cathen/11200c.htm>.

Dolan, Jay P. *The Irish Americans, A History*. New York:
Bloomsbury Press, 2008.

Hope, Arthur J. *The Story of Notre Dame – 100 Years*. Notre Dame:
University of Notre Dame Archives, 1943

Hullfish, William *The Canaller's Songbook: Words, Music and
Chords to over Thirty Canal Songs*. Manchester: American Canal
and Transportation Center, 1984

Klawitter, George *Adapted to the Lake: Letters by the Brother Founders of Notre Dame, 1841–1849*. New York: Peter Lang Publishing Co., 1993.

Koeppel, Gerard *Bond of Union: Building the Erie Canal and the American Empire*. Lebanon: De Capo Press, 2009

Laxton, Edward *The Famine Ships: The Irish Exodus to America*. New York: Henry Holt & Co., 1998

MacEoin, Gary *Basil Moreau-Founder of Holy Cross*. Notre Dame: Ave Maria Press, 2nd ed. 2007.

McGee, Thomas D'Arcy "A Popular History of Ireland: From the Earliest Period to the Emancipation of the Catholics." < <http://www.gutenberg.org/ebooks/6634>

O'Connell, Marvin R. *Edward Sorin*. Notre Dame: University of Notre Dame Press, 2001.

Scully, John and Tullio, Jim *Here Come the Irish*. University of Notre Dame, 1997.<https://strongofheart.nd.edu/profiles/john-scully-2010/>

Sorin, Edward *The Chronicles of Notre Dame du Lac*. Notre Dame: University of Notre Dame Press, 1992.

Tone, Theobold Wolfe *An Argument on Behalf of the Catholics of Ireland*. Belfast: Society of the United Irishmen of Belfast, 1791.

Wikipedia *"Battle of Tara Hill"* *<https://en.wikipedia.org/wiki/Battle_of_Tara_Hill>*

Wikipedia *"Daniel O'Connell"*
*<https://en.wikipedia.org/wiki/Daniel_O'Connell>*

Wikipedia *"The Irish Rebellion of 1641"*
*<https://en.wikipedia.org/wiki/Irish_Rebellion_of_1641>*

Wikipedia *"The Irish Rebellion of 1798"*
*<https://en.wikipedia.org/wiki/Irish_Rebellion_of_1798>*

## Chapter 3: The Wages of Whiteness

Bayor, Ronald H. and Meagher, Timothy J. *The New York Irish*. Baltimore: The Johns Hopkins University Press, 1996

Brownson, Orestes From orestesbrownson.org and/or ewtn.com

Brownson, Orestes "Mary Worship". 1853

Brownson, Orestes "Moral and Social Influence of Devotion to Mary". June, 1866

Brownson, Orestes "Slavery and the Church". October, 1862

Brownson, Orestes "Slavery and the War". 1861

Brownson, Orestes "State Rebellion-State Suicide". April, 1862

Capt, E. Raymond *Jacob's Pillar-Stone of Destiny*. Muskogee: Artisan Publishers, 2005.

Carew, Mairead *Tara and the Ark of the Covenant*. Dublin: Royal Irish Academy, 2003.

Corson, Dorothy V. *A Cave of Candles: The Story Behind Notre Dame's Grotto*. Nairobi: Evangel Publishing House, 2006.

Dolan, Jay P. *The Irish Americans, A History*. New York: Bloomsbury Press, 2008.

Hughes, Archbishop John "Exchange of correspondence with the French Journal des Debats concerning Slavery and Abolition." New York Times, 1862.

Kelly, Joseph "Charleston's Bishop John England and American Slavery" New Hibernia Review / Iris Éireannach Nua Vol. 5, No. 4 (Winter, 2001), pp. 48-56 Published by: University of St. Thomas (Center for Irish Studies) https://www.jstor.org/stable/20557774

Laxton, Edward *The Famine Ships: The Irish Exodus to America*. New York: Henry Holt & Co., 1998

Lee, J.J. and Casey, Marion R. *Making the Irish American: History and Heritage of the Irish in the United States*. New York:  New York University Press, 2006.

Lehrman, Lewis "Archbishop John J. Hughes (1797-1863)" <http://www.mrlincolnandnewyork.org/new-yorkers/archbishop-john-j-hughes-1797-1863>

Man, Albon P. Jr. "The Church and the New York Draft Riots of 1863" Records of the American Catholic Historical Society of Philadelphia Vol. 62, No. 1 (MARCH, 1951), pp. 33-50 Published

by: <u>American Catholic Historical Society</u>
<https://www.jstor.org/stable/44210148>


McAvoy, Thomas T. "Orestes A. Brownson and Archbishop John Hughes in 1860" *The Review of Politics* Vol. 24, No. 1 (Jan., 1962), pp. 19-47 Published by: Cambridge University Press for the University of Notre Dame du lac on behalf of Review of Politics <https://www.jstor.org/stable/1405454>


McGreevy, John T. *Catholicism and American Freedom*. New York: W.W. Norton & Co., 2003


Miller, Randall and Wakelyn, Jon *Catholics in the Old South*. Macon: Mercer University Press, 1999.


Panzer, Joel S. *The Popes and Slavery*. New York: Alba House, 1996.


Pope Eugene IV *Sicut Dudum,* 1435 Papalencyclicals.net


Pope Gregory XVI *In Supremo Apostolatus, 1839* Papalencyclicals.net


Pope Paul III *Sublimis Deus,* 1537 Papalencyclicals.net


Roediger, David R. *The Wages of Whiteness: Race and the Making of the American Working Class*. Brooklyn: Verso Books, 2007

Sorin, Edward *The Chronicles of Notre Dame du Lac*. Notre
Dame: University of Notre Dame Press, 1992.

Sorin, Edward *Miscellaneous Letter between Edward Sorin and
Southern Bishops pertaining to Slavery and the Civil War, etc.*
University of Notre Dame Archives, 1844-1882
<http://archives.nd.edu/cgi-bin/q-ead.pl?keyword=lynch+sorin>
and
<http://archives.nd.edu/cgi-bin/q-ead.pl?keyword=kenrick+sorin>


## **Chapter 4: We Were the Fighting Irish**

Corby, William *Memoirs of Chaplain Life*. New York: Fordham
University Press, 1992.

Costin, M. Georgia *Priceless Spirit-A History of the Sisters of the
Holy Cross, 1841-1893*. Notre Dame: University of Notre Dame Press,
1994.

Dike, Wm. L. *U.S.S. Red Rover, Civil War Hospital Ship*. Baltimore:
Publish America, 2004.

Dolan, Jay P. *The Irish Americans, A History*. New York:
Bloomsbury Press, 2008.

Hope, Arthur J. *The Story of Notre Dame – 100 Years*. Notre Dame:
University of Notre Dame Archives, 1943

Pritchard, Russ A. Jr. *The Irish Brigade*. Philadelphia: Courage
Books, 2004.

Sorin, Edward *The Chronicles of Notre Dame du Lac.* Notre Dame: University of Notre Dame Press, 1992.

Sorin, Edward *Miscellaneous Letter between Edward Sorin and Southern Bishops pertaining to Slavery and the Civil War, etc.* University of Notre Dame Archives, 1844-1882 <http://archives.nd.edu/cgi-bin/q-ead.pl?keyword=lynch+sorin> and
<http://archives.nd.edu/cgi-bin/q-ead.pl?keyword=kenrick+sorin>

————

Miscellaneous papers pertaining to the contributions of the Sisters and Priests of the Congregation of the Holy Cross in ministering to the soldiers who fought in the Civil War were provided courtesy of the Archives at the Sisters of the Holy Cross Library, Notre Dame, Indiana, including but not limited to:

Author Unknown "Absolution Under Fire: [Painting by] Paul Henry Wood, 1872-1892"

Connelly, James C.S.C. "Holy Cross Communities in the Civil War" Austin: 1993 Conference at St. Edward's University.

Wall, Barbara, RN, MS "Grace Under Pressure: The Nursing Sisters of the Holy Cross 1861-1865" Notre Dame: St. Mary's College, Havican Hall. (Undated)

## Chapter 5: Son of Erin, Father of Fighting Irish Football

DeHaven, George W. *Letter to Fielding H. Yost – First Football Encounter Between Michigan and Notre Dame in 1887.* Hollywood, 1939. (Courtesy of the Archives of the University of Michigan).

Klawitter, George *Adapted to the Lake: Letters by the Brother Founders of Notre Dame, 1841–1849.* New York: Peter Lang Publishing Co., 1993.

Kryk, John *Natural Enemies: Major College Football's Oldest, Fiercest Rivalry-Michigan vs. Notre Dame.* Lanham: Taylor Trade Publishing, 2007.

Obituary *"Patrick Connors 1849-1893."* South Bend Tribune, December 13, 1893.

Parrado, Nando *Miracle in the Andes.* New York: Broadway Books, 2006.

————

Miscellaneous papers and photos pertaining to Patrick Connors a/k/a Brother Paul of the Cross, and the beginnings of Notre Dame Football, were provided courtesy of the Archives at Notre Dame's Hesburgh Library, and the Archives at the Office of the Midwest Province for the Congregation of the Holy Cross. Notre Dame: 1865-1893, including materials from:

Ave Maria Magazine, circa 1878

Beach, Jim *A Story of a Proud Heritage: Notre Dame Football*. Manitowoc: Lakeshore Books, 1962

Beirne, Killian *From Sea to Shining Sea-The Holy Cross Brothers in the United States*. Valatie: Holy Cross Press, 1966.

Cohen, Richard M. et al. *The Notre Dame Football Scrapbook*. Indianapolis: Bobbs-Merril Publishing, 1977

Notre Dame Scholastic Magazine Excerpts, 1881-1893

O'Reilly, Aiden *The Story of Notre Dame - Brother Aiden's Extracts*. Notre Dame: University of Notre Dame Archives, 1951

**Chapter 6: Daughter of Misogyny, Mother of Blood Money**
Brinkman, Susan *The Kinsey Corruption*. West Chester: Ascension Press, 2004.

Burtchaell, James T. *Rachel Weeping-The Case Against Abortion*. San Francisco: Harper & Row, 1984.

Franks, Angela *Margaret Sanger's Eugenic Legacy: The Control of Female Fertility*. Jefferson: MacFarland & Co., 2005

Grant, George *Grand Illusions: The Legacy of Planned Parenthood*. Nashville: Cumberland House, 4th ed. 2000.

Grant, George *Killer Angel* Nashville: Highland Books, 2nd ed. 2001.

Gray, Madeline *Margaret Sanger: A Biography of the Champion of Birth Control*. New York: Richard Marek Publishers, 1979

Mayer, John *Daughters. Sony/ATV Music Publishing,* 2003. <https://songmeanings.com/songs/view/3530822107858489312/>

Planned Parenthood *Stand and Deliver Mission Statement, 2009.* <https://www.foxnews.com/world/planned-parenthood-pushes-intensive-sex-education-for-kids-as-young-as-10>

Planned Parenthood Statistics <https://www.all.org/>

Pope Pius XI *Casti Connubii* <http://www.papalencyclicals.net/pius11/p11casti.htm>

Reardon, David *Aborted Women: Silent No More.* Chicago: Loyola University Press, 1987

Reisman, Judith A. *Kinsey: Crime & Consequences.* Arlington: The Institute for Media Education, 1998.

Sanger, Margaret *The Margaret Sanger Papers Project.* New York University. <https://www.nyu.edu/projects/sanger/>

Sanger, Margaret *Woman and the New Race.* Middlesex: The Echo Library, 2006.

Wilke, Dr. & Mrs. J.C. *Abortion Questions & Answers.* Cincinnati: Hayes Publishing Co., 1985.

## Chapter 7: Notre Dame Our Mother

Burns, Robert E. *Being Catholic-Being American: The Notre Dame Story, 1934-1952*. Notre Dame: University of Notre Dame Press, 2000.

Dolan, Jay P. *The Irish Americans, A History*. New York: Bloomsbury Press, 2008.

Kryk, John *Natural Enemies: Major College Football's Oldest, Fiercest Rivalry-Michigan vs. Notre Dame*. Lanham: Taylor Trade Publishing, 2007.

Langford, Jim and Jeremy *The Spirit of Notre Dame*. New York: The Crossroad Publishing Company, 2005.

Rice, Charles E. *What Happened to Notre Dame?* South Bend: St. Augustine's Press, 2009.

Sperber, Murray *Shake Down The Thunder-The Creation of Notre Dame Football*. Bloomington: Indiana University Press, 2002.

Wallace, Francis *Notre Dame: Its People and Its Legends*. New York: David McKay Company, 1969

Ward, Arch *The Story of Notre Dame Football: Frank Leahy and The Fighting Irish*. New York: G. Putnam & Sons, 1944.

## Chapter 8: Weeds Among the Wheat

Alderman, Michael H. M.D. "White House Conference on Health." November 3-4, 1965, Washington, D.C.: Summary Report Public Health Reports (1896-1970) Vol. 81, No. 2 (Feb., 1966), pp. 111-120

Alinsky, Saul D. *Rules for Radicals: A Pragmatic Primer for Realistic Radicals.* New York: Vintage Books, 1989

Blantz, Thomas E. *George N. Shuster, On the Side of Truth.* Notre Dame: University of Notre Dame Press, 1993.

Burns, Robert E. *Being Catholic-Being American: The Notre Dame Story, 1934-1952.* Notre Dame: University of Notre Dame Press, 2000.

Burtchaell, James T. *Rachel Weeping-The Case Against Abortion.* San Francisco: Harper & Row, 1984.

"Catechism of the Catholic Church." *Libreria Editrice Vaticana.* 2nd ed. 1997.

Critchlow, Donald T. *Intended Consequences: Birth Control, Abortion, and the Federal Government in Modern America.* New York: Oxford University Press, 1999

Deedy, John "Catholics, Abortion, and the Supreme Court." Theology Today. October, 1973.

Gleason, Philip *Contending With Modernity: Catholic Higher Education in the Twentieth Century.* New York: Oxford University Press, 1995.

Green, Thomas H. *Weeds Among the Wheat*. Notre Dame: Ave Maria Press, 3rd ed. 1986.

Hendershott, Anne *Status Envy-The Politics of Higher Education*. New Brunswick: Transaction Publishers, 2009.

Hesburgh, Theodore M. *God, Country, Notre Dame*. New York: Doubleday, 1990.

Hesburgh, Theodore M. *Vision of a Great Catholic University in the World Today*. University of Notre Dame, 1967. <archives.nd.edu/Hesburgh/CPHS141-26-05.pdf>

Jones, F. Michael "Call to Action Turns Twenty: From Bicentennial Celebration to Excommunication." Culture Wars Magazine December, 1996 <https://ewtn.com/library/ISSUES/CTOA20.TXT>

Malone, Michael M. "From Orthodox to Heresy: The Secularizing of Catholic Universities" Catholic Citizens, September 8, 2008 <http://www.freerepublic.com/focus/f-religion/2261414/posts>

Mazza, Michael "Heart Attack: Catholic Academe Meets "Ex Corde Ecclesiae." South Bend: Fidelity Magazine, February 1995.

McGinley, Phyllis "Phyllis McGinley Papers". Special Collections Research Center at Syracuse University Library. 1897-1978. <https://library.syr.edu/digital/guides/m/mcginley_p.html>

Miscamble, William D. C.S.C. *American Priest: The Ambitious Life and Conflicted Legacy of Notre Dame's Father Ted Hesburgh.* New York: Image/Crown Publishing, 2019.

O'Brien, Michael *Hesburgh, A Biography.* Washington D.C.: The Catholic University of America Press, 1998.

Pope Leo XIII *Aeterni Patris,* 1879 <Papalencyclicals.net>

Pope Leo XIII *Testem Benevolentiae Nostrae,* 1899 <Papalencyclicals.net>

Pope Paul VI *Humanae Vitae,* 1968 <Papalencyclicals.net>

Pope Pius X *Pascendi Dominici Gregis,* 1907 <Papalencyclicals.net>

Rice, Charles E. *What Happened to Notre Dame?* South Bend: St. Augustine's Press, 2009.

Shuster, George N. *Catholic Education in a Changing World.* New York: Holt, Rinehart, and Winston, 1968.

Shuster, George N. *Like A Mighty Army.* New York: D. Appleton-Century Company, 1935.

Shuster, George N. *On the Side of Truth.* Notre Dame: University of Notre Dame Press, 1974.

Shuster, George N. *The Problem of Population: Practical Catholic Applications*. Notre Dame: University of Notre Dame Press, 1964.

Unknown Author *"Education: God and Man at Notre Dame."* Time, Feb. 1962.
http://content.time.com/time/magazine/article/0,9171,938327-1,00.html

Unknown Author "Suburban Rapture: Phyllis McGinley. New York Times Book Review, December 24, 20018

Wilke, Dr. & Mrs. J.C. *Abortion Questions & Answers*. Cincinnati: Hayes Publishing Co., 1985.

## **Chapter 9: Who Wrought Roe and What Roe Wrought**

Brinkman, Susan *The Kinsey Corruption*. West Chester: Ascension Press, 2004.

Burtchaell, James T. *Rachel Weeping-The Case Against Abortion*. San Francisco: Harper & Row, 1984.

Byrn, Robert M. "An American Tragedy: The Supreme Court on Abortion." 41 Fordham L. Review 807 (1972-73)

Corwin, Edward S. *The "Higher Law" Background of American Constitutional Law*. Ithaca: Cornell University Press, 1955.

Critchlow, Donald T. *Intended Consequences: Birth Control, Abortion, and the Federal Government in Modern America*. New York: Oxford University Press, 1999

Deedy, John "Catholics, Abortion, and the Supreme Court." Theology Today. October, 1973.

*Doe v. Bolton*, 410 U.S. 179 (1973)

Hendershott, Anne *Status Envy-The Politics of Higher Education.* New Brunswick: Transaction Publishers, 2009.

Jones, F. Michael "Call to Action Turns Twenty: From Bicentennial Celebration to Excommunication." Culture Wars Magazine December, 1996 <https://ewtn.com/library/ISSUES/CTOA20.TXT>

Lader, Lawrence *Abortion*. Boston: Beacon Press, 1967.

Lader, Lawrence *Breeding Ourselves to Death*. New York: Ballantine Books, 1971.

Malone, Michael M. "From Orthodox to Heresy: The Secularizing of Catholic Universities" Catholic Citizens, September 8, 2008 <http://www.freerepublic.com/focus/f-religion/2261414/posts>

McGinley, Phyllis "Phyllis McGinley Papers". Special Collections Research Center at Syracuse University Library. 1897-1978. <https://library.syr.edu/digital/guides/m/mcginley_p.htm>

Messall, Rebecca "The Long Road of Eugenics: From Rockefeller to Roe v. Wade." Human Life Review, Fall 2004. <http://www.orthodoxytoday.org/articles5/MessallEugenics.php>

Osborn, Frederick *The Future of Human Heredity: An Introduction to Eugenics in Modern Society*. California: Weybright and Talley, 1968.

Ponnuru, Ramesh *The Party of Death: The Democrats, The Media, The Courts, and the Diregard for Human Life*. Washington D.C.: Regnery Publishing, Inc., 2006

Reisman, Judith A. *Kinsey: Crime & Consequences*. Arlington: The Institute for Media Education, 1998.

Rice, Charles E. *What Happened to Notre Dame?* South Bend: St. Augustine's Press, 2009.

*Roe v. Wade,* 410 U.S. 113 (1973)

Reagan, Ronald *Abortion and The Conscience of the Nation*. Nashville: Thomas Nelson Publishers, 1984.

Unknown Author "Suburban Rapture: Phyllis McGinley. New York Times Book Review, December 24, 20018

Wilke, Dr. & Mrs. J.C. *Abortion Questions & Answers*. Cincinnati: Hayes Publishing Co., 1985.

## Chapter 10: Kennedy the Queen of Angels

Egg-Benes, Maria *When a Child is Different: A Basic Guide for Parents and Friends of Mentally Retarded Children*. New York: John Day Co., 1964

Haskins, James *A New Kind of Joy*. New York: Doubleday, 1976.

LoGiudice, Mary Ann and Grondahl, Paul *That Place Called Home.* Ann Arbor: Servant Publications, 2000.

McCallum, Jack "Small Steps, Great Strides." Sports Illustrated, December 8, 2008 [Feast of the Immaculate Conception of Mary] <https://www.si.com/vault/2008/12/08/105760282/small-steps-great-strides>

Shapiro, Joseph "Eunice Kennedy Shriver's Olympic Legacy." NPR.org, April 5, 2007. <https://www.npr.org/templates/story/story.php?storyId=9136962 >

Shriver Center. History. The Shriver Center. <https://shriver.umassmed.edu/about-us/history>

Shriver, Eunice Kennedy "How the Kennedy Family's Own Misfortune Spurred the Fight against Widely Misunderstood Affliction." Saturday Evening Post, September 22, 1962. http://www.eunicekennedyshriver.org/articles/article/148

Shriver, Eunice Kennedy 1921-2009 Bio. <http://www.eunicekennedyshriver.org/bios/eks>

Shriver, Maria Statement responding to President Obama's comments about the Special Olympics. March 20, 2009 <https://latimesblogs.latimes.com/washington/2009/03/obama-gaffe.html>

Shriver, Mrs. Sargent "The Sun Has Burst Through." Parade Magazine, February 2, 1964
<http://www.eunicekennedyshriver.org/articles/article/68>

Shriver "Statement From the Shriver Family." Hyannis Port, August 11, 2009.
<http://www.eunicekennedyshriver.org/articles/article/171>

## Chapter 11:  Kennedy the Cowardly Lion

Day, Kristen *Democrats for Life*. Green Forest: New Leaf Press, 2006.

*Planned Parenthood v. Casey, 505 U.S. 833 (1992)*

Ponnuru, Ramesh *The Party of Death: The Democrats, The Media, The Courts, and the Diregard for Human Life*. Washington D.C.: Regnery Publishing, Inc., 2006.

Reagan, Ronald *Abortion and The Conscience of the Nation*. Nashville: Thomas Nelson Publishers, 1984.

*Roe v. Wade,* 410 U.S. 113 (1973)

Sirico, Rev. Robert A. "Kennedy the Catholic." Acton Institute, August 27, 2009.

## Chapter 12: Cuomo Catholicism Comes To Campus

"Catechism of the Catholic Church." *Libreria Editrice Vaticana.* 2nd ed. 1997.

Corwin, Edward S. *The "Higher Law" Background of American Constitutional Law*. Ithaca: Cornell University Press, 1955.

Cuomo, Mario "Religious Belief and Public Morality: A Catholic Governor's Perspective." University of Notre Dame, September 13, 1984. <http://archives.nd.edu/research/texts/cuomo.htm>

Day, Kristen *Democrats for Life*. Green Forest: New Leaf Press, 2006.

Hendershott, Anne *Status Envy-The Politics of Higher Education*. New Brunswick: Transaction Publishers, 2009.

Mazza, Michael "Heart Attack: Catholic Academe Meets "Ex Corde Ecclesiae." South Bend: Fidelity Magazine, February 1995.

Planned Parenthood Statistics <https://www.all.org/>

*Planned Parenthood v. Casey*, 505 U.S. 833 (1992)

Ponnuru, Ramesh *The Party of Death: The Democrats, The Media, The Courts, and the Diregard for Human Life*. Washington D.C.: Regnery Publishing, Inc., 2006.

Pope John Paul II *The Splendor of Truth*. Boston: St. Paul Books, 1994.

Pope John Paul II *Springtime of Evangelization*. San Diego: Basilica Press, 1999.

Reagan, Ronald *Abortion and The Conscience of the Nation*. Nashville: Thomas Nelson Publishers, 1984.

Rice, Charles E. *What Happened to Notre Dame?* South Bend: St. Augustine's Press, 2009.

*Roe v. Wade,* 410 U.S. 113 (1973)

**Chapter 13: Casey the Champ**

Casey, Robert et al. "A New American Compact: Caring About Women, Caring for the Unborn.  New York Times, November 1992. <https://www.firstthings.com/article/1992/11/005-a-new-american-compact-caring-about-women-caring-for-the-unborn>

Casey, Robert P. *Fighting for Life*. Dallas: Word Publishing, 1996.

Day, Kristen *Democrats for Life*. Green Forest: New Leaf Press, 2006.

Ginsburg, Justice Ruth Bader "Interview: New York Times Magazine. July 2009.< http://aarontallent.com/?p=1153>

*Planned Parenthood v. Casey, 505 U.S. 833 (1992)*

Wikipedia "Alphonsus Liguori" <https://en.wikipedia.org/wiki/Alphonsus_Liguori>

**Chapter 14: Teresa the Teacher**

Chaliha, Jaya and Le Joly, Edward *The Joy in Loving: A Guide to Daily Living by Mother Teresa*. New York: Random House, 2000.

Collopy, Michael *Works of Love are Works of Peace*. San Francisco: 2016.

Kolodiejchuk, Brian M.C. *Come Be My Light: The Private Writings of the Saint of Calcutta*. New York: Doubleday, 2007

Mother Teresa Address at the National Prayer Breakfast. Washington D.C. February 3, 1994.
<https://www.ewtn.com/library/issues/prbkmter.txt>

Mother Teresa Amicus Curiae Brief to the United States Supreme Court. Washington D.C. February, 1994.
<http://haroldcassidy.com/mother-teresa.html>

Muggeridge, Malcom *Something Beautiful for God*. New York: Harper and Row, 1971.

Porter, David *Mother Teresa, The Early Years*. Grand Rapids, William B. Eerdmans Publishing Co., 1986.

State v. Loce, 267 N.J. Super 102 (Law.Div. 1991), aff'd. as modified, 267 N.J. Super 10 (App. Div. 1993)

*Wikipedia "Mother Teresa"*
< https://en.wikipedia.org/wiki/Mother_Teresa>

## Chapter 15: John Paul the Great

Chaput, Charles J. *Render Unto Caeser-Serving the Nation by Living Our Catholic Beliefs in Political Life*. New York: Doubleday, 2008.

Conley, James "Toasting the Conscience." First Things, October, 2015. <https://www.firstthings.com/web-exclusives/2015/10/toasting-the-conscience>

Mazza, Michael "Heart Attack: Catholic Academe Meets "Ex Corde Ecclesiae." South Bend: Fidelity Magazine, February 1995.

Pope John Paul II *Ex Corde Ecclesiae*. Rome: The Vatican, 1990

Pope John Paul II *The Splendor of Truth*. Boston: St. Paul Books, 1994.

Pope John Paul II *Springtime of Evangelization*. San Diego: Basilica Press, 1999.

Papal Encyclicals and Writings republished at Papalencyclicals.net, usccb.org, newadvent.org/library, and/or ewtn.com/library/papaldoc:

Pope Leo XIII *Testem Benevolentiae Nostrae*, 1899

Pope Pius X *Pascendi Dominici Gregis*, 1907

Pope Paul VI Gaudium et Spes, 1965

Pope Paul VI *Humanae Vitae*, 1968

Pope John Paul II *Ex Corde Ecclesiae*, 1990

Pope John Paul II *Evangelium Vitae*, 1995

## Chapter 16: Benediction

Chaput, Charles J. *Render Unto Caeser-Serving the Nation by Living Our Catholic Beliefs in Political Life.* New York: Doubleday, 2008.

Pope Benedict XVI *Caritas In Veritate,* 2009 <http://www.usccb.org/beliefs-and-teachings/who-we-teach/adults/caritas-in-veritate-resource-material.cfm>

Pope Benedict XVI "Meeting with Catholic Educators." April 17, 2008. <http://w2.vatican.va/content/benedict-xvi/en/speeches/2008/april/documents/hf_ben-xvi_spe_20080417_cath-univ-washington.html>

Ratzinger, Joseph Cardinal *God in the World: Believing and Living in our Time.* San Francisco: Ignatius Press, 2002.

## Chapter 17: "Big Mistake"

Alinsky, Saul D. *Rules for Radicals: A Pragmatic Primer for Realistic Radicals.* New York: Vintage Books, 1989

Beckwith, Francis "Barack Obama and Notre Dame: Juris Doctor Honoris." First Things, March 31, 2009 <https://www.firstthings.com/web-exclusives/2009/03/barack-obama-and-notre-dame-ju>

Bramwell, Bevil OMI "Notre Dame's Useful Service." The Catholic Thing, May 19, 2009. This column first appeared on the website *The Catholic Thing* (www.thecatholicthing.org). Copyright 2009. All

rights reserved. Reprinted with permission.
<https://www.thecatholicthing.org/2009/05/19/notre-dames-useful-service/>

Brown, Francis F. *Abortion and Slavery: History Repeats.*
University of Notre Dame Archives, 1984.
http://archives.nd.edu/cgi-bin/q-ead.pl?keyword=abortion+and+slavery

Bush, Alex and Jalsevac, John "Notre Dame President Sits on Board of Directors of Pro-Abortion, Pro-Contraception Organization." LifeSiteNews.com, May 13, 2009. <
https://www.lifesitenews.com/news/notre-dame-president-sits-on-board-of-directors-of-pro-abortion-pro-contrac>

Chaput, Archbishop Charles J. *Render Unto Caeser-Serving the Nation by Living Our Catholic Beliefs in Political Life.* New York: Doubleday, 2008.

Chaput, Archbishop Charles J. "Notre Dame: The Issues That Remain." Catholicculture.org, May 19, 2009
<https://www.catholicculture.org/culture/library/view.cfm?recnum=8963>

Daley, Mary K. "Letter to Rev. John I. Jenkins, C.S.C. on behalf of the Notre Dame Response Student Coalition." Notre Dame, April 10, 2009

D'Arcy, Bishop John "Statement to the Faithful." Fort Wayne: April 21, 2009. <http://bdstatements.blogspot.com/2009/04/letter-to-faithful.html>

D'Arcy, Bishop John "The Church and the University". American Magazine, August, 31, 2009.

Dempsey, William "How Pro-Life is Notre Dame?" Sycamore Trust, November 18, 2009 <https://wp.me/p9235P-q7>

Dolan, Archbishop Timothy "Installation Mass Homily." St. Patrick's Cathedral, New York, April 15, 2009

Freddoso, David *The Case Against Barack Obama: The Unlikely Rise and Unexamined Agenda of the Media's Favorite Candidate.* Washington, D.C.: Regnery Publishing, 2008

Glendon, Mary Ann "Letter to the Rev. John I. Jenkins, C.S.C., April 27, 2009." <https://www.firstthings.com/blogs/firstthoughts/2009/04/declining-notre-dame-a-letter-from-mary-ann-glendon/>

Johnson, Douglas and Muskett, Susan, NLRC *Memorandum Re: Why the Hyde Amendment will not prevent government funding of abortion..."* Washington D.C., September 3, 2009.

Kirsanow, Peter "Clarifying Obama's Vote on Born Alive." National Review, February 10, 2012 <https://www.nationalreview.com/corner/clarifying-obamas-vote-born-alive-peter-kirsanow/>

Mazza, Michael "Heart Attack: Catholic Academe Meets "Ex Corde Ecclesiae." South Bend: Fidelity Magazine, February 1995.

McGurn, William "Obama Scored Big at Notre Dame." Wall Street
Journal, May 19, 2009.
<https://www.wsj.com/articles/SB124269063343832561>

McIlhern, Patrick "Milwaukee's Loss is God's Gift to Gotham." New
York Post, February 24, 2009
<https://nypost.com/2009/02/24/milwaukees-loss-is-gods-gift-to-
gotham/>

Miscamble, William D. C.S.C. et al. "Work to Maintain Catholic
Traditions." Notre Dame: The Observer, April 8, 2009

Reilly, Naomi Schaefer "Catholicism, Inc." Wall Street Journal, April
12, 2008 <https://www.wsj.com/articles/SB120796155333509621>

Rice, Charles E. *Open Letter to Rev. John I. Jenkins, C.S.C.,
President, University of Notre Dame, September 21, 2009.*
<https://insightscoop.typepad.com/2004/2009/09/open-letter-
from-dr-charles-e-rice-to-fr-john-i-jenkins.html>

Rice, Charles E. *What Happened to Notre Dame?* South Bend: St.
Augustine's Press, 2009.

Stanek, Jill "Obama's Connections on Notre Dame Board of
Trustees." JillStanek.com, May 13, 2009
<http://www.jillstanek.com/archives/2009/05/obamas_friendly.ht
ml>

Stanek, Jill "Top 10 Reasons Obama voted against the Illinois Born
Alive Infant Protection Act." Illinois Review, January 10, 2008
<https://illinoisreview.typepad.com/illinoisreview/2008/01/top-10-
reasons.html>

Walker, Frank "No Likely Support From Notre Dame's Board of Trustees For Rescinding Obama Invite." Pewsitter.com, May 10, 2009. <https://www.all.org/notre-dame-trustees-and-father-jenkins-final-word/>

Weigel, George "Obama and the 'Real' Catholics." National Review, May 18, 2009. <https://www.nationalreview.com/2009/05/obama-and-real-catholics-george-weigel/>

Westin, John Henry "Editorial: A False Theology: Obama's Appeal to Faith Runs Contrary to Christian Faith." LifeSiteNews.com, May 20, 2009. <https://www.lifesitenews.com/news/editorial-a-false-theology-obamas-appeal-to-faith-runs-contrary-to-christia>

## **Chapter 18:  Where are the Fighting Irish?**

Brejcha, Thomas Notre Damee 88. Catholic News Agency. <https://www.catholicnewsagency.com/news/judge_on_notre_dame_88_case_allows_appeals_court_to_decide_recusal_issue>

Bush, Alex and Jalsevac, John "Notre Dame President Sits on Board of Directors of Pro-Abortion, Pro-Contraception Organization." LifeSiteNews.com, May 13, 2009. < https://www.lifesitenews.com/news/notre-dame-president-sits-on-board-of-directors-of-pro-abortion-pro-contrac>

Chaput, Charles J. *Render Unto Caeser-Serving the Nation by Living Our Catholic Beliefs in Political Life*. New York: Doubleday, 2008.

D'Arcy, Bishop John "The Church and the University". American Magazine, August, 31, 2009.

Dempsey, William "Father Hesburgh's Intervention in the Pro-Life Health Care Dispute." Sycamore Trust, April 19, 2010. <https://sycamoretrust.org/hidden-agendas/>

Dempsey, William "How Pro-Life is Notre Dame?" Sycamore Trust, November 18, 2009 <https://wp.me/p9235P-q7>

Dempsey, William "ND 88 Free at Last." Sycamore Trust, May 5, 2011. <https://sycamoretrust.org/nd-88-free-at-last/>

Notre Dame, University of "What Would You Fight For" Videos. <https://fightingfor.nd.edu/>

NOW v. Scheidler, 510 U.S. 249 (1994

Rice, Charles E. *Open Letter to Rev. John I. Jenkins, C.S.C., President, University of Notre Dame, September 21, 2009.* <https://insightscoop.typepad.com/2004/2009/09/open-letter-from-dr-charles-e-rice-to-fr-john-i-jenkins.html>

Rice, Charles E. *What Happened to Notre Dame?* South Bend: St. Augustine's Press, 2009.

## Chapter 19: Will Notre Dame Reclaim the Glory of Her Name?

Diaz, Elizabeth and Horowitz, Jason "Pope Defrocks Theodore McCarrick, Ex-Cardinal Accused of Sexual Abuse." New York Times, February 16, 2019.

<https://www.nytimes.com/2019/02/16/us/mccarrick-defrocked-vatican.html>

DiNardo, Cardinal Daniel "Letter to House of Representatives on Health Care." March 20, 2010 <http://www.usccb.org/issues-and-action/human-life-and-dignity/health-care/letter-to-house-of-representatives-from-dinardo-murphy-wester-on-health-reform-bill-2010-03-20.cfm>

Dolan, Archbishop Timoty "Commencement Address-University of Notre Dame-May 19, 2013 Pentecost Sunday." <http://blog.archny.org/images/2013/05/CardinalDolan_CommencementAddress_NotreDame.pdf>

Editorial Board "Little Sisters Back in Court." Wall Street Journal, January 18, 2019. <https://www.wsj.com/articles/little-sisters-back-in-court-11547856751>

Ertelt, Steven *Email to Lifenews.com subscribers – Health Care Bill Prompts New Planned Parenthood Abortion Center in Michigan."* *April 29, 2010*

Gardey, Ellie "Panel of Notre Dame Professors Defend 'Abortion Rights'." IrishRover.net, February 6, 2019. <https://irishrover.net/2019/02/panel-of-notre-dame-professors-defend-abortion-rights/>

Gilbert, Kathleen "Obama Admin to Mandate Contraception, Sterilization Coverage under Health Care Law." LifeSiteNews.com, August 1, 2011. <https://www.lifesitenews.com/news/breaking-obama-admin-to-mandate-contraceptive-sterilization-coverage-under>

Green, Emma "Notre Dame Switches Its Position on Birth Control Coverage-Again." TheAtlantic.com, February 7, 2018. <https://www.theatlantic.com/politics/archive/2018/02/notre-dame-switches-its-position-on-contraception-coverage-again/552605/>


Jenkins, Rev. John I. C.S.C. "Letter on Health Care Coverage." University of Notre Dame, February 7, 2018. <https://president.nd.edu/writings-addresses/2018-writings/letter-on-health-care-coverage/>

Jenkins, Rev. John I. C.S.C. "Who is Next?" University of Notre Dame, February 7, 2019. <https://news.nd.edu/news/who-is-next-statement-by-rev-john-i-jenkins-c-s-c-president-of-the-university-of-notre-dame/>

Mena, Adelaide "Pro-Life Congressman, wife honored with Notre Dame Award." CatholicNewsAgency.com, April 9, 2014. <https://www.catholicnewsagency.com/news/pro-life-congressman-wife-honored-with-notre-dame-award>

Newton, Cara "Notre Dame Re-files Obamacare Contraception Lawsuit [originally filed in May of 2013]." USA Today, December 7, 2013. <https://www.usatoday.com/story/news/nation/2013/12/07/notre-dame-obamacare-lawsuit/3893845/>

Notre Dame News "Statement on Theodore McCarrick." February 16, 2019. <https://news.nd.edu/news/statement-on-theodore-mccarrick/>

Pashman, Manya Brachear "Students Sue Notre Dame and Trump Administration over Contraceptive Coverage." Chicago Tribune, June 26, 2018 <https://www.chicagotribune.com/news/ct-met-notre-dame-contraceptive-lawsuit-20180626-story.html>

Pecknold, Chad "Behind Ted McCarrick's Fall: The Wrong Kind of 'Openness'." New York Post, February 14, 2019

*Planned Parenthood v. Casey, 505 U.S. 833 (1992)*

Simon, Richard and Fiore, Faye "Healthcare Victory Could Bolster Pelosi." Los Angeles Times, March 23, 2010. <http://irishwatchdog.blogspot.com/2010/03/did-fr-ted-get-healthcare-passed.html>  See also, >http://irishwatchdog.blogspot.com/2010/03/did-fr-ted-get-healthcare-passed.html>

Wikipedia "[President Obama] Executive Order 13535" <https://en.wikipedia.org/wiki/Executive_Order_13535>

Wikipedia "Stupak-Pitts Amendment" <https://en.wikipedia.org/wiki/Stupak%E2%80%93Pitts_Amendment>

Woodward, Kenneth L. "Andrew Cuomo and the Sad Inheritance of 'Personal Opposition' to Abortion." American Magazine, February 12, 2019.

# Bibliography

<u>Books</u>

Alinsky, Saul D. *Rules for Radicals: A Pragmatic Primer for Realistic Radicals.* New York: Vintage Books, 1989

Bayor, Ronald H. and Meagher, Timothy J. *The New York Irish.* Baltimore: The Johns Hopkins University Press, 1996

Blantz, Thomas E. *George N. Shuster, On the Side of Truth.* Notre Dame: University of Notre Dame Press, 1993.

Brinkman, Susan *The Kinsey Corruption.* West Chester: Ascension Press, 2004.

Burns, Robert E. *Being Catholic-Being American: The Notre Dame Story, 1934-1952, Parts I and II* Notre Dame: University of Notre Dame Press, 1999, 2000.

Burtchaell, James T. *Rachel Weeping-The Case Against Abortion.* San Francisco: Harper & Row, 1984.

Cahill, Thomas *How the Irish Saved Civilization.* New York: Anchor Books, 1995.

Cahill, Thomas *The Gifts of the Jews.* New York: Anchor Books, 1999.

Capt, E. Raymond *Jacob's Pillar-Stone of Destiny*. Muskogee: Artisan Publishers, 2005.

Carew, Mairead *Tara and the Ark of the Covenant*. Dublin: Royal Irish Academy, 2003.

Casey, Robert P. *Fighting for Life*. Dallas: Word Publishing, 1996.

**Chaliha, Jaya and Le Joly, Edward *The Joy in Loving: A Guide to Daily Living by Mother Teresa*. New York: Random House, 2000.**

Chaput, Charles J. *Render Unto Caeser-Serving the Nation by Living Our Catholic Beliefs in Political Life*. New York: Doubleday, 2008.

Collopy, Michael *Works of Love are Works of Peace*. San Francisco: 2016.

Corby, William *Memoirs of Chaplain Life*. New York: Fordham University Press, 1992.

Corson, Dorothy V. *A Cave of Candles: The Story Behind Notre Dame's Grotto*. Nairobi: Evangel Publishing House, 2006.

Corwin, Edward S. *The "Higher Law" Background of American Constitutional Law*. Ithaca: Cornell University Press, 1955.

Costin, M. Georgia *Priceless Spirit-A History of the Sisters of the Holy Cross, 1841-1893*. Notre Dame: University of Notre Dame Press, 1994.

Critchlow, Donald T. *Intended Consequences: Birth Control, Abortion, and the Federal Government in Modern America.* New York: Oxford University Press, 1999

Cuomo, Mario Religious *Belief and Public Morality: A Catholic Governor's Perspective.* New York, Megan Sassi, 1987.

Day, Kristen *Democrats for Life.* Green Forest: New Leaf Press, 2006.

Dike, Wm. L. *U.S.S. Red Rover, Civil War Hospital Ship.* Baltimore: Publish America, 2004.

Dolan, Jay P. *The Irish Americans, A History.* New York: Bloomsbury Press, 2008.

Egg-Benes, Maria *When a Child is Different: A Basic Guide for Parents and Friends of Mentally Retarded Children.* New York: John Day Co., 1964

Franks, Angela *Margaret Sanger's Eugenic Legacy: The Control of Female Fertility.* Jefferson: MacFarland & Co., 2005

Freddoso, David *The Case Against Barack Obama: The Unlikely Rise and Unexamined Agenda of the Media's Favorite Candidate.* Washington, D.C.: Regnery Publishing, 2008

Gleason, Philip *Contending With Modernity: Catholic Higher Education in the Twentieth Century.* New York: Oxford University Press, 1995.

Grant, George *Grand Illusions: The Legacy of Planned Parenthood*. Nashville: Cumberland House, 4th ed. 2000.

Grant, George *Killer Angel* Nashville: Highland Books, 2nd ed. 2001.

Gray, Madeline *Margaret Sanger: A Biography of the Champion of Birth Control*. New York: Richard Marek Publishers, 1979

Green, Thomas H. *Weeds Among the Wheat*. Notre Dame: Ave Maria Press, 3rd ed. 1986.

Haskins, James *A New Kind of Joy*. New York: Doubleday, 1976.

Hendershott, Anne *Status Envy-The Politics of Higher Education*. New Brunswick: Transaction Publishers, 2009.

Hesburgh, Theodore M. *God, Country, Notre Dame*. New York: Doubleday, 1990.

Hullfish, William *The Canaller's Songbook: Words, Music and Chords to over Thirty Canal Songs*. Manchester: American Canal and Transportation Center, 1984

Klawitter, George *Adapted to the Lake: Letters by the Brother Founders of Notre Dame, 1841–1849*. New York: Peter Lang Publishing Co., 1993.

Koeppel, Gerard *Bond of Union: Building the Erie Canal and the American Empire*. Lebanon: De Capo Press, 2009

Kolodiejchuk, Brian M.C. *Come Be My Light: The Private Writings of the Saint of Calcutta.* New York: Doubleday, 2007

Kryk, John *Natural Enemies: Major College Football's Oldest, Fiercest Rivalry-Michigan vs. Notre Dame.* Lanham: Taylor Trade Publishing, 2007.

Lader, Lawrence *Abortion.* Boston: Beacon Press, 1967.

**Lader, Lawrence *Breeding Ourselves to Death.* New York: Ballantine Books, 1971.**

Langford, Jim and Jeremy *The Spirit of Notre Dame.* New York: The Crossroad Publishing Company, 2005.

LoGiudice, Mary Ann and Grondahl, Paul *That Place Called Home.* Ann Arbor: Servant Publications, 2000.

Lee, J.J. and Casey, Marion R. *Making the Irish American: History and Heritage of the Irish in the United States.* New York:  New York University Press, 2006.

MacEoin, Gary *Basil Moreau-Founder of Holy Cross.* Notre Dame: Ave Maria Press, 2nd ed. 2007.

**McGreevy, John T. *Catholicism and American Freedom.* New York: W.W. Norton & Co., 2003**

Miller, Randall and Wakelyn, Jon *Catholics in the Old South.* Macon: Mercer University Press, 1999.

Miscamble, William D. C.S.C. *American Priest: The Ambitious Life and Conflicted Legacy of Notre Dame's Father Ted Hesburgh.* New York: Image/Crown Publishing, 2019.

Muggeridge, Malcom *Something Beautiful for God.* New York: Harper and Row, 1971.

O'Brien, Michael *Hesburgh, A Biography.* Washington D.C.: The Catholic University of America Press, 1998.

O'Connell, Marvin R. *Edward Sorin.* Notre Dame: University of Notre Dame Press, 2001.

Osborn, Frederick *The Future of Human Heredity: An Introduction to Eugenics in Modern Society.* California: Weybright and Talley, 1968.

Panzer, Joel S. *The Popes and Slavery.* New York: Alba House, 1996.

Parrado, Nando **Miracle in the Andes.** New York: Broadway Books, 2006.

Ponnuru, Ramesh *The Party of Death: The Democrats, The Media, The Courts, and the Diregard for Human Life.* Washington D.C.: Regnery Publishing, Inc., 2006.

Pope John Paul II *The Splendor of Truth.* Boston: St. Paul Books, 1994.

Pope John Paul II *Springtime of Evangelization.* San Diego: Basilica Press, 1999.

Porter, David *Mother Teresa, The Early Years*. Grand Rapids, William B. Eerdmans Publishing Co., 1986.

Pritchard, Russ A. Jr. *The Irish Brigade*. Philadelphia: Courage Books, 2004.

Ratzinger, Joseph Cardinal *God in the World: Believing and Living in our Time*. San Francisco: Ignatius Press, 2002.

Reagan, Ronald *Abortion and The Conscience of the Nation*. Nashville: Thomas Nelson Publishers, 1984.

Reardon, David *Aborted Women: Silent No More*. Chicago: Loyola University Press, 1987

Reisman, Judith A. *Kinsey: Crime & Consequences*. Arlington: The Institute for Media Education, 1998.

Rice, Charles E. *What Happened to Notre Dame?* South Bend: St. Augustine's Press, 2009.

Roediger, David R. *The Wages of Whiteness: Race and the Making of the American Working Class*. Brooklyn: Verso Books, 2007

Saint Luke *Holy Bible, New Testament, Gospel of Luke, 1:41-55*

Sanger, Margaret *Woman and the New Race*. Middlesex: The Echo Library, 2006.

Shuster, George N. *Catholic Education in a Changing World*. New York: Holt, Rinehart, and Winston, 1968.

Shuster, George N. *Like A Mighty Army*. New York: D. Appleton-Century Company, 1935.

Shuster, George N. *On the Side of Truth*. Notre Dame:  University of Notre Dame Press, 1974.

Shuster, George N. *The Problem of Population: Practical Catholic Applications*. Notre Dame: University of Notre Dame Press, 1964.

Sorin, Edward *The Chronicles of Notre Dame du Lac*. Notre Dame: University of Notre Dame Press, 1992.

Sperber, Murray *Shake Down The Thunder-The Creation of Notre Dame Football*. Bloomington: Indiana University Press, 2002.

Tone, Theobold Wolfe *An Argument on Behalf of the Catholics of Ireland*. Belfast: Society of the United Irishmen of Belfast, 1791.

Wallace, Francis *Notre Dame: Its People and Its Legends*. New York: David McKay Company, 1969

Ward, Arch *The Story of Notre Dame Football: Frank Leahy and The Fighting Irish*. New York: G. Putnam & Sons, 1944.

Wilke, Dr. & Mrs. J.C. *Abortion Questions & Answers*. Cincinnati: Hayes Publishing Co., 1985.

## Encyclopedias

"Catechism of the Catholic Church." *Libreria Editrice Vaticana.* 2nd ed. 1997.

## Magazine and Newspaper Periodicals

Byrn, Robert M. "An American Tragedy: The Supreme Court on Abortion." 41 Fordham L. Review 807 (1972-73)

D'Arcy, Bishop John "The Church and the University". American Magazine, August, 31, 2009.

Hughes, Archbishop John "Exchange of correspondence with the French Journal des Debats concerning Slavery and Abolition." New York Times, 1862

Mazza, Michael "Heart Attack: Catholic Academe Meets "Ex Corde Ecclesiae." South Bend: Fidelity Magazine, February 1995.

Obituary *"Patrick Connors 1849-1893."* South Bend Tribune, December 13, 1893.

Miscamble, William D. C.S.C. et al. "Work to Maintain Catholic Traditions." Notre Dame: The Observer, April 8, 2009

Unknown Author "Suburban Rapture: Phyllis McGinley. New York Times Book Review, December 24, 20018.

Deedy, John "Catholics, Abortion, and the Supreme Court." Theology Today. October, 1973.

## Letters and Memorandums

Daley, Mary K. "Letter to Rev. John I. Jenkins, C.S.C. on behalf of the Notre Dame Response Student Coalition." Notre Dame, April 10, 2009

DeHaven, George W.  *Letter to Fielding H. Yost regarding the first football game between Michigan and Notre Dame in 1887.* Hollywood, 1939. (Courtesy of the Archives of the University of Michigan).

Ertelt, Steven *Email to Lifenews.com subscribers – Health Care Bill Prompts New Planned Parenthood Abortion Center in Michigan."* April 29, 2010

King, Martin Luther Jr., *A Letter from a Birmingham Jail.* Birmingham, 1963.

Johnson, Douglas and Muskett, Susan, NLRC *Memorandum Re: Why the Hyde Amendment will not prevent government funding of abortion..."* Washington D.C., September 3, 2009.

## Miscellaneous Materials from Archives

Miscellaneous papers and photos pertaining to Patrick Connors a/k/a Brother Paul of the Cross, the beginnings of Notre Dame Football, and the early history of Notre Dame, were obtained courtesy of the Archives at Notre Dame's Hesburgh Library, and the Archives at the Office of the Midwest Province for the Congregation of the Holy Cross. Notre Dame: 1865-1893, including but not limited to materials from:

Ave Maria Magazine, circa 1878

Beach, Jim *A Story of a Proud Heritage: Notre Dame Football.* Manitowoc: Lakeshore Books, 1962

Beirne, Killian *From Sea to Shining Sea-The Holy Cross Brothers in the United States.* Valatie: Holy Cross Press, 1966.

Brown, Francis F. *Abortion and Slavery: History Repeats.* University of Notre Dame Archives, 1984.

Cohen, Richard M. et al. *The Notre Dame Football Scrapbook.* Indianapolis: Bobbs-Merril Publishing, 1977
Corson, Dorothy V. *The Spirit of Notre Dame: Notre Dame Legends and Lore.* University of Notre Dame Archives, 1953

Corson, Dorothy V. *The Spirit of Notre Dame: Notre Dame Legends and Lore.* University of Notre Dame Archives, 1953

Hesburgh, Theodore M. *Vision of a Great Catholic University in the World Today.* University of Notre Dame, 1967.

Hope, Arthur J. *The Story of Notre Dame – 100 Years.* University of Notre Dame Archives, 1943

Notre Dame Scholastic Magazine Excerpts, 1881-1893

O'Reilly, Aiden *The Story of Notre Dame - Brother Aiden's Extracts.* Notre Dame: University of Notre Dame Archives, 1951

Sorin, Edward *Miscellaneous Letter between Edward Sorin and Southern Bishops pertaining to Slavery and the Civil War, etc.* University of Notre Dame Archives, 1844-1882 <http://archives.nd.edu/cgi-bin/q-ead.pl?keyword=lynch+sorin> and <http://archives.nd.edu/cgi-bin/q-ead.pl?keyword=kenrick+sorin>

———

Miscellaneous papers pertaining to the contributions of the Sisters and Priests of the Congregation of the Holy Cross in ministering to the soldiers who fought in the Civil War were obtained courtesy of the Archives at the Sisters of the Holy Cross Library, Notre Dame, Indiana, including but not limited to:

Author Unknown "Absolution Under Fire: [Painting by] Paul Henry Wood, 1872-1892"

Connelly, James C.S.C. "Holy Cross Communities in the Civil War" Austin: 1993 Conference at St. Edward's University.

Wall, Barbara, RN, MS "Grace Under Pressure: The Nursing Sisters of the Holy Cross 1861-1865" Notre Dame: St. Mary's College, Havican Hall. (Undated)

**<u>Internet Publications</u>**

Alderman, Michael H. M.D. "White House Conference on Health." November 3-4, 1965, Washington, D.C.: Summary Report Public

Health Reports (1896-1970) Vol. 81, No. 2 (Feb., 1966), pp. 111-120 Sage Publications, Inc. DOI: 10.2307/4592660 <https://www.jstor.org/stable/4592660>

Beckwith, Francis "Barack Obama and Notre Dame: Juris Doctor Honoris." First Things, March 31, 2009 <https://www.firstthings.com/web-exclusives/2009/03/barack-obama-and-notre-dame-ju>

Bramwell, Bevil OMI "Notre Dame's Useful Service." The Catholic Thing, May 19, 2009. This column first appeared on the website *The Catholic Thing* (www.thecatholicthing.org). Copyright 2009. All rights reserved. Reprinted with permission. <https://www.thecatholicthing.org/2009/05/19/notre-dames-useful-service/>

Brejcha, Thomas Notre Damee 88. Catholic News Agency. <https://www.catholicnewsagency.com/news/judge_on_notre_dame_88_case_allows_appeals_court_to_decide_recusal_issue>

Brownson, Orestes From orestesbrownson.org and/or ewtn.com

Brownson, Orestes "Mary Worship". 1853

Brownson, Orestes "Moral and Social Influence of Devotion to Mary". June, 1866

Brownson, Orestes "Slavery and the Church". October, 1862

Brownson, Orestes "Slavery and the War". 1861

Brownson, Orestes "State Rebellion-State Suicide". April, 1862

Burton, Edwin, Edward D'Alton, and Jarvis Kelley. "Penal Laws." The Catholic Encyclopedia. Vol. 11. New York: Robert Appleton Company, 1911. 18 Feb. 2019 <http://www.newadvent.org/cathen/11611c.htm>.

Bush, Alex and Jalsevac, John "Notre Dame President Sits on Board of Directors of Pro-Abortion, Pro-Contraception Organization." LifeSiteNews.com, May 13, 2009. <https://www.lifesitenews.com/news/notre-dame-president-sits-on-board-of-directors-of-pro-abortion-pro-contrac>

Chaput, Archbishop Charles J. "Notre Dame: The Issues That Remain." Catholicculture.org, May 19, 2009 <https://www.catholicculture.org/culture/library/view.cfm?recnum=8963>

Conley, James "Toasting the Conscience." First Things, October, 2015. <https://www.firstthings.com/web-exclusives/2015/10/toasting-the-conscience>

D'Arcy, Bishop John "Statement to the Faithful." Fort Wayne: April 21, 2009. <http://bdstatements.blogspot.com/2009/04/letter-to-faithful.html>

Dempsey, William "How Pro-Life is Notre Dame?" Sycamore Trust, November 18, 2009 <https://wp.me/p9235P-q7>

Dempsey, William "Father Hesburgh's Intervention in the Pro-Life Health Care Dispute." Sycamore Trust, April 19, 2010. <https://sycamoretrust.org/hidden-agendas/>

Dempsey, William "ND 88 Free at Last." Sycamore Trust, May 5, 2011. <https://sycamoretrust.org/nd-88-free-at-last/>

Diaz, Elizabeth and Horowitz, Jason "Pope Defrocks Theodore McCarrick, Ex-Cardinal Accused of Sexual Abuse." New York Times, February 16, 2019.
<https://www.nytimes.com/2019/02/16/us/mccarrick-defrocked-vatican.html>

DiNardo, Cardinal Daniel "Letter to House of Representatives on Health Care." March 20, 2010 <http://www.usccb.org/issues-and-action/human-life-and-dignity/health-care/letter-to-house-of-representatives-from-dinardo-murphy-wester-on-health-reform-bill-2010-03-20.cfm>

Dolan, Archbishop Timothy "Installation Mass Homily." St. Patrick's Cathedral, New York, April 15, 2009
<https://archny.org/news/archbishop-dolans-homily-mass-of-installation>

Dolan, Archbishop Timoty "Commencement Address-University of Notre Dame-May 19, 2013 Pentecost Sunday."
<http://blog.archny.org/images/2013/05/CardinalDolan_CommencementAddress_NotreDame.pdf>


Editorial Board "Little Sisters Back in Court." Wall Street Journal, January 18, 2019. <https://www.wsj.com/articles/little-sisters-back-in-court-11547856751>

Gardey, Ellie "Panel of Notre Dame Professors Defend 'Abortion Rights'." IrishRover.net, February 6, 2019. <https://irishrover.net/2019/02/panel-of-notre-dame-professors-defend-abortion-rights/>

Gilbert, Kathleen "Obama Admin to Mandate Contraception, Sterilization Coverage under Health Care Law." LifeSiteNews.com, August 1, 2011. <https://www.lifesitenews.com/news/breaking-obama-admin-to-mandate-contraceptive-sterilization-coverage-under>

Ginsburg, Justice Ruth Bader "Interview: New York Times Magazine. July 2009.< http://aarontallent.com/?p=1153>

Glendon, Mary Ann "Letter to the Rev. John I. Jenkins, C.S.C., April 27, 2009." <https://www.firstthings.com/blogs/firstthoughts/2009/04/declining-notre-dame-a-letter-from-mary-ann-glendon/>

Casey, Robert et al. "A New American Compact: Caring About Women, Caring for the Unborn.  New York Times, November 1992. <https://www.firstthings.com/article/1992/11/005-a-new-american-compact-caring-about-women-caring-for-the-unborn>

Green, Emma "Notre Dame Switches Its Position on Birth Control Coverage-Again." TheAtlantic.com, February 7, 2018. <https://www.theatlantic.com/politics/archive/2018/02/notre-dame-switches-its-position-on-contraception-coverage-again/552605/>

Jenkins, Rev. John I. C.S.C. "Letter on Health Care Coverage." University of Notre Dame, February 7, 2018.

<https://president.nd.edu/writings-addresses/2018-writings/letter-on-health-care-coverage/>

Jenkins, Rev. John I. C.S.C. "Who is Next?" University of Notre Dame, February 7, 2019. <https://news.nd.edu/news/who-is-next-statement-by-rev-john-i-jenkins-c-s-c-president-of-the-university-of-notre-dame/>

Kirsanow, Peter "Clarifying Obama's Vote on Born Alive." National Review, February 10, 2012 <https://www.nationalreview.com/corner/clarifying-obamas-vote-born-alive-peter-kirsanow/>

Lehrman, Lewis "Archbishop John J. Hughes (1797-1863)" <http://www.mrlincolnandnewyork.org/new-yorkers/archbishop-john-j-hughes-1797-1863>

Malone, Michael M. "From Orthodox to Heresy: The Secularizing of Catholic Universities" Catholic Citizens, September 8, 2008 <http://www.freerepublic.com/focus/f-religion/2261414/posts>

Man, Albon P. Jr. "The Church and the New York Draft Riots of 1863" Records of the American Catholic Historical Society of Philadelphia Vol. 62, No. 1 (MARCH, 1951), pp. 33-50 Published by: American Catholic Historical Society <https://www.jstor.org/stable/44210148>

Mayer, John *Daughters. Sony/ATV Music Publishing*, 2003. <https://songmeanings.com/songs/view/3530822107858489312/>

McAvoy, Thomas T. "Orestes A. Brownson and Archbishop John Hughes in 1860" *The Review of Politics* Vol. 24, No. 1 (Jan., 1962), pp. 19-47 Published by: Cambridge University Press for the University of Notre Dame du lac on behalf of Review of Politics <https://www.jstor.org/stable/1405454>

McCallum, Jack "Small Steps, Great Strides." Sports Illustrated, December 8, 2008 [Feast of the Immaculate Conception of Mary] <https://www.si.com/vault/2008/12/08/105760282/small-steps-great-strides>

McGee, Thomas D'Arcy "A Popular History of Ireland: From the Earliest Period to the Emancipation of the Catholics." < <http://www.gutenberg.org/ebooks/6634>

McGinley, Phyllis "Phyllis McGinley Papers". Special Collections Research Center at Syracuse University Library. 1897-1978. <https://library.syr.edu/digital/guides/m/mcginley_p.htm>

McGurn, William "Obama Scored Big at Notre Dame." Wall Street Journal, May 19, 2009. <https://www.wsj.com/articles/SB124269063343832561>

McIlhern, Patrick "Milwaukee's Loss is God's Gift to Gotham." New York Post, February 24, 2009 <https://nypost.com/2009/02/24/milwaukees-loss-is-gods-gift-to-gotham/>

Mena, Adelaide "Pro-Life Congressman, wife honored with Notre Dame Award." CatholicNewsAgency.com, April 9, 2014. <https://www.catholicnewsagency.com/news/pro-life-congressman-wife-honored-with-notre-dame-award>

Messall, Rebecca "The Long Road of Eugenics: From Rockefeller to Roe v. Wade." Human Life Review, Fall 2004. <http://www.orthodoxytoday.org/articles5/MessallEugenics.php>

Minges, Parthenius. "Blessed John Duns Scotus." The Catholic Encyclopedia. Vol. 5. New York: Robert Appleton Company, 1909. 18 Feb. 2019 <http://www.newadvent.org/cathen/05194a.htm>.

Mother Teresa Address at the National Prayer Breakfast. Washington D.C. February 3, 1994. <https://www.ewtn.com/library/issues/prbkmter.txt>

Mother Teresa Amicus Curiae Brief to the United States Supreme Court. Washington D.C. February, 1994. <http://haroldcassidy.com/mother-teresa.html>

Newton, Cara "Notre Dame Re-files Obamacare Contraception Lawsuit [originally filed in May of 2013]." USA Today, December 7, 2013. <https://www.usatoday.com/story/news/nation/2013/12/07/notre-dame-obamacare-lawsuit/3893845/>

Notre Dame, University of "What Would You Fight For" Videos. <https://fightingfor.nd.edu/>

Notre Dame News "Statement on Theodore McCarrick." February 16, 2019. <https://news.nd.edu/news/statement-on-theodore-mccarrick/>

Papal Encyclicals and Writings republished at Papalencyclicals.net, usccb.org, newadvent.org/library, and/or ewtn.com/library/papaldoc:

Pope Benedict XVI *Caritas In Veritate,* 2009

Pope Eugene IV *Sicut Dudum,* 1435

Pope Gregory XVI *In Supremo Apostolatus,* 1839

Pope John Paul II *Ex Corde Ecclesiae,* 1990

Pope John Paul II *Evangelium Vitae, 1995*

Pope Leo XIII *Aeterni Patris,* 1879

Pope Leo XIII *Testem Benevolentiae Nostrae,* 1899

Pope Paul III *Sublimis Deus,* 1537

Pope Paul VI Gaudium et Spes, 1965

Pope Paul VI *Humanae Vitae,* 1968

Pope Pius X *Pascendi Dominici Gregis,* 1907

Pope Pius XI *Casti Connubii,* 1930

Pope Benedict XVI "Meeting with Catholic Educators." April 17, 2008. <http://w2.vatican.va/content/benedict-xvi/en/speeches/2008/april/documents/hf_ben-xvi_spe_20080417_cath-univ-washington.html>

Pashman, Manya Brachear "Students Sue Notre Dame and Trump Administration over Contraceptive Coverage." Chicago Tribune, June 26, 2018 <https://www.chicagotribune.com/news/ct-met-notre-dame-contraceptive-lawsuit-20180626-story.html>

Pecknold, Chad "Behind Ted McCarrick's Fall: The Wrong Kind of 'Openness'." New York Post, February 14, 2019

Peters, Edward "Father Jenkins discovers canon law. Not." In the Light of the Law, April 22, 2009. <https://canonlawblog.wordpress.com/2009/04/09/fr-jenkins-discovers-canon-law-not/>

Planned Parenthood *Stand and Deliver Mission Statement, 2009.* <https://www.foxnews.com/world/planned-parenthood-pushes-intensive-sex-education-for-kids-as-young-as-10>

Planned Parenthood Statistics <https://www.all.org/>

Reilly, Naomi Schaefer "Catholicism, Inc." Wall Street Journal, April 12, 2008 <https://www.wsj.com/articles/SB120796155333509621>

Rice, Charles E. *Open Letter to Rev. John I. Jenkins, C.S.C., President, University of Notre Dame, September 21, 2009.* <https://insightscoop.typepad.com/2004/2009/09/open-letter-from-dr-charles-e-rice-to-fr-john-i-jenkins.html>

Sanger, Margaret *The Margaret Sanger Papers Project.* New York University. <https://www.nyu.edu/projects/sanger/>

Scully, John and Tullio, Jim *Here Come the Irish.* University of Notre Dame, 1997. <https://strongofheart.nd.edu/profiles/john-scully-2010/>

Shapiro, Joseph "Eunice Kennedy Shriver's Olympic Legacy." NPR.org, April 5, 2007. <https://www.npr.org/templates/story/story.php?storyId=9136962>

Shriver "Statement From the Shriver Family." Hyannis Port, August 11, 2009. <http://www.eunicekennedyshriver.org/articles/article/171>

Shriver, Eunice Kennedy 1921-2009 Bio. <http://www.eunicekennedyshriver.org/bios/eks>

Shriver, Eunice Kennedy "How the Kennedy Family's Own Misfortune Spurred the Fight against Widely Misunderstood Affliction." Saturday Evening Post, September 22, 1962. http://www.eunicekennedyshriver.org/articles/article/148

Shriver Center. History. The Shriver Center. <https://shriver.umassmed.edu/about-us/history>

Shriver, Maria Statement responding to President Obama's comments about the Special Olympics. March 20, 2009 <https://latimesblogs.latimes.com/washington/2009/03/obama-gaffe.html>

Shriver, Mrs. Sargent "The Sun Has Burst Through." Parade Magazine, February 2, 1964 <http://www.eunicekennedyshriver.org/articles/article/68>

Simon, Richard and Fiore, Faye "Healthcare Victory Could Bolster Pelosi." Los Angeles Times, March 23, 2010. <http://irishwatchdog.blogspot.com/2010/03/did-fr-ted-get-healthcare-passed.html> See also, >http://irishwatchdog.blogspot.com/2010/03/did-fr-ted-get-healthcare-passed.html>

Sirico, Rev. Robert A. "Kennedy the Catholic." Acton Institute, August 27, 2009. < https://blog.acton.org/archives/11882-nro-kennedy-the-catholic.html>

Stanek, Jill "Obama's Connections on Notre Dame Board of Trustees." JillStanek.com, May 13, 2009 <http://www.jillstanek.com/archives/2009/05/obamas_friendly.html>

Stanek, Jill "Top 10 Reasons Obama voted against the Illinois Born Alive Infant Protection Act." Illinois Review, January 10, 2008 <https://illinoisreview.typepad.com/illinoisreview/2008/01/top-10-reasons.html>

Unknown Author *Education: God and Man at Notre Dame.* Time, Feb. 1962. <http://content.time.com/time/magazine/article/0,9171,938327-1,00.html>

Walker, Frank "No Likely Support From Notre Dame's Board of Trustees For Rescinding Obama Invite." Pewsitter.com, May 10, 2009. <https://www.all.org/notre-dame-trustees-and-father-jenkins-final-word/>

Weigel, George "Obama and the 'Real' Catholics." National Review, May 18, 2009. <https://www.nationalreview.com/2009/05/obama-and-real-catholics-george-weigel/>

Westin, John Henry "Editorial: A False Theology: Obama's Appeal to Faith Runs Contrary to Christian Faith." LifeSiteNews.com, May 20, 2009. <https://www.lifesitenews.com/news/editorial-a-false-theology-obamas-appeal-to-faith-runs-contrary-to-christia>

Wikipedia "Alphonsus Liguori" <https://en.wikipedia.org/wiki/Alphonsus_Liguori>

Wikipedia *"Battle of Tara Hill"* *<https://en.wikipedia.org/wiki/Battle_of_Tara_Hill>*

Wikipedia *"Daniel O'Connell"* *<https://en.wikipedia.org/wiki/Daniel_O'Connell>*

*Wikipedia "Mother Teresa"* < https://en.wikipedia.org/wiki/Mother_Teresa>

Wikipedia "[President Obama] Executive Order 13535" <https://en.wikipedia.org/wiki/Executive_Order_13535>

Wikipedia "Stupak-Pitts Amendment" <https://en.wikipedia.org/wiki/Stupak%E2%80%93Pitts_Amendment>

*Wikipedia "The Irish Rebellion of 1641"* *<https://en.wikipedia.org/wiki/Irish_Rebellion_of_1641>*

Wikipedia *"The Irish Rebellion of 1798"*
*<https://en.wikipedia.org/wiki/Irish_Rebellion_of_1798>*

Woodward, Kenneth L. "Andrew Cuomo and the Sad Inheritance of 'Personal Opposition' to Abortion." American Magazine, February 12, 2019.

## Court Decisions

*Doe v. Bolton,* 410 U.S. 179 (1973)

*Dred Scott v. Sandford,* 60 U.S. 393 (1857)

NOW v. Scheidler, 510 U.S. 249 (1994)

*Planned Parenthood v. Casey, 505 U.S. 833 (1992)*
*Roe v. Wade, 410 U.S. 113 (1973).*

*State v. Loce,* 267 N.J. Super 102 (Law.Div. 1991), aff'd. as modified, 267 N.J. Super 10 (App. Div. 1993)

www.ingramcontent.com/pod-product-compliance
Lightning Source LLC
Chambersburg PA
CBHW031047250726
48655CB00004B/1341